A PEOPLE WHO LIVE APART

A PEOPLE WHO LIVE
APART

jewish identity and the future of israel

ELS van DIGGELE

translated by JEANNETTE K. RINGOLD

Prometheus Books

59 John Glenn Drive
Amherst, New York 14228-2197

Published 2003 by Prometheus Books

Inquiries should be addressed to
Prometheus Books
59 John Glenn Drive
Amherst, New York 14228–2197
VOICE: 716–691–0133, ext. 207
FAX: 716–564–2711
WWW.PROMETHEUSBOOKS.COM

07 06 05 04 03   5 4 3 2 1

Library of Congress Cataloging-in-Publication Data

Diggele, Els van, 1967–
  [Volk dat alleen woont. English]
  A people who live apart : Jewish identity and the future of Israel / by Els van Diggele ; translated by Jeannette K. Ringold.
    p. cm.
  Includes bibliographical references (p.) and index.
  ISBN 1–59102–076–X (cloth : alk. paper)
  1. Jews—Israel—Identity. 2. Orthodox Judaism—Relations—Nontraditional Jews. 3. Israel—Social conditions—20th century. I. Title.

DS143.D5413 2003
305.6'9605694—dc21

                                                                2003001752

Printed in Canada on acid-free paper

CONTENTS

CONTENTS

FOREWORD

The initial impulse for this book about the struggle for the Jewish identity of the state of Israel came about in 1997 when a settler said to me, "We, the Jews, have won our last election, and the Israelis, the Jews who have forgotten what it means to be Jewish, have lost. We are the real Jews and we will not give up the struggle for the Jewish identity of our own state."

At that time I was staying in Tel Aviv with a laptop, a number of books about the history of Israel and the Jewish people, and a Bible. I intended to write some articles. However, nothing came of that because of the encounter with this settler whose statement referred to the 1996 election results. I took his words seriously because they made me aware of the evident tension between secular and Orthodox Jews that was prevalent in the country. Of course I had heard that the murder of Yitzhak Rabin in November 1995 by an Orthodox Jew signified a turning point in Israel's history and that the underlying polarization between secular and Orthodox Jews had come to the surface because of this event. But now I realized that the mutual alienation and fear which I had not experienced in such a direct manner during my previous visits vexes Israeli society in political and social respects.

During those conversations, I jotted down some statements such as: "Since the murder of Rabin I'm ashamed to be Jewish"; "If we get peace here, a civil war will break out"; "I worry about Jewish anti-Semitism"; "Our Jewish democracy is theocratic and our Israeli democracy is anarchistic"; "We shouldn't become so democratic that it makes us worse." These sorts of statements that I heard from the mouths from many in the streets, in cafés, and in stores without even trying didn't just make me curious—above all they spurred me on to search for the causes of this mutual hostility.

Because during that period I was primarily confronted by secular points of view, I began to read religious papers, and my circle of friends expanded to include Orthodox Jews. In my conversations with them and with secular Jews, I focused on how Jewish religion influences everyday life, what different Jews mean by Judaism, and where the border between modernity (secularism) and tradition (Orthodox Judaism) could be drawn. In the company of religious Jews I usually tried to cultivate understanding for the way of life of secular Jews, and, in the same way, I tried to explain the religious points of view when I was with secular Jews. But the Jews who emphasize their Jewish identity and those Jews who emphasize their Israeli identity seemed to be unable or unwilling to understand one another.

I became increasingly convinced of the seriousness of this *Kulturkampf* (culture war), which didn't seem to be a short-lived struggle but instead had the characteristics of a long-standing family feud. These conversations convinced me that Israel at the eve of the new century had become the arena for the fight about the "true" meaning of Judaism and the Jewish content that a Jewish state should have. While many Jews had discussions about this subject among themselves, my plans to write a book about it began to take shape.

Dressed soberly—this is what religious Jews call the outfit consisting of a long skirt, a high-necked blouse with long sleeves, and pantyhose—I set off to Orthodox and ultra-Orthodox families, yeshivas, synagogues, Orthodox and ultra-Orthodox marriages and funerals, and to the West Bank. In most cases I had an appointment with an Orthodox or a Reform rabbi, but sometimes I would drive to a religious neighborhood or area just to look around, to go shopping, or to check out the atmosphere. For example, I went to an Orthodox hairdresser, I went shopping in Bnei Brak, an Orthodox suburb of Tel Aviv where I went into wig stores and then talked about the culture war. I did the same thing in cities where problems had occurred about such matters as the sale of pork or the construction of a religious school in a secular neighborhood. Most of the time the makeup of the population in these cities, the combination of Moroccan Jews, Russian immigrants and religious Ashkenazi Jews was the cause of conflicts. During these kinds of visits I spoke about the situation with all the parties involved. I was very well-informed about the situation by hitchhikers for whom I almost always stopped when I was on the road.

In the car I often had animated conversations with these hitchhikers who were usually yeshiva students. There was mutual curiosity; on my part, I was curious about their background, their study, their way of life. These young men wondered about the world I represented, a world that they had never had contact with. After they noticed my interest in Judaism, they often asked me if I was Jewish or perhaps had a Jewish family member, and if I had plans to "come out." Most observant Jews are surprised that someone with a non-Jewish background is interested in Judaism, but we would eventually discuss the subject I was interested in: the culture war. I found their questions and comments interesting because they revealed something about their background and their way of thinking. For example, after I had closed the windows and turned on the air-conditioning, one of these young men asked me if I could open the window. He explained that it is written that a man is not allowed to be in a closed space with a woman.

During these meetings, which often took place in someone's home, I often felt like an intruder but especially like an outsider. The first contact was usually by telephone; sometimes a first meeting took place during an official gathering. In these circumstances, my knowledge of Hebrew was very useful because modern Hebrew is more than just a language: it's an ideology, an expression of national identity. Someone who makes the effort to master it belongs. An explanation of the subject that interested me was usually superfluous because all the people I approached played a role in it themselves. Usually I expressed the opinion that Israel is a country like no other and cannot be otherwise, an opinion of many religious Jews. Yet people often said to me, "Are the goyim in the Netherlands interested in this subject?" In spite of this skepticism, no one ever refused to talk to me, although it was more difficult to get in touch with the Sephardic leaders.

The most striking thing was that the conversations usually started out much less pleasantly than they ended. The turning point was usually the moment when the interviewees realized that they were dealing with someone who was trying to understand Judaism and its role in Israel, who was not hostile to Jews, and even more important, someone who was informed about the history of this subject and about the present situation. This last point is of great importance because of the extremely complex issues at the heart of the subject of this book, which was, of course, the main topic of our discussion. People prefer not having to explain the situation to an outsider—in this case not only a foreigner but—especially—a non-Jew. Jews often feel misunderstood by "the others," and in this respect Orthodox Israeli Jews are more reserved and less approachable than secular Jews. I should like to emphasize that this should not be surprising in view of the extremely complex issues that are involved in the centuries-old struggle for Jewish identity.

The method of my research consisted of the journalistic interview and report and historical research, and it took me to people who had dealt with these problems for a long time and in-depth. After a sigh, they often tried with many "ifs" and "buts" to formulate an answer that could never be complete. In addition we should remember that in Israel no answer is ever complete and free from value judgments. The integrity of answers is often obscured by the political meaning of such things as the head covering of the speaker, his or her place of residence, the part of Jewish tradition maintained, and sometimes the university to which he or she is connected. In other words, I had a double task: it was important to know the background of the person to whom I was speaking as well as his or her opinions about a certain subject. It became apparent rather quickly that my research would raise as many questions as it would answer.

Before I started the research, I was already somewhat familiar with the complexity of the Jewish psyche and the sensitivities in the country. Since my first long visit to Israel in 1986 I have never broken off my contact with the Holy Land. Between that visit and February 1998, when I decided to live there temporarily, I have witnessed the development of religious-nationalistic fanaticism and I have seen the ultra-Orthodox community come out of its isolation. As a result of this last development, the tension between modernity and tradition was more clearly tangible in Israel in 1998 than in 1986. Why it came about that Israel was "different" and what was so "abnormal" and why the religious influence in a predominantly secular country could not be lessened were questions that preoccupied me from the first visit.

The media still pay little attention to the culture war. Newspaper readers or television viewers can check daily on news reports about the progress of the peace process in the Middle East through regular news reports, analyses, and background articles. There seems to be an overabundance of news from Israel, but it is one-sided and has for years consisted of the next step in the peace process; this news seems to be more of the same. All the attention of the many correspondents in Israel—and I have been able to observe this from close up during the past few years—is monopolized by the progress of discussions between Palestinians and Israelis. Yet, it is only when the peace talks between the Palestinians and the Israelis, which always have the most prominent place in newspapers in Western Europe and in the United States, are at a standstill that the news media have time to concentrate on this "civil war," which is what the culture war actually is. The same thing is true of Israeli politicians as well, and this has been the case for fifty years. It is only when external war and peace temporarily disappear from the political agenda—a rarity in Israeli politics—that the second great Israeli problem (the domestic war) comes to the surface.

Now that the peace process is practically at a standstill, this culture war is still topical but dormant—as was the case during the first decades after the creation of the state. It seems likely that an artificial Jewish unity, directed toward the Palestinians, will temporarily suppress the expression of internal Jewish differences of opinion.

The Dutch version of this book was written in the period from May 1998, the fiftieth anniversary of the state of Israel, to Passover of 2000. My purpose was to show the nature of the conflicting opinions in this country. My purpose was to show, without passing judgment, that numerous and almost insoluble and sensitive problems determine the domestic problems, and that there is a tug-of-war between secular and Orthodox Jews that prevents a convincing development in either direction. I have tried to reveal as much as possible the roots of the present domestic discussions and to place the current events in their historical context.

I have tried to do this by emphasizing certain developments as well as the long-term unchanged situation in view of events that took place during the above-mentioned period. In this way the reader sees how changeable the situation is in Israel but that there are nevertheless constant factors that point to the continuity of the problems. The paradox is that the new facts that can be reported since the publication of the Dutch edition of this book in October 2000—for example, the fall of the government of Barak and Sharon's government taking office—don't shed any new light on the gradual development that is taking place below the surface in Israeli society.

Therefore, in preparing the text for the English language translation of this book, I strove to keep the original text as much as possible. I have left the verb tenses unchanged, and I have added no new facts. After all, the very insight that this problem has been an issue for centuries and changes only very slightly would be lost if the emphasis were too much on current events. The topic of this book is not subject to great changes—it is rather a question of more of the same. The dates in the chapters that follow the historical overview and the names of the politicians and other players in the "game" that are no longer current could be misleading. The point of this book is not the present situation but rather the views and opinions that representatives of certain groups in Israeli society have held for a long time.

This last point is especially true for the residents of the West Bank who speak out in the last chapter, "The West Bank: A False Messiah?" To be sure, some of them no longer play an important role in present-day Israel, but their positions are still of great importance for a good understanding of the contemporary history of religious-Zionist ideology, the subject of that chapter. Because the conflict between Israel and the Palestinians is not the subject of the final chapter, I have retained the original text as much as possible. Since this chapter is not about peace negotiations but the meaning of the "Jewish country" for the religious-Zionist identity, it doesn't matter that the people are talking about the Oslo agreement, or the Wye agreement, about Prime Minister Benjamin Netanyahu and his successor Ehud Barak, and not about Camp David and Prime Minister Ariel Sharon. The above-mentioned peace negotiations have actually become interchangeable, and the opinions of prime ministers Netanyahu, Barak, and Sharon don't (or hardly) influence the opinions of the people who express their ideas in this final chapter, or the description of religious-Zionist ideas.

I have tried to be as clear as possible, and therefore I have used the names of the current ministers where relevant and have used the terms *current, previous, under Barak,* and *under Sharon* as much and as consistently as possible. This was necessitated by the relatively quick shifts and changes on the political stage in the past (that will most likely continue in the future).

The above-mentioned paradox, whose importance I would like to emphasize once more, is that these quick surface changes don't really influence the issues treated in this book. The policy of a new minister of education can have a short-term effect, but fundamentally the problems and the opinions have remained the same, and in the meantime no answer has been found for any of the dilemmas treated in this book. I have therefore chosen to alert the reader in the epilogue to various developments that started to take shape more clearly in the period during which the translation of this book was being done.

I am very grateful to Mark Edersheim and Benno Gitter who made possible the realization of this translation via the Benal Fund. In addition I want to express my appreciation for the support I received from the Foundation for the Promotion and Translation of Dutch Literature and the Levi Lassen Foundation. I also want to thank Rabbi Lody van de Kamp and Prof. Dan Michman for the useful comments they made about the original publication.

In addition I would like to thank Clinton Bailey for the interest he has always shown in the results of my interviews and my reports that we often discussed afterward when we encountered each other in Tel Aviv or Jerusalem. I also want to thank him for pointing me to many publications, but especially to the book *Perpetual Dilemma* by S. Zalman Abramov at an early stage of my work. In this book Abramov uncovers the roots of Israel's domestic problems during his time (he published the book in 1976) as well as in the present. His book strengthened my conviction that the Jewish state, exactly because of these deep roots, is a different and special state. If I had not read this book (a subject to which I will return in detail in the epilogue) I would not have been able to write *A People Who Live Apart*.

In addition I would like to express my appreciation for the support I have received from René Kruis during the last years. He saw the first version of this book expand into the book as it is now. From the very beginning until the end he has been a great support for me because of his constant involvement and commitment. He has encouraged me by editing my new versions, by making notes on them, and by pointing out publications of interest about the subject. Our exchange of views about the subject matter has encouraged and stimulated me. For all this I am very grateful to him.

In conclusion I thank Gert Kampman for the understanding and patience he showed for the fact that I preferred spending my free time at my desk instead of doing something with him. I thank him for the peace and quiet he gave me and the favorable circumstances he created during which I was able to entrust my acquired knowledge and collected information to paper. I am very grateful to him for all this.

Els van Diggele
Jerusalem, August 2001

INTRODUCTION

THE CELEBRATION OF ISRAEL'S FIFTIETH BIRTHDAY on May 15, 1998, turned into a conflict between secular and Orthodox Jews about freedom of expression and the related principle of religious freedom. The occasion was an artistic striptease that the Israeli dance company Batsheva was going to perform in Tel Aviv during the birthday party. The performance never took place, however, because during the dress rehearsal the scene in which the dancers take off their clothes to accompany a text from the Jewish Passover service and continue to dance in their underwear did not go down well with the Orthodox. They demanded—successfully—that the company be pulled out of the celebration because of blasphemy. In this way, the celebration that was supposed to bring together all Jews was overshadowed by a reminder of the deep-rooted *Kulturkampf* (culture war) that has divided the Jewish people for more than two centuries.

A few days later, secular Jews demonstrated on Rabin Square in Tel Aviv against censorship and religious tyranny and in favor of drafting a constitution that would include separation of religion and state. The following Saturdays, confrontations took place in Jerusalem between secular and religious Jews at cafés and restaurants that are open on the Sabbath. (This is legally prohibited, but a blind eye has been turned to this practice for years.) The birthday seems to have set the tone for the *Kulturkampf*, which in the fifty-first year of the state of Israel has increasingly taken on the characteristics of a conflict between a number of irreconcilable parties. On the street, in stores, on the road (via bumper stickers), while reading the papers or watching television, Israelis were more than ever reminded of this division because of ads and announcements from both parties. In December 1998, for example, an ad appeared in the national papers and on street posters; its text was "*Yes* to differing opinions, *no* to civil war."

For years this problem didn't engage the Israelis very much at all because searching for a solution to the conflict with its Arab neighbors and with the Palestinians was more urgent. This situation continues, although during the period of relative peace that preceded the second *intifada* it appeared that 80 percent of Israelis considered the problems of Jews among themselves the greatest problem in Israel.

For the first time in the history of Israel, the struggle between Orthodox and secular Jews about the character of the state also seemed to play a principal role in the campaigns for municipal elections at the end of 1998 and in the campaigns for national elections in 1999. Perhaps the mutual contempt came into the open once again because peace talks with the Palestinians had reached an impasse during that very period. The secularists called the Orthodox "parasites," "power-mad," "unproductive," and the Orthodox in turn answered with "anti-Semites," "Jew haters," "wicked." Slogans like "money for universities, not for yeshivas," "stop the *haredim*, they divide the Jewish people," "being free in our own country," "being Jewish in our own country," and "the ultra-Orthodox are the source of all problems" persuaded the Israelis once more of the need to find a solution for this problem in the coming years.

Shahar Ilan, the reporter on religious affairs for the highly regarded Israeli newspaper *Ha'aretz*, published a series of articles about the ultra-Orthodoxy in 1998 and in the early part of 1999. These articles were considered unreliable in strict religious circles, while the author was awarded a prize in journalism by the secular side. Through these articles the secularists were reminded once again of the use of their tax money for the Orthodox, and the ultra-Orthodox considered the articles as another demonstration of "anti-Jewish agitation of the secular newspaper editors who spread nothing but lies" about them.

According to the Orthodox, one of these lies is that it's a shame that 51 percent of the average income of the ultra-Orthodox families—more than half of whom live below the poverty line—comes from public funds. The strict Orthodox feels that he has no other choice but to preserve the halakhah and the Jewish people by studying the Talmud. After all, as a Jew he carries the burden of the whole Jewish people on his shoulders.

In 1997 it was made public that the annual financial support of the government to the yeshivas had been increasing for a number of years, as had the number of yeshiva students. For the secular Jews this increase was another reason for concern about the use of their tax money and the increasing influence of the Orthodoxy. According to the Orthodox Jews, this increase (from 159,000 in 1996 to 209,000 in 2001) is a good sign, and the ultra-Orthodoxy is entitled to the financing of the yeshivas by the state because universities are subsidized as well. The secularists have been incredibly annoyed at ultra-Orthodox men who don't serve in the army and are unemployed. This raised the percentage of nonworking Israeli men between the ages of 25 and 44 to 15 percent, the highest in the world. (In Western countries, this percentage varies from five to seven.) In 2001 one secular family supported an ultra-Orthodox family, but the secularists, who no longer seem willing to accept this situation, fear that in the future one secular family will support five ultra-Orthodox families if the situation doesn't change.

However, according to the Orthodox community, it is not at all unreasonable that in spite of the tight Israeli treasury the budget of the minister of religious affairs increased and that numerous ultra-Orthodox agencies are financed by the Orthodox minister of finance. In his articles Ilan calls this "illegal patronage," but journalists from religious newspapers feel that they have a right to this and that the secularists "live too lavishly and should forgo buying a second car or having a dog."

Another great source of dissatisfaction in Israel is the exemption from military service of the approximately thirty thousand students of Talmud seminaries (7.5 percent of the total number of potential draftees in Israel). For the secularists it is inconceivable that eighteen-year-old religious Jews would throw in their lot as full-time yeshiva students and choose to be dependent on the advice of rabbis. For them it is incomprehensible that a complete community is plunged in prayer day-in and day-out and immersed in Talmud study which, moreover, is too difficult for many of these young men. Yet they enroll again every year in order to support the yeshiva financially (yeshivas receive a yearly sum per student from the state). These young ultra-Orthodox, called *shababs* in Hebrew, hang around in the streets and don't look for jobs because as soon as they do, they forfeit their exemption from military service. After all, these "conscientious objectors"—16 percent of the total number of yeshiva students—have grown up with the idea that they live in spiritual *Eretz Yisrael*, a land that needs no defense, where the study of the Torah is the highest good and where rabbis represent the highest authority.

Meanwhile, the hostility of many secular Israeli taxpayers who have the feeling that they are supporting a flourishing enterprise has reached the level of national consensus. They emphasize the importance of equality in a democracy, but the question remains whether forcing yeshiva students to fulfill military service will result in this equality. After all, it is known that almost half of the secular Israelis of military age don't serve in the army. In spite of this, the student strike that broke out in mid-October of 1998 and lasted almost a month turned fiercely against the Orthodox minister of finance who, according to the students, "seems to have money for fraudulent yeshiva students, but not for students who fulfill their military service, learn a trade, support themselves, and ask for a reduction of college tuition." The students lost the struggle, and for many secularists that was the umpteenth proof that the ultra-Orthodox community increasingly influences Israel.

Fifty years after the founding of the state, the question still remains where the balance between Israel as Jewish state and Israel as democratic state can be found. The Jews returned to Palestine to found a Jewish state, whatever that might mean, but not to establish a pluralistic country or a haven for the persecuted. Judaism in the diaspora maintained itself by the separation of religion and state, but most Jews realized that the return to the old land would change the way of life of the Jewish people as a Jewish community. After all, the establishment of a Jewish state would mean interference of politics in religious affairs. All public buildings and almost all private homes have mezuzot on their doorposts. The Jews are glad about that, not because they all subscribe to the religious meaning of the mezuzah, but because it affirms the Jewish identity, like a flag or a coat of arms.

For many Europeans, but also for Jewish Israelis who want to assume a Western identity, it is difficult to understand that someone who is not religious attaches importance to symbols that have a religious meaning. Europeans are usually able to keep questions of collective identity outside religion. Their cultural and political tradition, in contrast to the Jewish cultural and political tradition, is largely determined by secular elements to which their ethnic and cultural identity is almost completely subordinated.

The attempt of Jewish Israelis to be "European" and to separate the synagogue from the state feels forced because they try to see Orthodox Judaism as a universal abstraction without historical and geographic connections. In this effort they overlook (or ignore) that Jews are a people with a certain collective consciousness and not just a group of individuals. Many Jews have always been aware of their separate place in the world, and Jewish identity is rooted in this awareness.

Israel may be defined as a Jewish democracy, but the question of the true identity of the country and of the democracy (Jewish or Western) is obvious. Is Israel a secular state as in the Zionists' vision, or is Israel a theocratic state as the Orthodox Jews wish? Is Israel a state for all its citizens, or has Israel actually become a Jewish democracy as was stated in the Declaration of Independence of 1948? And if the latter is the case, can a state in which every fifth citizen is a non-Jew be both Jewish and democratic? And who is a Jew?

All these questions sound abstract, but they have become concrete in the daily lives of Israeli Jews; the secularists and the Orthodox have been fighting about them for over fifty years. In the history of Israel this fight has become known as the *Kulturkampf*. According to the secularists, the solution to this conflict lies in the separation of religion and state. The weakness of this solution is that the secularists start from different principles than the Orthodox, whose all-consuming concern after the disaster of the years

1940–1945 was preserving the core of Judaism in its original purity. Biblical scholars and other ultra-Orthodox, who seem to belong to another world from the secular, live in the fear that the age-old system that they are protecting will collapse if even the smallest change is introduced. This fear explains, at least partially, the influence of the synagogue on public life, its guardianship of the "Jewish state" inspired by God.

Before proceeding to the contents of each chapter, I would like to comment about the terminology used, the interviewees, and the structure of the chapters.

A core idea of this book is the German word *Kulturkampf*, translated as "culture war," which in Israel and in relation to the diaspora indicates the struggle between secular and Orthodox Jews about the identity of the state.

I have alternated the words "ultra-Orthodox" and the Hebrew equivalent *haredi* (plural: *haredim*) as much as possible. Since the Jewish enlightenment, the *Haskalah* (1780–1880), both terms have been used for Jews who keep religious Jewish traditions and don't modernize. Nowadays, many in Israel don't call those who are faithful to tradition "Orthodox"—although that's what they are in the strict sense of the word—but rather "ultra-Orthodox" because of their extremely strict observance of Jewish law.

The word *hared*, which means "fear" or "tremble," appears in biblical Hebrew in Isaiah (66:5) when the prophet addresses his people with the words: "Hear the word of the Lord, Ye that tremble at His word." This text, which today is still read aloud in the synagogue, depicts the God-fearing, the *haredim*, as the only Jews who defend the faith and obey the law. They continue to maintain their exclusive relationship with God because they never turned away from the faith, even during the time when Jewish historical awareness became secular.

In modern Hebrew the word *haredim* at first referred to all Orthodox and observant Jews. Later, when differences in observing the law became more defined in Israel, the term *dati* (plural: *datim*) was created as general designation of "religious." But *datim* increasingly referred to Orthodox Jews who had to a great extent adapted their lives to modern life. Therefore, the word *haredim* is used more exclusively for those who have not adjusted in that way.

One reason for the use of the term *haredim* is that it simplifies the distinction between several types of Orthodox Jews. Besides, the term is more neutral than the term "ultra-Orthodox," which refers to the extent of other people's religiosity. Another reason to use this term is Jewish ethnic pride. When the Jews returned to their biblical homeland and revived their old language, they no longer needed foreign names. Although the terms "Orthodox" and "ultra-Orthodox" are used in Hebrew, they come from a language that is foreign to the Jewish experience. On the other hand, *hared* is a typically "Jewish" word. The Hebrew language is an expression of national identity, therefore in Israel "Orthodox" becomes *dati* and "ultra-Orthodox" *hared*, just like Isaac becomes Yitzhak and Rebecca became Rivka.

Fourteen percent of Israeli Jews call themselves *haredim*, strictly observant; 24 percent say they are "to a great extent observant" and call themselves *dati*. Forty-one percent of Jewish Israelis say they are "somewhat observant" and are called *masorti*, which means "traditional." Twenty-one percent say they are "absolutely not observant" and call themselves *hiloni*, which means "nonbelieving."

In every chapter, historical passages, reports, and interviews alternate. As regards the interviews, one should not lose sight of the fact that Israel is a society that is not easy to define because it is made up of countless groups and many experts in the field, like the professors to whom I spoke, are members of one of these groups. I realize that the opinions of the Israelis who did speak might, for this reason, not find broad support, and that the representativeness of their opinions is therefore limited.

The Israelis who were willing to answer my questions (see the list of interviewees on p. 293) were chosen for a number of reasons, different for each person. Perhaps they represent the opinion of a certain Jewish Israeli faction (Gush Emunim, Netivot Shalom, Yesha); maybe they hold an important position (mayor, chief rabbi, member of the Knesset), or they hold a view opposite to that stated in the chapter. In each chapter, conversations with the principal actors and reports alternate with the knowledge of an expert in the field. For statistical data I have used the *Israel Yearbook & Almanac 2000* and research published in 1992 by the Guttman Institute of Jerusalem. This institute studies religious ceremonies, beliefs, and behavior of Israeli Jews and their thoughts about the role that Judaism should play in public life. According to the results of this research, the division of Jewish Israelis into "secular" and "Orthodox" is an exaggerated polarization, and division according to degree of religiosity gives a more accurate picture of reality. Although I think that even in the lives of secular Jews in Israel there is often a certain measure of religiosity, I have nevertheless chosen to use this division of Orthodox and secular for the simple reason that many Jews call themselves secularist.

The title of the first chapter, "The Time Bomb of Ben Gurion," refers to the Status Quo, the agreement that Ben Gurion made in 1948 with the Orthodox about the separation of religion and state. In accordance with this agreement, with which Ben Gurion thought he had found a reasonable demarcation between Israeli modernity and Jewish traditionalism, the Orthodox received certain privileges that enabled them to live an observant life in the new state. Contrary to the intention of this agreement—maintaining unity among Jews—the Status Quo is causing a schism in Israeli society.

This chapter presents the agreement in its historical context, starting in Eastern Europe during the Jewish enlightenment (the *Haskalah*) when conflicts about religious subjects arose. This review continues until the last decade of the twentieth century and sheds light on events that caused tensions between Orthodox and secular Jews. Menachem Begin's coming to power in 1977 receives special attention since during his regime the Orthodoxy managed to become an influential movement. As a result of this development secular Jews, who had formerly shown willingness to negotiate compromises with the Orthodox for the sake of Jewish unity, turned increasingly against the Orthodoxy. The founding of Shas, the ultra-Orthodox Sephardic party, receives special attention in this chapter.

The last developments described in this chapter show the increasing power of Shas and its consequences for Israeli society. One of these developments was the large ultra-Orthodox demonstration in February 1999 against the interference of the Supreme Court in religious affairs. Another was the electoral victory of Shas, which in the elections of May of that year managed to increase its number of Knesset seats to seventeen. This victory expressed the deep anger of the Sephardic community after its leader, Aryeh Deri, was given a four-year prison sentence because of fraud. Although this affair was not officially a religious question, it made clear how the support of Shas can increase when there is an appeal to the feelings of inferiority that the Sephardic community has experienced ever since its reception in Israel in the fifties by the Ashkenazi community.

Ehud Barak (and this is also true of Ariel Sharon and, at the time, Yitzhak Rabin) ruled with a coalition in which Shas as well as Meretz, the most explicitly antireligious party, participated. The prime ministers were repeatedly confronted by crises because these two hostile parties consistently gave higher priority to their own "religious" agenda than to the most important aims of the government. Barak's government fell in December 2000 largely as a result of insolvable internal tensions. It seems that these internal tensions are playing no role during the government of Ariel Sharon because of the second *intifada*.

The second chapter, "Is a Jewish Democracy Possible?" deals with the greatest paradox of the state of Israel as a Jewish democracy. Can "Jewishness" and "democracy" go together as the most important characteristics of the state? This chapter illustrates the strongly polarized Israeli political culture in which most attention is paid to religious parties, their political and social demands, and their position with respect to the secular parties. This chapter describes the so-called politics of compromise that became characteristic of the Israeli political arena where secular and religious demands collide.

The participation of Orthodox parties in politics has blurred the distinction between political and spiritual leaders in Orthodox communities. The political involvement of the latter, together with the increasing influence of the ultra-Orthodox minority on everyday life, has made the effort of the secularists to formulate a constitution almost impossible. Moreover the two rival secular parties, the Labor Party and Likud, are silent about this sensitive subject. They are afraid of antagonizing the Orthodox parties to such an extent that it will no longer be possible to form a coalition with them and in this way exclude other parties. This is why political pilgrimages to spiritual leaders to obtain their support have become the trademark of secular political leaders. In this chapter, representatives of secular and religious political parties and political scientists who specialize in Orthodox and ultra-Orthodox politics comment on the problems of the Jewish democracy.

The third chapter, "Who Is a Jew? The Orthodox Monopoly on Judaism," deals with the question of Jewish identity that has preoccupied the state of Israel for the past four decades. This question, rooted in the age-old conflict between religious and secular Jews, is today part of the "religious war" in Israel about which interpretation of the divine biblical revelation is the true one: the Orthodox, the Reform, or the Conservative. These matters are described in light of some actual social problems around the performance of marriages and divorces, the conducting of funerals, and the approval of conversions. All these actions can officially be performed only by Orthodox Jews, and this causes the other movements within Judaism to feel frustrated in their rabbinic calling. The Reform and Conservative Jews are trying to break the monopoly of the Orthodoxy on Judaism through the Supreme Court. They have recently been supported by a number of prominent secular Jews who consider this expression of support a part of the struggle to transform Israel into a secular country.

The fourth chapter, "The Russians in Israel: Is Being Israeli Jewish Enough?" examines the problems that arose at the end of the last decade of the twentieth century as a result of the massive immigration of secular Jews from the former Soviet Union. The large number of immigrants, most of whom are not Jewish or half-Jewish, live in a small Russian state inside Israel and, according to many, they endanger the preservation of the Jewish character of the state of Israel. Through the Law of Return they have the right to Israeli citizenship, yet many of them are unable to marry in Israel. And this is because the Orthodoxy, which has a monopoly in this area, does not recognize many of the Russian immigrants as Jews. In the long term, these immigrants can bring about the era of "normality" desired by the secularists because by their sheer numbers they would be able to extort the above-mentioned rights as citizens of the state of Israel. This would, among other things, mean the abolition of the Law of Return and the legalization of civil marriage and nonreligious funerals.

This chapter will remain particularly relevant in the coming years. On the one hand the Russian immigrant party, Israel ba'Aliyah, and many "ordinary" Russians speak up, and on the other hand representatives from the Sochnut (the Jewish Agency) and a specialist in the area of Soviet Jewry present their ideas about this subculture that has given the *Kulturkampf* (culture war) an extra dimension.

The fifth chapter, "Crossing the Line: New Orthodox and New Secular Jews," offers insight into Orthodox Jewish life through the new secularists, those who have renounced the faith, and through Jews who have converted to Judaism, the new believers. This chapter depicts the way of thinking of the ultra-Orthodox and shows how strictly secular as well as strictly religious education can promote contempt and lack of understanding of the other. For example, the experience of a newly secular ultra-Orthodox yeshiva student who has practically no contact with his family since he has become secular shows that mutual interest and understanding between secular and religious Jews are minimal. The immensity of this chasm is also evident from the changes a newly religious person has to undergo in order to become Orthodox. These changes affect eating and dressing habits, rhythm of life, and even language. The newly secular also needs to learn a new code of behavior in order to feel at home in the "modern world."

Because the new secularist often feels like an immigrant in his own country, the Hillel organization has been created. In the year 2000 this organization received a subsidy from the minister of education for the first time while organizations that educate the new believers have been receiving government support for many years. Therefore the problems resulting from this phenomenon have social as well as political consequences. For this reason the subject of the newly religious and the newly secular are included in this book.

The sixth chapter, "The West Bank: A False Messiah?" is about Orthodox nationalistic settlers who live on the West Bank of the Jordan. This is a territory that Israel occupied in the Six-Day War in 1967 and to which they refer with the biblical names Judea and Samaria. In their view, their Jewishness and the Jewish identity of the state mean that the people Israel must take care that all of the biblical land remains in Jewish hands. According to them, giving up parts of Judea and Samaria is in conflict with Jewish belief. This chapter shows how and why the religious-Zionist movement had a revival after 1967, and it describes how it went through more difficult times after the Palestinian *intifada* of 1987.

While I was writing the initial Dutch version of this book, the future development of the religious-Zionist community was by and large uncertain. Many religious Zionists seemed to moderate their positions and resign themselves to the decision of the democratically elected government to hand over parts of the West Bank—initially claimed for the Jews—to the Palestinian authority. However, the far-reaching territorial concessions of Prime Minister Ehud Barak in Camp David in August 2000, the failure of the negotiations, and the start of the second *intifada* have shown that the extreme positions of some residents of the West Bank have not at all died out. The actual situation has changed, but at the same time there is nothing new under the sun.

The most important question of this final chapter remains whether the fight of the settlers and other extreme religious Zionists has become a rearguard action or whether they will still be able to stop territorial concessions to the Palestinians. In addition, there is a legitimate question about whether the residents of the West Bank will in the long run become isolated or will get support from a part of the other Jews in Israel.

In this final chapter a number of West Bank residents are quoted frequently. Some of them use biblical stories to justify their settlement as God's will. The religious Zionists, among whom there are moderates and extremists, corroborate the confusion and disorganization in their ranks although they don't say it in so many words. At the end of this chapter a political scientist from Bar Ilan University in Ramat Gan gives a number of concluding remarks.

ONE

THE TIME BOMB OF BEN GURION

"I do not know when I shall die, but Zionism will never die. Since those days in Basel, the Jewish people has a national representation once again; as a result the Jewish state will once more rise in its own country."

—Theodor Herzl

"Herzl forged the Jewish people into a national power, a creative and fighting power, for the first time since it went into exile. . . . Herzl was the creator of a renewed Jewish policy. In two clear, simple and at the same time emotional words he determined the political goal of the Jewish people: a Jewish state."

—David Ben Gurion

FOR A CLEAR UNDERSTANDING OF THE creation of the state of Israel and of its present domestic problems, it is necessary to go back to an earlier phase in the history of Judaism. After all, before proclaiming the state of Israel in 1948, Ben Gurion had to deal with an abundance of opposing opinions about the meaning of Judaism in the life of a Jew and therefore in the daily life of the future Jewish state. These views were in large part rooted in a crucial period of Jewish history. In the eighteenth century being a Jew was for the first time no longer considered as a self-evident fate but as a choice. Many Jews chose the status of ordinary citizen and even held political offices, and some of them behaved as Jews only at home. This meant that for the first time in the history of Judaism a distinction was made between the public and private life of Jews, and being Jewish had become an option.

The emancipation of the Jews in Central and Eastern Europe and in France (where the Jews were granted civil rights in 1791) and anti-Jewish measures in Russia stimulated Jewish intellectual life around 1800. Eastern Europe, where the greatest concentration of Jews lived from 1700–1940, became a center of Jewish culture. Afraid of the effect of the secular "unclean" knowledge that had entered Jewish culture starting at the time of the *Haskalah* (Jewish Enlightenment) around 1780, a few emigrated to Palestine and many Jews withdrew into their community, where they clung to their religion. Many Orthodox Jews felt that the *Haskalah* had a destructive influence on the community, and adults feared that their children would choose the goyish world and science and that they would no longer see the age-old accepted Jewish truths as a solution for contemporary problems.

The *Haskalah* was a social and cultural movement in Middle and Western Europe that wanted to develop Jewish learning to show that Judaism was more than a religion. Under the leadership of this anti-Orthodox movement of the *maskilim*, the enlightened Jews of the *Haskalah*, the Hebrew language experienced a philological revival as a secular spoken language. The Orthodox Jews were against this movement because the *maskilim* did not revive the Hebrew language in order to study biblical texts but to do modern science. Therefore, from the beginning of the *Haskalah*, the revival of Hebrew was part of a broader scientific pursuit. For the Orthodox, the word *maskil* (from the Hebrew word *sechel*, meaning "reason, intellect") was an insult.

The Orthodox felt that in a modernizing society, in which Jewish assimilation reached a peak, Jews should not try to be German, British, or any other sort of citizen. They should instead keep their minds on keeping alive the halakhah, and the chosen quality that they had inherited from their ancestors, who in difficult times had always found support in the religion that God had chosen for them as a "kingdom of priests" and a "holy nation" (Exod. 19:6). In long black coats with "Jewish caps" and on Saturdays a *shtreimel* (black broad-brimmed hat) on their heads, Jewish men hurried through the streets. Their sideburns were unshaven according to God's commandment (Lev. 19:27), and the tzitzit, although not visible, served as a warning against sensual temptations: "Look at it and recall all the commandments of the Lord (. . .) so that you do not follow your heart and eyes in your lustful urge" (Num. 15:39). They lived as transients in a secular world because God had "set them apart from other peoples" (Lev. 20:26). The Jewish dietary laws, the purity laws, the laws for cleansing, and the dress rules made them into strangers and symbolized the age-old thought that Jews had a special destiny. Those Jews who assimilated were called "Jewish goys," "deserters," and they were "confused" rather than "enlightened." For fear of "perishing among the nations" (Lev. 26:38) and in an attempt to rescue Jewish traditional life which was in a crisis, the established Orthodoxy in the diaspora forbade the Jews from following "unclean" schooling and insisted on intensification of Talmud studies and stricter observance of the laws. Striving for an intense religious life would protect the inner life against the threats of reality. The best protection against "foreign knowledge" was the study of the Torah, the highest Jewish value that causes a Jew to approach God's revelation most closely. Study brought them back to the foot of the mountain in the Sinai desert, and this realization became ever stronger because of the danger of assimilation and secularization of the Jews around them. At home the father taught his child to believe in God, entirely according to the Jewish tradition. Later, when his mind was fully developed and he would be able to reflect on these matters, he would not renounce his faith but instead continue to fear God for "the fear of the Lord is the beginning of wisdom" (Ps. 111:10).

The prominent place that some emancipated Jews had started to take in society was one of the causes of modern anti-Semitism. It surfaced mainly in countries of Middle and Western Europe where Jews thought they had cut all their Jewish roots in order to assimilate completely. Jewish despair was best summed up in the questions "Do we have to leave, and where do we go?" and "Can we still stay, and for how long?" Assimilation, the initial answer to these questions, had failed. Therefore flight seemed obvious as a new answer. Between 1881 and 1930 more than two and one-half million Ashkenazi Jews, primarily nonbelieving Jews, fled pogroms in Czarist Russia and anti-Semitism in Western Europe. One hundred eighty thousand of them fled to Palestine where this wave of immigration was called the first aliyah. These immigrants set up the new *yishuv* (settlement, derived from the Hebrew verb *l'hityashev*, which means "to settle") in Palestine, which was at that time part of the Ottoman empire. They strove to create a "normal" life for the Jewish people. The old *yishuv*, the Jewish community as it had developed in Palestine from the sixteenth century to the end of the nineteenth century, consisted exclusively of Orthodox communities in Jerusalem, Tiberias, Hebron, and Safed. Its members turned from secular daily life and advocated the study of Torah in yeshivas.

The Orthodox Jews of the old *yishuv* had a great fear of the renewal that was caused by the first aliyah. Orthodox life reached a peak of religious fervor never before experienced by a Jewish community in modern times. Some rabbis turned out to be real zealots, a new phenomenon in the history of modern Judaism. They excluded every form of modernism by pronouncing a curse. This curse might be pronounced against someone who had, for example, suggested setting up a religious agricultural community in order to let Talmud students earn their keep.

Even Eliezer Ben Yehuda (1857–1922), the man who gave the impulse to enrich and renew old Hebrew and who now has a street named after him in every city in Israel, was a threat for these zealots. Ben Yehuda had come from Russia to Palestine in 1881 and regretted "not having been born in Jerusalem and not even in the land of Israel." He lived in Jerusalem, wore traditional clothing, and conformed to traditional Jewish life. The fact that he was nevertheless condemned as a heretic is characteristic of the contrasts that existed and the tensions these produced. In 1886 he was banished from the Jewish community, and in 1893 he was imprisoned for a year because as chairman of the Organization for the Revival of Israel he had wanted to teach trades to yeshiva students.

In addition Ben Yehuda, whose original name was Eliezer Perlman and who was the first Jew in Palestine to Hebraize his name, touched a sore spot with his initiative to infuse new life into Hebrew.

He spoke only Hebrew with his son Itamar, who grew up in isolation because of this. At the time this "language of the Zionists" was spoken by very few. Yiddish and Arabic were spoken in the old *yishuv*, yet speaking Hebrew was forbidden. The official argument was that Hebrew was a holy language that could not be spoken until the arrival of the Messiah. But in reality the old *yishuv* forbade Hebrew because it was the language of the *maskilim* who had wanted to make Hebrew into a colloquial and scientific language.

Moreover, Ben Yehuda had objections against studying the Torah without also earning a living. This was done in the old *yishuv*, and in the eyes of the Jews from the diaspora this was a new phenomenon: after all, they had always worked in addition to their study. The *halukkah*, the Jewish trusteeship for the poor whose headquarters had been in Amsterdam since 1809, enabled mystics and "scholars" who lived or went to live in Palestine for spiritual reasons to lead an absolutely observant life. It regularly gave money to the Palestinian Ashkenazi community, which provided for the necessities of life but which also paid for the necessities of spiritual life. The *halukkah* was a controversial institution. Heinrich Grätz (1817–1891), who studied the old *yishuv* in 1872, criticized the students who called themselves rabbis "no matter how meager their knowledge of the Talmud" and in this capacity "feel they have the right to large sums of money." He doubted that "these men who all think they are scholars actually are scholars because they do nothing but study the Torah." He observed that "they don't know what to do with all their free time" and that "their laziness and their uselessness aren't very promising for the future." In contrast, the Sephardic Jews who had been living in the area since the seventeenth century had developed their own financial distribution system. But they freed themselves from this quickly because, despite their deep-rooted traditionalism, they didn't at all shun modernization. These Jews sent their children to mixed-sex nonreligious schools founded by Europeans, something that was inconceivable in Ashkenazi circles.

Meanwhile European Jews still wrestled with the question "Should we leave, and where to?" In addition to assimilation, which had largely failed, and—until then—uncoordinated flight, the idea of founding a Jewish state began to take shape at the end of the nineteenth century. The socialist-oriented nationalists wanted to found a "normal Jewish state" and be done with the idea of Jews being the chosen. In other words, they contrasted cosmopolitanism with Jewish particularism. For them secular folkloric *Yiddishkeit* was the principal constituent of Jewish identity. In contrast, the religious Zionists strove for a religious Jewish state in which the "true chosen Jewish soul" would flower in the Messianic era. After all, for the majority of the Orthodox, emigration to Palestine at that time was false messianism, and those Jews who emigrated disqualified themselves as "good Jews." In their eyes, waiting for God's redemption, for the Messiah, was the only solution.

The aspiration to return to the homeland was given shape by (among others) Theodor Herzl (1860–1904), a journalist who was born in Budapest and grew up in Vienna. This man in tails and tie, this "possessed man with his pale face and his full black beard," as he was often described, founded the World Zionist Organization in which, it was hoped, all Jewish nationalist groups would be able to find a place. Herzl, an ambitious man, broke through the Orthodox dogma that the appearance of the Messiah had to precede the resurrection of the Kingdom of Israel. At first Herzl's ideas encountered a lot of resistance. In the eyes of Eastern European Jews, his plan was insufficiently rooted in the traditions of the Jewish people, and some considered his plans "too much of a romantic sport." People looked up to Western European Jews and to Herzl, who talked with kings. In the impoverished East, people would never do such a thing, and in some circles he was therefore regarded as a kind of messiah.

Herzl had come to Zionism from a life that was so completely outside Jewish tradition that he imagined the Jewish state as a reflection of Western society, without a specifically Jewish character. He would have preferred to transfer his nonreligious intellectual milieu to a new Jewish homeland—which at first didn't have to be Palestine. Among other things he suggested going to Argentina, but gradually the goal became a "Vienna in the Middle-East." His only motive for Zionism was wounded pride, because he didn't have a love of Zion as such. He was filled with the ideals of the emancipation period, although the nonexistence of the Jewish people was its core. He didn't have much knowledge of Jewish culture or religious Judaism, and he didn't want Hebrew to become the official language of the Jewish state because he didn't want the Jews to fall back into a ghetto mentality. He couldn't really imagine the pogroms in Poland and Russia because he came from a bourgeois Jewish milieu in which assimilation was the highest good. It took time for Herzl to break away from this assimilationist atmosphere, but he wanted to rescue the Jewish people from their hostile environment. In the end the Dreyfuss affair opened his eyes. This scandal caused him to feel Jewish once again. His efforts to emancipate, to modernize, and to assimilate into German culture had failed, and his disappointment about this showed him the way back to the national Jewish rebirth after the Dreyfuss affair.

Despite their initial aversion to the ideas of nonreligious Herzl, religious Eastern European Jews sought refuge in his Zionism. In 1897 he convened the first World Zionist Congress in Basel, Switzerland, where he decided to "create a national home for the Jewish people." And he added: "As yet we carry a flag without a country, but after us others will carry this flag that will fly over a happy Israel." After several meetings of the World Zionist Organization, where he was confronted by Orthodox Jewish points of view for the first time in his life, Herzl became increasingly convinced that it was impossible to ignore the wishes of the Orthodox any longer. Henceforth when there were differences of opinion, Herzl would choose their side because he wanted to prevent creating a divided and weak Jewish home. Herzl, who later said that he would not "shrink from joining up with beggars and the hungry if the purpose is justice," announced during the Congress in 1898 that with political Zionism he also meant the spiritual renewal of the Jewish people and that he would not make any decisions that were contrary to Jewish beliefs. Within a short time this struggle between secular and Orthodox Jews resulted in the creation of three Jewish political parties that would later play an important role in Israel. Herzl encouraged the formation of these parties, although he hoped for the sake of Jewish unity that these parties would continue to be part of his organization.

The first party, the Democratic party, was founded during the fifth Zionist Congress in 1901 in Basel. Martin Buber (1874–1965), the Galician philosopher, Bible translator, and writer of Hasidic tales, and Chaim Weizmann (1874–1952), the nonreligious liberal bourgeois, regretted Herzl's indifferent cultural interests and his exclusively political Zionism. Especially Buber, who included the Torah in his ideas about the state but was not Orthodox, argued for *"Kulturzionismus,"* for the study of the Hebrew language and literature, the foundation of a Jewish university, and the education of the Jewish people in the spirit of Jewish nationalism. He indicated also that he did not want the Jewish people to "go the way of all other peoples." Buber urged the Jews to work on building a new Jewish culture, first in Germany or in other countries that had become theirs. Even though Buber had for a long time devoted himself to Zionism as the editor of *Die Welt*, the Zionist weekly established by Herzl in 1897, it was logical that Buber stayed in Germany until 1938.

Buber shared Weizmann's view that the future Jewish state should be a collectivist state. Weizmann, the first president of Israel, came from Motol, a small town near Minsk that was part of the so-called pale of settlement, the limited area where Jews were allowed to live in Czarist Russia. Weizmann described this area as "the darkest and most remote corner of the village." He said he found it "difficult" to give Westerners even a "vague idea" of the "horrible life" of the Jews in Motol, about their special trades, their efforts, and their terrible isolation. Although Weizmann was an antisocialist liberal, as a Zionist he nevertheless worked for a socialist state. "You don't have to be crazy to be a Zionist," he wrote, "but it does help." He felt that the Zionists should not "start behaving like Prussian noblemen in the Jewish state," which, according to him, should be as Jewish as Great Britain is British. And above all—and in this he disagreed with Herzl—this new state should not become the umpteenth average nation state.

A year later, in 1902, a group of Eastern European Jews with Torah in hand founded the Zionist party Mizrachi (an acronym of the Hebrew words *Mercaz Ruchani*: spiritual center; in Israel this party would become the National Religious Party). Their traditional way of living, praying, and *lernen* was no longer able to hold its own against the power of Jewish secularization and anti-Semitism. On the day of the party's founding, twenty-four rabbis announced that "they wanted to take the people of Israel and the Torah back to the land of milk and honey." Their longing for Zion was stimulated by the spiritual impoverishment of Judaism in their surroundings and by assimilation. It seemed better to them to serve the interests of religious Judaism through participation in Herzl's organization and thereby prevent the creation of a secular Jewish state. It was irrelevant to them whether Jewish law would offer suitable solutions for problems that occur in modern times.

The modern Jewish *Kulturkampf* (culture war) is among other things rooted in three views about the educational system to be established in the Jewish state. The secular Zionists had secular public education in mind for their children; this education would be directed at the new Jew who would speak Hebrew and who would study his own history and not that of other people. The Bible should be taught as folk literature and as national history, but not as a holy book. In contrast, the Mizrachi felt that the Bible should in the first place be taught as the word of God and as national history. This new second trend, which would later be known in Israel as "religious public education," started from secular nationalist education, but oral Jewish tradition was also part of the school program.

A number of Mizrachi members who were dissatisfied with the education that went "outside the Talmudic paths" organized a third party that was called Agudat Israel (its shortened name is Aguda) that remained under the wings of Herzl's organization. This worldwide pluralistic federation of Orthodox communities would in the future play an important role in Palestine and in Israel. For example, the party introduced independent "emancipated" education that focused exclusively on Jewish religious education. These schools were not subsidized because they did not allow the authorities to influence the curriculum. The schools made great financial sacrifices in order to maintain the long school day and to keep the curriculum as Orthodox as possible. The rivalry among these three views of Jewish education would be a recurring theme in the history of Israel.

Bringing together all these rival Eastern European rabbis was no small task, because Jewish customs differed from country to country. Later in Israel, Aguda would be organized into different communities under the leadership of the Polish rabbi Yitzhak Meir Levin. All these communities undertook to preserve a lost Jewish past. Levin, who would later negotiate with Ben Gurion about the Declaration of Independence and about the role of Judaism in the state of Israel, was born in 1894 in Gora Kalvaria (near Warsaw), called "Gur" by the Jews. His grandfather was the Hasidic rabbi in Gur, an intelligent and energetic rabbi who as a vehement opponent of Zionism founded the Polish branch of the Aguda. In 1940 Meir Levin became the leader of Agudat Israel in Palestine. When the state was founded he was a relative newcomer in the country, and he always spoke poor Hebrew despite being a member of the Knesset and a minister of welfare.

The first meeting of Aguda took place in 1912 in Katowice (Silesia) where three hundred mainly German ultra-Orthodox Jews declared that "the Jewish people is in essence different from all other peoples in the world" and "that it should always let itself be guided by the Torah." Aguda kept up with the events in Palestine, and the discussion about Zionism was part of the struggle for the formation of Jewish identity in the diaspora. For many Aguda members, living in the Holy Land was a divine task and forcing God's hand was in conflict with Jewish tradition; that is why they advised against emigration to Palestine. Many joined Aguda as an answer to their anxiety about the increasing popularity of the secular movement among Jews, including the Zionist movement.

Many rabbis, including the so-called protest rabbis, criticized Herzl who had become poor around 1900 and had a heart condition. Among them was the chief rabbi of France, Zadoc Kahn (1839–1905), a friend of Herzl. With his questions he articulated the problems regarding the relations between Orthodox and secular Jews that present-day Israel still has to contend with. As a proponent of a theocratic constitutional body and an opponent of emigration, Kahn explained to Herzl that Orthodox Judaism and nationalism couldn't coexist: "Our law doesn't belong in a modern state, and in their impossible struggle the religious Zionists are trying to reconcile divine Jewish law and the democratic form of government. Where is freedom of speech when the Jewish state becomes a theocracy?" he asked. "And how Jewish can a Jewish state be? Jews always try to reconcile opposite tendencies, but a Jewish state cannot be secular and religious at the same time. We Jews always try to maintain our own culture—Judaism—but we also want to be like the majority, that is to say like other modern states, by founding a democracy. But only a state rooted in religious Judaism can be Jewish."

Notwithstanding the criticism of the protest rabbis, democrats, socialists, liberals, and the Orthodox, Herzl won in favor of the Jewish-national rebirth. He let it be known that he wanted to prevent "all theocratic tendencies of rabbis" and to "limit their influence to the synagogue" in the future state. Herzl died in 1904 of his heart condition. He had become tired from running—until then mostly in vain—to presidents, kings, and diplomats to win them over to his cause with his refined Viennese manners. He was especially disillusioned after a visit to arid Palestine. Nor was he able to find rest at home. After his death his wife sighed: "The Zionists have robbed me of my husband." In his last speech Herzl said: "Although I was originally a *Judenstaatler*, I later took up the banner of Zionism and became *chovev Tsion* (a friend of Zion). Palestine is the only land where our people can settle." The enthusiasm that Herzl aroused in the Jews in the diaspora appeared to be sufficient to accomplish his Zionist revolution in Palestine. Based on the unity in feeling and deed that Herzl had forged, a new style of Jewish living and awareness came about that made it possible for his "pupils" to get to the Balfour Declaration.

Many Eastern European Jews were already in Palestine at that time; they had come with the second aliyah (1904–1914). Together with the third aliyah (1920–1922), the New Yishuv counted a total of 45,000 immigrants in the early 1920s. The 60,000 Orthodox Jews of the Old Yishuv, soon numerically dominated by the newcomers, looked on with sorrow at how the "rebels against God" had signed a declaration, namely the Balfour Declaration, that held out the prospect of submission to a secular regime! And they wondered how an Orthodox Jew would ever be able to live in such a state. And how should the strictly religious Jew interpret this far-reaching diplomatic victory theologically? After all, only through a miracle would it finally be possible to establish the traditional religious "Kingdom of Israel" on earth. How was it possible that these godless people would receive a godless state from God "at the wrong moment," as they called it, while the Orthodox watched? The Jews who believed in Divine Providence were almost obliged to believe that even "this heretic Declaration" was a revelation of God's will.

In the end, largely as a result of the Holocaust, Aguda accepted the state as a provisional social structure that would offer them many practical and material advantages. This meant that from a spiritual viewpoint they lived in *Eretz Yisrael* (the land of Israel), and not in *Medinat Yisrael* (the state of Israel). Living in a Jewish state that was not based on the Torah was unacceptable as long as the Messiah had not yet come. This paradoxical attitude is typical of the position of a large part of the ultra-Orthodox community in Israel today. Mizrachi considered the establishment of the state as the beginning of the Messianic era and decided to fight secularization from within. According to its members, participation in politics was the best way to make the best of a bad situation. Their only concern was to make the character of the state as Jewish as possible by making sure that in the future as many religious laws as possible would be adopted.

The new immigrants of the second and third aliyah had unintentionally encouraged the hostility between the Orthodox and the secular communities in Palestine. These tanned pioneers had high hopes for reconciliation with the pale yeshiva boys and their leaders. But the Orthodox had many objections to these hippies "avant la lettre" who walked around Palestine and worked the land in shorts, rough cotton shirts, and simple or no shoes. In their opinion, a free-and-easy farmer who didn't spend his days bent over holy texts was not a real Jew. A "farming" Jew was less Jewish than a praying Jew. Their customs and ideas were fatal for pure Judaism, and in addition they were laying the foundations for a modern democratic society in which there was no room for Orthodox Jews. Their Zionist ideology was a dangerous alternative to the traditional Jewish identity, among other things because of its emphasis on the importance of the Hebrew language and on settling in Palestine as a value in itself and not as a part of a system of religious obligations. Yet, from that moment on the only mitzvah, the new belief, was tilling the land. The new Jew, the sabra, built cities, encouraged agriculture, opened secular elementary schools and high schools, formed political parties, founded the first kibbutzim, and started the first newspapers. For these sabras God was a literary hero; many of them explained biblical references to the divine as mythology; they ignored kashrut; and the Sabbath was violated on a large scale. The resulting Sabbath war was a big problem during the British Mandate (1918 to 1947); during this period the Chief Rabbinate (1922) and a Parliament (1926), the *Knesset Yisrael*, were created and a Provisional Administration (1928) was formed. During that time, as a reaction to the above-mentioned unconventional behavior of the new immigrants, the Old Yishuv presented itself increasingly as an isolationist, sectarian movement. This caused the differences between the two groups to become ever greater. Finally these differences culminated in the question about the identity of the future Jewish state and the identity of the new Jew—a question that became unavoidable in specifically Jewish surroundings for the first time since the Jewish Enlightenment.

The questions confronting the Jewish inhabitants of Palestine were not new, but now they needed an urgent answer. What should the new Jewish society look like? "Normal" as Herzl wished, "theocratic-socialist" as Buber wished, or "secular-socialist" as Weizmann championed? Or should the Jewish home "safeguard the continuity of Jewish history and nationalize religious rites and symbols" and also be "the moral example for all of humanity and . . . 'a light unto the nations'" as Ben Gurion wished?

Ben Gurion (1886–1973), pioneer and adventurer par excellence, walked from Tel Aviv to Beersheba in Palestine and later in Israel. In 1906 he gave up his studies and came with his rucksack as a twenty-year-old from Plonsk (a small town northwest of Warsaw) to Palestine. As a young man in Plonsk, Ben Gurion had already led a division of the socialist-Zionist movement (*Po'alei Tsion*), and in Palestine he worked for a Jewish organization free from revolutionary Russian influences. This practical man, who said he wanted to make the desert bloom (and for that reason settled there later on), made a "civil religion" out of Judaism by nationalizing and secularizing the holidays and even of the Jews being the chosen people. He observed Jewish commemorations and fostered historic places and nationalistic ceremonies. He believed in Jewish moral and intellectual superiority and said that he based his convictions on his knowledge of the Jewish people and not on a mystic belief. Later, his pronouncement "*Lo chashuv ma yagidu ha goyim, ela ma ya'asu ha'yehudim*" (it doesn't matter what the goyim say, but what the Jews do) would be quoted frequently. He had great interest in the Jewish religion, but also said that "the glory of God's presence in the Jewish people is in their hearts." This individualistic view of the meaning of religion was at odds with that of the Orthodox Jews who during that period consolidated their position by the above-mentioned creation of the Chief Rabbinate.

In this conflict of interests an influential role was played on the secular side by Histadrut, the trade union established by Ben Gurion in 1921 that continued to have an important influence on the economy of the country until the last decade of the twentieth century. Meanwhile, Ben Gurion studied law in Constantinople (1911–1914), and upon his return to Palestine in 1914 he was arrested by the Turkish government and exiled to the United States where he founded the pioneer organization Hechalutz (the pioneer) and returned to Palestine in 1918. Partly because of these experiences he became a great champion of organizing workers. It is therefore not surprising that he had an important voice in the Histadrut, which played an important role in the formation of the state of Israel and was controlled by the pioneer party Mapai (abbreviation of *Mifleget Po'alei Eretz Yisrael*; literally, "Workers' Party of Palestine," which became "Workers' Party" in 1968). In 1930 Ben Gurion founded Mapai as the successor of the socialist party Mapam (abbreviation of *Mifleget haPo'alim haMe'uchedet*; literally, "United Workers Party"). Under Ben Gurion's inspiring leadership (he was secretary as well as party leader of Mapai), Histadrut and Mapai developed into influential organizations that set the tone for the future political barter and created a political atmosphere that tended toward the Machiavellian principle of the end justifying the means.

Ben Gurion determined the economic and political policies of the Histadrut, and meanwhile he used his position in the World Zionist Organization to attain his goal (he was a member of its executive body since 1933 and in 1935 he became chairman of the Jerusalem division). First he made Histadrut into a kind of state, led by union leaders who were chosen in democratic elections. Through political haggling Mapai had become the most powerful political party in the Zionist World Organization. Ben Gurion offered the members of Mizrachi material advantages in exchange for political support. In this way he laid the foundation for the coalition of Mapai and Mizrachi that would continue for many years in Israel between the successors of both parties, the Labor Party and the National Religious Party. He was able to hold on to the religious Zionists of Mizrachi by the cheap health care of the Histadrut, and about 80 percent of the population profited from this. Later he had other means, but at the time he offered some Histadrut members, who were still bivouacked in tents like many other pioneers, parcels of land for permanent settlement that were bought by the Zionist World Organization, as well as money to maintain these settlements.

In this way Ben Gurion developed gradually into the leader of Zionism in Palestine at the expense of Weizmann, who resumed his scientific work in London from 1931 to 1935. Ben Gurion considered Weizmann's conciliatory attitude to the Palestinian Arab population that resisted the settlement of the Jews in Palestine a danger for the Zionist movement. During the early forties he called on the Jewish community to resist England and in 1942, during an "emergency conference" that he had convened in New York, he decided on the establishment of a Jewish Commonwealth in Palestine after the war. To the satisfaction of many Jews, Ben Gurion was successful in giving leadership to the Jewish community in the struggle against the British Mandate. In 1946 he formally took over the position as leader of the Zionists.

Meanwhile, the Chief Rabbinate was established in 1922. During his visits to Palestine in 1918 and 1921 Weizmann had in vain called for the establishment of a central rabbinic authority. London had imposed several limitations on the administration of the mandate: it involved the way marriages and divorces were performed and the control of the organization of religious bodies. For this reason, the administration of the British Mandate kept the Turkish system that gave religious and cultural autonomy to every community. However, the problem with this was that the *chacham* (wise man) appointed by the Turkish sultan was recognized only by the Sephardic Jews. Therefore the Ashkenazi Jews had no central religious authority and their religious courts had no official status. A commission set up by the mandate administration found a solution for this problem: the election of a Sephardic and an Ashkenazi rabbi who, together with some assistants, would constitute the Chief Rabbinate. In this way Orthodox Judaism became the established religion for the Jews in Palestine.

The first Ashkenazi Chief Rabbi, Abraham Kook, was an extraordinarily original religious thinker and one of the most important rabbis in Jewish history, as well as the most important authority of the religious Zionists. Abraham Kook (Lithuania 1859–Palestine 1935) permitted cooperation with non-Orthodox and even with antireligious Jews for the sake of the new Jewish state in *Eretz Yisrael.*

Kook came to Palestine in 1904, became rabbi of Jaffa, and in 1922 accepted the function of first chief rabbi of Palestine. According to him, the spirit of the nonreligious pioneers was "healthier" than that of the Orthodox who, according to him, did not yet realize that the era of redemption had begun. He embraced the pioneers, not because he saw them as heralds of a new Jewish spirituality but because they were busy reclaiming the land for the Jewish people. The Holy Land could temporarily play the role of a modern secular society, but Kook didn't believe that such a Jewish state would be of an enduring nature. The holiness of the land would ultimately get the upper hand. That is why in Kook's view the Zionists, who revived the language and tilled the land as part of the rebirth of Jewish life, were, without knowing it, the players in a performance directed by God.

The United Nations proposal in 1947 to divide the British Mandate territory into a Jewish and an Arab state presented new theological worries to the Orthodox. Could such a "physical redemption" take place at a moment other than the "spiritual redemption"? Rabbi Levin, who held the point of view that these two were inextricably bound, negotiated with Ben Gurion as the representative of Aguda about the position and the role of the Orthodox community in the future state. At the very last moment, when Ben Gurion had already put together a Provisional Government, Levin threatened to frustrate Ben Gurion's Zionist ideal to found a Jewish state. In 1947 Levin intended to present himself to the United Nations independent from Ben Gurion's Provisional Government because his religious belief didn't permit him to accept a secular state. After many nighttime discussions with Ben Gurion, Levin reached agreement with him and with the thirteen secular members of the Provisional Government.

Because Levin kept expressing his uncertainty about the feasibility for him and for other Orthodox Jews to continue leading their religious lives, Ben Gurion—many of whose letters have been preserved—assured him in writing. Ben Gurion wrote, "In my view, despite all differences of opinion about spiritual matters, and these are not to be neglected, there is one subject about which there cannot be any difference of opinion: any form of anti-religious tyranny is unthinkable, as is religious tyranny." Earlier he informed Levin that the latter had no reason to complain because this Provisional Government had done more to give the population and the army a Jewish character than all the religious organizations in the world: "This government is not trying to make a theocracy of the state of Israel," wrote Ben Gurion, "but this government in which you participate declares that there will not be any anti-religious tyranny. I cannot imagine any other government that has more understanding of your religious feelings and those of others and is as devoted to the values of Judaism as this government." The Orthodox ministers seemed to agree with Ben Gurion: "Our life styles differ in many small and large matters, but ultimately all these matters constitute a binding factor that leads us along the same road. No doubt one of them is as objective an evaluation as possible of all these explosively controversial subjects."

Tom Segev, a historian and journalist, describes this episode in the history of Israel in his book *1949, the First Israelis*. He writes that Levin spoke about "sober and inspired thinking" that was motivated by the "genuine fear" that a cultural conflict would explode that would split the Jewish people into two peoples and would cause such a deep chasm that it would never again be bridged. As a result of this thinking, which resulted from fear on the part of both sides, the Orthodox and the secularists could finally agree and were able to sign the Declaration of Independence. During the negotiations about the Declaration of Independence, Mizrachi, which still had problems seeing the creation of the Jewish state as separate from the Messiah, said that the word "the King of Israel" or the name of God had to be included in the document. Although Ben Gurion was aware of this issue, he could agree to Mizrachi's demand only with the consent of the nonreligious in the Provisional Government. Obviously this demand encountered great opposition from Mapam, the party that demanded that the declaration be signed on the Sabbath—during the night from Friday to Saturday around midnight, at the exact moment when the British Mandate would end. This demand, considered as confrontational by many, was ignored by a number of members of the Provisional Government. But everyone realized that a Declaration of Independence in which the Almighty was not mentioned would have little chance of succeeding, which is why there was a rush to search for a compromise. Ultimately, on behalf of Agudat Israel, Levin also proclaimed the state of Israel on May 14, 1948, with the words: "With faith in the Rock of Israel we sign this declaration." The expression "Rock of Israel" (*Tsur Yisrael*: a biblical phrase that in general referred to God) served to replace the word *God* and was approved by both Orthodox and nonreligious Jews. Ben Gurion agreed with the compromise, which he described as a "good pact of Jewish solidarity." He once wrote that "the Rock of Israel" is in the state of Israel and in the "Book of Books." Ben Gurion found his roots in the Bible and linked the national state of Israel to the biblical Hebrews. He said that he would later "have no trouble explaining to his children who are not religious why he approved this sentence without qualms." During the ceremony he let Rabbi I. L. Maimon of Mizrachi say the traditional Jewish prayer of thanks, but he listened to the prayer with uncovered head.

Ben Gurion was not a religious man. Like many others he had maintained the *Yiddishkeit* of his youth. He was disgusted by the mitzvot and by Jewish life in the diaspora, but for him the Bible was a moral standard and in this respect Israel was to be an example for other nations. His habit of politicizing the Bible for contemporary purposes would later infuriate the Orthodox, but he enjoyed arguing with them. He slighted the importance of the postbiblical Mishnah and the Talmud: "I don't have a high regard for the Talmud—these writings cannot be compared to the *Tanakh*." When asked during one of these discussions, he acknowledged that he didn't believe that God ever spoke with Moses: "I think that Moses heard a human voice in his heart. Most Jews see God as someone with a long beard on a heavenly throne." Despite his unbelief in God, he—like many of his contemporaries—had a Polish Jewishness that he couldn't shake.

Soon after signing the Declaration of Independence, Ben Gurion granted the religious community of Israel a number of privileges that together have come to be called the Status Quo. Ben Gurion entered into these agreements with Levin because he wanted to make the life of Orthodox Jews bearable in the liberal democracy that the pioneers strove for. Among the privileges (which will be discussed in detail later in this chapter) were the following: in public places the rules of kashrut would be observed; the Sabbath would be a day of rest; and the Orthodox who wanted to consecrate their lives to studying God's word would be exempted from military service. In these matters Ben Gurion was governed by political pragmatism and a feeling of national responsibility, but not by Jewish sentiments. According to a religious Knesset member at the time, Ben Gurion understood that the Orthodox would leave the country if he did not give in to their wishes. Ben Gurion understood that the need for religious education and religious organizations were national needs, and he insisted that these services be financed by the state. Ben Gurion reasoned that once the state had taken the responsibility upon itself to finance religion, the state would also be the source of authority. He once said: "I want to keep religion in the palm of my hand." Yeshayahu Leibowitz (Riga 1903–Jerusalem 1994), the controversial intellectual to whom Ben Gurion made this remark, considered this a misuse of religion for the sake of personal power and political interests. But Ben Gurion believed that the share of national responsibility that he gave to the Orthodox would prevent them from rebelling. Moreover, and this was no less important, he thought that he had lessened the tensions between Orthodox and secularists with the Status Quo. Fear for the consequences of these increasing tensions kept him from separating state and religion at that moment.

Ben Gurion suggested at the time that a compromise between the Orthodox and the secularists was impossible. He wrote: "The very existence of a religious party indicates, intentionally or unintentionally, a desire to impose rabbinic laws and traditions on the country. The religious parties which demand freedom of religion for themselves are unwilling and unable to offer the same to the other parties and to those who don't think like them." Not everyone understood this statement at the time. Years later Zerah Wahrhaftig (1906, Krakow), a member of Mizrachi and the first minister of religious affairs of the state of Israel, said that Ben Gurion "hated religion" but he praised Ben Gurion for his understanding of "religious psychology": "He reproached us that we weren't willing to make concessions, but he understood that we couldn't make concessions." Still, Ben Gurion realized that the Orthodox would be able to do this under certain circumstances, and that is why he thought he would be able to solve the religious problem later: "At this moment there is no need to search for a solution to the religious problems about which we will be divided in the future." He thought that a discussion about the place of religion in the state was "idiotic" and according to him it would cause a national explosion. Moreover he thought that Orthodox Judaism would die out after the Holocaust.

The Status Quo was in general meant to offer a guarantee of a balance between secular and religious Jews in the new state and to prevent excesses in the future. Nevertheless, this agreement could not prevent tension between Orthodox and secular Jews in the young state. Not more than a year after the signing of the Declaration of Independence, the secularists and the Orthodox in Jerusalem came to blows on Saturdays, just like during the British Mandate. The Orthodox demonstrated and shouted "Sabbath!" and recited prayers aloud in front of movie theaters where the first show started forty-five minutes before the end of the Sabbath. There were efforts

at reconciliation that consisted of asking the owners of the movie
theaters to sell tickets the day before and to let the movies start later,
but these efforts failed. The government decided to investigate the
movie riots during which the police were sometimes unable to control the demonstrators, stones were thrown, and people were
wounded. But the investigation came to nothing.

In addition to the movie riots, there were in 1949 also demonstrations by the Orthodox against the road to the Mandelbaum Gate
(the passage between the Israeli and Jordanian halves of Jerusalem)
that ran straight through the ultra-Orthodox district of Mea
Shearim. Many drivers who used the road disrupted the quiet Saturday of the Orthodox. The latter started demonstrations not only
on behalf of their own community but also on behalf of Judaism in
general. They felt that the desecration of the Sabbath in public was
more serious than desecration in private. A prominent rabbi and
Knesset member characterized it as follows: "He who desecrates the
Sabbath in public uses a sword to stab through the heart of the religious Jew."

The observance of the Sabbath was, and in religious circles in
Israel still is, a holy command: "But if ye will not hearken unto Me
to hallow the Sabbath day . . . then will I kindle a fire. . . ." (Jer.
17:27). In Orthodox views, neglecting to observe the Sabbath can
have disastrous consequences. Even in the young state, the struggle
about the Sabbath rest became a religious struggle that was sometimes fought until blood flowed. (In 1954 there were ten Sabbath
demonstrations, and in 1965, nineteen—with one death.) During
debates in the Knesset, Levin tried to foster understanding for the
Orthodox: "Why don't you understand our fear? Isn't it under-
standable that someone who has for thousands of years learned
from the prophets to observe the Sabbath cannot do anything but
shout 'Sabbath' from the bottom of his heart whenever he sees that
this day is being violated on a large scale by Jews. Don't you understand that for us the Sabbath means the existence of the Jewish
people and that the violation of this day means the end of the state
and the ruin of the nation? For us this discussion is a matter of life
and death."

From the Orthodox point of view, the problem was that the state
of Israel permitted its citizens to violate the Sabbath rest in public as
well as in private. After all, the state itself violated this rest by

allowing electric power stations and industry to keep running, to let radio broadcasts take place, operate telephone services, expand diplomatic activities, and to let the police and the army take action if necessary. The Orthodoxy resisted all this but realized that Israel would never become a theocratic state. Still, in the course of time some adjustments were made so that the Orthodox would feel more comfortable in the modern secular state. Synagogues were opened on army bases, and some technical innovations made modern life possible without violating religious laws. But the greatest problem remained unsolved: the Orthodox Jews did not produce a significant reformer, and the religious laws were not adapted to the state. Some, like the modern Orthodox, learned to compromise with reality without scruples, but the strict believers, the most exacting of whom belong to "Neturei Karta" ("city guards," in Aramaic), continued to resist the Zionist movement. They were convinced that they were not allowed to violate the three agreements that, according to legend, the Almighty had made with them: not to revolt against the nonbelievers among whom they lived, not to try to conquer the Holy Land with force, and not to try to hasten the coming of the end of time.

The tension between the Orthodox and the secularists continued to increase. Most Israelis saw themselves as Jews, but the definition of Jewish identity was unclear. The following anecdote can perhaps shed light on this situation: One Saturday at the end of the 1920s, three men were sitting and talking on a bench on Allenby Street while smoking a cigarette. This was a violation of religious law. An Orthodox Jew passed and reproached them for violating the law. Two of the three men put out their cigarettes while the third answered. "I'm not a Jew." His name was Uriel Halperin, the man who would later become known in Israel as the Canaanite poet Yonathan Ratish, a man with an adamantly antireligious attitude. Later Halperin said that perhaps he himself didn't know what his remark meant, but the Orthodox man didn't know it at all. "I knew only that I wasn't religious at all. I didn't have any respect for religion."

In the fifties Halperin was the leader of the Canaanite movement, which made a distinction between the Jewish community and the Hebrew nation. The Canaanites saw themselves as Hebrews and not as Jews and fought harder against Zionism than against Judaism. As Jews they wanted to integrate with the other Semites in the Middle East. They were convinced that the Jewish problem, as they called the fighting of Jews among themselves, would ultimately resolve itself. Halperin asserted that it was but a question of time before the Jews with side curls and long black coats would disappear from the world; after all, every community in the world had a backward group in its midst. He brushed aside the influence of the ultra-Orthodox and was convinced that this group would disappear of its own accord. He said that he would resist them only if they "try to impose their way of life on us."

Another public figure who was known at that time for his strong antireligious attitude was Knesset member Eri Jabotinsky, the son of Ze'ev Jabotinsky. One day he insisted on being served a ham and cheese sandwich in the Knesset. Yet his attitude toward Judaism was ambiguous and might even be called typical for that time. According to him, the task of Judaism was not to adapt the institutions of the state of Israel to Judaism but to spread the ideals of Judaism and Jewish morality throughout the world.

At that time it was clearer in Israel than it is now that many Israelis were not able to break away from religion. Many Jews who were building the state had grown up near a mother or grandmother who lit candles on Friday night at the start of the Sabbath and a father or grandfather who regularly went to the synagogue. At least such an experience produced a positive attitude toward Judaism. It was this attitude that made the coexistence of the Orthodox and the secularists more or less possible during the early years of the state. Although only 16 of the 120 Knesset members were religious in 1949, the majority of the representatives of the secular parties had religious grandparents and had themselves had a religious education. To be sure, many of them rebelled against their past and called themselves atheists, but they had a "Jewish *neshomme* [soul]" and cherished their upbringing.

Meanwhile, as was mentioned earlier, there were large-scale violations of the Sabbath rest. Local rabbis, religious councils, and the representatives of religious parties in city councils joined forces to prevent this violation. Since the thirties this struggle had been a regular activity that was led by the Public Council for the Sabbath, which was linked to the Department of Religious Affairs. This council concentrated its activities primarily in non-Orthodox districts and cities and had as its purpose to strengthen the religious character of life in the state. Most members of the Council were members of Mizrachi. The council tried not to enforce the observance of the Sabbath in private situations, but where there were no city laws to guarantee Sabbath rest, the members tried everything possible—not always successfully—to pass such laws. In some cities the council suggested appointing yeshiva students as "Sabbath overseers." The council acted only on the local level and used personal contacts. In one year the council reported that it had prevented three hundred violations of the Sabbath, an average of six per week. A quarter of the cases concerned public transportation—trains, buses, and aviation. In 1952 the Council reported: "When it became clear that El Al did not adhere to the agreement not to fly on the Sabbath, the Council protested to the Department of Religious Affairs and demanded that all flights be stopped on the Sabbath." The department answered that from then on El Al would fly on the Sabbath only if it were unavoidable. The council was concerned with many cases that involved movie houses, theaters, and other places of entertainment that opened their doors to the public on Friday evening. In addition the council dealt with industries that worked on Saturdays, street merchants, stores, and restaurants. Mayors who were not dependent on coalitions with religious parties tried to ignore the activities of the council and made no effort to enforce the Sabbath laws.

In 1949 the "Sabbath League"—among its members were the two chief rabbis of Israel at the time—drafted a Sabbath law and tried to get it passed (unsuccessfully) as bylaw in Jerusalem. The law contained a list of actions that could be carried out only with the permission of a "Sabbath Commission" that was to be created. Anyone who violated the Sabbath could expect a fine, three months of prison, or both. The forbidden actions included all forms of labor, turning lights on or off, smoking, making noise with machines, musical instruments and other instruments, professional meetings, exhibitions, and sports activities.

In the fifties and sixties, many who had renounced their faith in the twenties and thirties and seemed to have chosen secular life felt the need to express their connection with Judaism once again. Many kibbutzim and other villages and cities lost their secular character and started to introduce Judaism into everyday life. As a reaction, the Association to Prevent Religious Tyranny was established in Jerusalem in 1951. The association declared that it wanted to put its energy primarily into fighting religious legislation by the Knesset. The activists published ads in the newspapers, distributed pamphlets, organized meetings, and tried to influence politicians. Their influence remained extremely limited, and eventually they disappeared from the stage. They came to the conclusion that they were too late; after all, the decision not to separate religion and state had been made long ago. Moreover, the quantity of religious rituals and traditions that Judaism prescribed for the individual and for the community meant that the separation between religion and state could be made only if the secular population would rise against the Orthodox and minimize their influence; most Israelis didn't want to go that far.

At that time the great difference—still obvious to the attentive observer in Israel—between the secular and the Orthodox camps manifested itself: the Orthodox were (and are) prepared to fight for their way of life while the secularists took (and take) little notice that they couldn't go to the movies on Friday evening (this is possible today). Most Israelis attended soccer matches in droves on Saturdays, but they didn't demonstrate against the ban on showing movies on Friday evenings. Many secularists were not yet able to separate their Jewish identity from religious Judaism. They still felt connected to their Jewish heritage and preserved a number of rituals and laws. (These observations still apply to the present situation in Israel, although the displeasure of the secularists as regards the terror—as they express it—of the religious way of life has increased.)

As was mentioned before, it may have been this very respect for the religious education of their parents and grandparents—that many of them had enjoyed themselves—that made the close coexistence of the Orthodox and the secularist possible at that time. The above-mentioned mother or grandmother who lights candles and the father or grandfather who goes to the synagogue became increasingly rare in Israel as the years passed. This decreased the mutual understanding between the Orthodox and the secularists and the willingness to reach a compromise. A total lack of understanding and even hate was evident during the scuffles between the Orthodox and the secularists that took place in Jerusalem during the opening on Saturday of a supermarket in February 1999. The *haredi* Jerusalem weekly *Yom Hashishi* called this supermarket a "time bomb." In the past years approximately a hundred bars, restaurants, cafés, and newspaper stands have opened their doors on that day. Yet the Orthodox aren't giving up the struggle for the Sabbath: a supermarket owner was informed by telephone that the threat of a second "Bar Ilan Street situation" was occurring in the street where his supermarket was located. The controversy over Bar Ilan Street in Jerusalem (whether this street should be closed on the Sabbath) symbolized for the Orthodox the increasing influence of the secularists, and for the secularists just the opposite, the increasing influence of the Orthodox. After disturbances had taken place on this street for several Saturdays in a row, the Court decided in May 1997, as a compromise, to close the street only during the hours of prayer.

How did it get to the point that the Orthodox and the secularists stand facing each other in a struggle that has come to be called the *Kulturkampf* (culture war) in Israel? What has happened to the pioneers' striving for freedom and democracy since the signing of the Declaration of Independence in 1948? And how was it possible for things to come to the point that the religious factions in Israel are endangering the democracy?

First of all, the answers to these questions must in part be found in 1977, the year that Menachem Begin of Likud came to power and with him the *haredi* parties. Part of the answer must be sought in the consolidation of power of the Sephardic Jews, who always felt close to Herut (Herut was the party of Menachem Begin, founded in 1948, and in 1977 together with a number of small parties it formed Likud under Begin's leadership). But in 1984 the Sephardic Jews established their own party—a development that will be treated in detail in this and the following chapter.

The answers to the above-mentioned questions must be sought in the previously mentioned agreement that Ben Gurion entered into in 1948 with the Orthodox part of the population.

With this he made the biggest mistake in Jewish history, at least according to many secular Israelis. Without being aware of it, he enabled the Orthodox to build up a religious empire in exchange for their political support. For that matter, he assumed that Orthodoxy would disappear before long, or at any rate that the number of its adherents would diminish. Therefore he had no difficulty in giving privileges to the ultra-Orthodox community to involve it in the otherwise secular Jewish state. He decided that the Sabbath would by law be the day of rest for the Jewish citizens of the new state, that all public institutions should observe the rules of kashrut, that the laws pertaining to the civil registry would be regulated according to the halakhah, that the Orthodox would be exempted from military service, and finally that the Orthodox and the ultra-Orthodox would have a separate school system. This agreement, known as the Status Quo, turned out to be a time bomb under the foundations of the state and has meanwhile become the greatest source of irritation of the secular community of Israel. It is true that Ben Gurion safeguarded the Jewish character of Israel, but over the years this Status Quo, which turned out to be a sop, was undermined; nevertheless, the ultra-Orthodox insist that its content be maintained.

The question is whether Ben Gurion could have done or would have wanted to do anything differently after the Holocaust. Was he guided by his respect for the Torah and for his observant fellow Jews? Or was it naïveté that caused him to be unaware of the consequences of this agreement? When he was much older, when his speeches were less flamboyant, Ben Gurion would say during radio interviews, "I didn't dance in 1948." By this statement he meant that on the day of the proclamation of statehood, when crowds of people were dancing in the streets, he had a heavy heart because he supposedly was aware of the internal and external dangers that were lurking.

The second error that Ben Gurion made, according to many leftist Israelis, was to postpone indefinitely drafting the constitution that was mentioned in the Declaration of Independence. A democratic constitution was mentioned in the official Partition Plan of Palestine (UN resolution 181), and on June 13, 1950, the Knesset was getting ready to draft it. But Ben Gurion felt that "at this time" it would be impossible to reach a consensus about the spiritual character of the state because the "controversy about the constitution would almost certainly turn into a *Kulturkampf* [culture war]." After all, for the Orthodox the Torah was the law, and Ben Gurion felt that a worldly constitution would only increase the animosity between the secularists and the Orthodox because a constitution would hinder the implementation of the halakhah. Maintaining the unity of the Jewish people was essential for him and for most Israelis. Moreover—and this was an argument to which Ben Gurion attached much importance—only a small fraction of Jews had settled in Israel. According to him, future immigrants should also be able to identify with a yet-to-be drafted constitution.

The discussion about the constitution was one of the most important debates for the future of the state and also in the parliamentary history of Israel. During the debates in which the Orthodox were entirely at odds with the secularists, Ben Gurion wanted to know from the Orthodox exactly what their objections were. The Orthodox believed that the only way to ensure the survival of the state was to uphold God's law, the halakhah, whereas a constitution was drawn up by human beings. But Ben Gurion then asked, "Isn't the whole state of Israel a human creation?" He also wanted to know if the Orthodoxy respected the principle of sovereignty of a people. From these debates it generally turned out that life in the state of Israel had brought to the surface the ambivalence of the Orthodox with respect to life in a secular but still Jewish country. On the one hand the Orthodox embraced the state that would give shelter to the survivors of the Holocaust, but on the other hand they realized that the return of Israel to the Holy Land would not mean the coming of the Kingdom of Heaven. After all, the majority of the Jews in Israel had lost touch with Jewish law.

It is worth mentioning the part played in this discussion by Zerah Wahrhaftig, a Mizrachi member and chairman of the Commission for the Constitution. In May of 1948 he opened the debate in the Knesset with religious arguments that don't surprise anyone in Israel today. Defending Mizrachi's anticonstitutional point of view, Wahrhaftig stated, "A constitution isn't *formed* but is *given* by the Almighty." Instead of the constitution, he proposed drafting a set of Basic Laws. According to him, the Torah had been given to the Jewish people "chapter by chapter," and it took forty years for the Jewish people to receive the whole Torah—therefore they should now be patient. Rabbi Meir David Levinstein, Wahrhaftig's Aguda colleague, agreed with him in the discussion. He thought that a constitution would lead to an "unsolvable fight, a *Kulturkampf* [culture war], a struggle without compromise because religion knows no compromise." Another Aguda colleague, Rabbi Yitzhak Meir Levin, reminded the audience that "the Torah should not be adapted to life, but that life should be adapted to the Torah." Levin said that he would not tolerate a constitution that was imposed from the secular side: "For centuries life was made bitter for the Jews in exile. Do nonreligious Knesset members think that they can achieve with the power of government what our enemies could not do with blood and fire?"

This is how the decision was made to indefinitely postpone drafting a constitution. For the religious Zionists of the National Religious Party this was a victory. In the coalition with Mapai (and later with the Labor Party) whose attitude toward the Orthodox was sympathetic, socioeconomic issues were of minor importance. Although the coalition was never an easy one, it lasted for almost thirty years. From the beginning, the National Religious Party always got two ministerial posts, and from 1959 on the party always occupied three: Ministry of Religious Affairs, Ministry of the Interior, and Ministry of Social Services. The coalition managed to last this long because the preservation of Jewish unity was more important than anything for Mapai, and that is why Ben Gurion did not dismantle the Status Quo; it was even expanded during his time. At the time the religious Zionists were focused exclusively on attaining their religious goals, and for the National Religious Party every concession made by Mapai was a "permanent gain" that became part of the Status Quo. During the course of the years, thanks to the sympathetic attitude of Mapai, the National Religious Party was able to extend the Status Quo and to prevent acceptance of a constitution.

This meant that Ben Gurion actually chose a "constitution in installments," that is to say, the Knesset would gradually accept a number of Basic Laws that would, according to him, "one day" result in a constitution. During the course of the years, eleven Basic Laws have been passed that form the foundation of the Israeli state; all of these laws have been amended several times. However, Ben Gurion's "day" when these laws will actually be transformed into a full-fledged constitution is still awaited. (During the debates of each new Knesset session the coming of this day is always mentioned, but usually the Knesset members stay away from drafting new Basic Laws because of the sensitivity of the subject.)

The controversial Orthodox intellectual Yeshayahu Leibowitz was the greatest proponent of constitutional democracy—and therefore of the separation of religion and state—that Israel has ever known. He was born in Riga and had training in Switzerland and Germany from where he fled to Palestine in 1935. He taught chemistry, physics, philosophy of history, and history at the Hebrew University in Jerusalem and has many books and articles to his name. He has four doctorates. Many coreligionists condemned him as an anti-Zionist because he criticized the occupation in 1967 and because he disapproved of the veneration of the Wailing Wall by Orthodox nationalistic Israelis. He called the Wailing Wall the "discotheque of the believers" otherwise known as the "diskotel" (*kotel* is Hebrew for "Wailing Wall"), and he called *Shalom Achshav* (the "Peace Now" movement) a "pacifier." For many Israelis it was a thorn in their side when in 1992 he was awarded the most prestigious award in Israel, the "Israel Prize," which he declined to accept because Prime Minister Yitzhak Shamir had said that he found Leibowitz disgusting.

Leibowitz, one of the few Orthodox Jews who combined his faith with intellectual liberalism, thought that separation of religion and state was needed to keep Judaism pure. In his book *The Torah and Religious Laws in Our Time*, published in the fifties, he had already started the debate: "Separation is necessary to prevent the use of Judaism as an extension of the government in order to obtain power. Religion as the instrument of a secular authority is the opposite of true belief." Forcing nonbelievers to live according to Jewish laws was, according to Leibowitz, a greater threat to the continued existence of pure Judaism than the separation of religion and politics. Moreover there was no greater incoherence imaginable than a religious political party that demanded a state set up according to the Torah without having a concrete plan for the organization of this state. As an example he mentioned the exemption from military service that the Orthodox demanded or could demand only because they knew that there were sufficient secular Jews to defend the country. In the same way the religious could expect religious farmers to let their lands lay fallow only because they knew that the whole agrarian sector would not observe the Sabbath year.

Leibowitz felt that Israel was not a Jewish state but a state for Jews who were tired of life among the goyim. He stated that it was "superfluous" to link Israel to the Jewish (halakhic) tradition: "Israel is based on nonreligious foundations: the identity card and the passport, the military service of our children, the civil and criminal laws—all these are recognized by the religious community in Israel. The Torah and the mitzvot separate us Orthodox from the secularists. But for the safety of the country it is of no importance whether the commander-in-chief of the army keeps the mitzvot and puts on his tefillin in the morning. Judaism has fallen into a crisis that can be overcome only by someone who doesn't see religion as a collective national political demonstration." For Leibowitz the essence of Judaism was the observance of the commandments: "But that's a personal obligation that I have to God, and the state has nothing to do with it."

In 1992, two years before his death, his book *Judaism, Human Values and the Jewish State* was published. In this book Leibowitz declared himself once again in favor of a constitution that had to hold together a pluralistic society. He also declared that Jewish identity must come from society and that the state should not impose it. Leibowitz was repeatedly called the "conscience of Israel" by the secularists and was at the same time vilified by the orthodox authorities. In the 1930s when he was still a Mizrachi, he had pointed out that the halakhah would be unsuitable as the basis for Jewish life in Israel. He declared "after all the halakhah originated in the Diaspora where Jews are dependent on non-Jews for services rendered." He felt that the religious authorities who kept striving for a Jewish state based on halakhah and therefore didn't accept the separation of religion and state were "parasites."

The answers to the above questions about the origins of the culture war can also be found—as has already been stated—in the developments that took place in 1977. In that year the National Religious Party left the government before the elections, and this brought an end to the traditional coalition between it and the Labor Party. The reason for this break was the arrival of a number of airplanes on Friday evening as the Sabbath was starting. With an eye on the coming elections, Likud formed an electoral alliance under its own name with a number of smaller parties. This alliance was led by Menachem Begin (Brest-Litovsk 1913–Israel 1992) who won the elections.

With Begin's taking office, the ultra-Orthodox won an accepted place in Israeli society. As a neglected community, the Sephardic Jews felt a special affinity with Begin's party, which was still talking about the necessity of solving socioeconomic problems of the Oriental Jews. While in the opposition, Likud remained populist and sensitive to the religious and traditional Jewish mentality. This Likud rhetoric was short-lived and in the eighties was taken over by Shas (the Sephardic Guardians of the Torah), a new ultra-Orthodox Sephardic political party.

The formation of Shas in 1984 and the swift growth of this party, whose supporters are sometimes called modern Israeli ultra-

Orthodox, have drastically changed the political and social landscape of Israel. Its founder, Rabbi Ovadia Yossef (Baghdad 1920), who was the chief Sephardic rabbi of Israel from 1972 to 1982, wanted to break the monopoly of the Ashkenazi yeshivas where many Sephardic Jews had felt inferior for years. This feeling of inferiority had actually existed among many traditional Sephardic Jews ever since they settled in Israel in the fifties. At that time the young state had to contend with economic problems, problems at the borders, building roads, and the construction of housing for new immigrants.

In the Ashkenazi hegemony, which counted many survivors of the Holocaust, there was at that time a certain contempt for the Sephardic newcomers who had very different cultural baggage. Moreover, this lack of understanding was magnified because Sephardic Jews were not well-informed about the Holocaust, which influenced in large measure the behavior and opinions of the Ashkenazi leaders of the time. These leaders were culturally attached to their mostly European countries of origin. The national educational curriculum that they drew up was intended for the development of the new Israeli: the anti-diaspora Jew who would speak Hebrew and would have his cultural roots in European civilization. The Sephardic culture was ignored and it never managed to gain a full-fledged place in the young state. Nor were the Sephardic Jews able to get a hold on European culture. These traditional newcomers who had looked forward to emigrating to Israel were unhappy with this position of the Ashkenazi leaders, and the conviction that they were not welcome began to take on a life of its own. However, this feeling had never before led to a public debate or to the initiative to found a party.

In 1984 Rabbi Ovadia Yossef mentioned for the first time in public the humiliations he had suffered at the hands of the Ashkenazi rabbis; with this he addressed the whole Sephardic community. It was not difficult for this *haredi* rabbi to have numerous traditional Sephardic Jews, many of whom had returned to religion, side with him. Yossef announced that he was convinced that only a Sephardic party would be able to increase the influence of the Orthodoxy in the secular country that was run by Ashkenazi Jews. After all, Ashkenazi Jews were strange, had a shtetl mentality, wore strange clothes, had strange hairstyles, and spoke Yiddish. Orthodox Sephardic Jews spoke Hebrew, were better integrated, and they looked like "ordinary" Israelis. In this way Shas, the party that was originally known

for its mildness and tolerance, took over the struggle against secularization from the ultra-Orthodox Ashkenazi Jews.

In the year of its establishment the party gained four seats, and the
support increased in the years that followed. In 1988 the party gained
eight seats, in 1992 and 1996 it gained ten, and in 1999 the number of
seats increased to seventeen. The party proved to be an attractive combination of ultra-Orthodox piety, Sephardic traditionalism, and political opportunism. The secret of Shas is the extensive social, political,
and educational network that for many Sephardic Jews (mostly from
Morocco) has increasingly taken the role of an alternative to the secular Ashkenazi society. Thousands of children from poor Oriental
families are picked up at home and go to Shas schools where they
receive free meals and where they hear that they have an inferior position in Israel and that only religion can offer a solution. Shas has
sparked a revolution in Israeli politics. With the appearance of Shas,
the anti-Zionists have become more Zionist and more Israeli. The
ultra-Orthodox, who twenty years ago were committed anti-Zionists
and wanted to be left alone, became increasingly involved in political
decision making. This was more because of opportunistic considerations than because they had discarded their anti-Zionist ideology.

Shas looks increasingly like a protest movement. Tens of thousands of poor and nonreligious Oriental Jews express their need to
get back their self-respect by voting for Shas. It has gradually
become clear that the party leaders are not developing an alternative
system with religious laws that the party wants to impose on the
rest of the population. Instead, the leaders seem interested in organizing a state within a state, a sort of "anti-state," and in obtaining the
financial means needed for this purpose. The spiritual leader
Ovadia Yossef, who always appears in a traditional long black robe
with gold embroidery, his head covered by a black spherical hat,
wearing sunglasses because of an eye disease, has increasingly been
filling the role of political and labor union leader. He developed a
strategy though which the party would—in a democratic way—get
control over certain governmental budgets in order to strengthen
Shas's "anti-state." Resistance to Sephardic culture is still seen in
Sephardic circles as a new attempt by the Ashkenazi establishment
to undermine their culture. The message that the party conveys to
the Israeli society during these confrontations is: "We won't let ourselves be oppressed a second time."

During the last five years of the twentieth century it was primarily the *Kulturkampf* that divided Israel rather than the peace negotiations with the Palestinians and its Arab neighbors. In striving for a more religious state, the ultra-Orthodox tried to preserve the Status Quo of Ben Gurion by resisting such things as public transportation and commercial activities on the Sabbath, the import of non-kosher meat, civil marriages, non-Jewish funerals, and military service for ultra-Orthodox Jews—all topical subjects in Israel. In short, they are against all measures that, according to the Orthodox, are a threat to the Jewish character of Israel. From the secular point of view, the Orthodox resist all measures that could make Israel into a "normal" democracy in which it is not the law of God that has power, but the law formulated by men.

In February 1999 these differences of opinion came to a head in the largest ultra-Orthodox demonstration up to that point, which was directed to the Supreme Court, and a secular counterdemonstration that took place on the same day in Jerusalem. A large part of the Israeli population was fearful of the possible violent consequences of the announced demonstration and worried about a civil war. This religious agitation together with ethnic polarization caused the level of social solidarity to sink to a dangerous low. That is why President Ezer Weizmann, as head of state, visited Rabbi Ovadia Yossef and figuratively threw himself at his feet to plead for cancellation of the demonstration or at least for postponement until after the elections that were supposed to take place on May 17 of that year. But Weizmann returned home empty-handed, and the demonstration, which took place a day later, proceeded peacefully.

The 250,000 demonstrators, most of whom were ultra-Orthodox with a minority of Orthodox, rebelled against interference from the state and especially from the Supreme Court in religious affairs. Barely one kilometer away, approximately sixty thousand secularists held a counterdemonstration "in order to protect the constitutional state against the tyranny of the Orthodox." In the Orthodox demonstration the God-fearing men, dressed in long black coats, were separated from the women. On a stage, old rabbis and Bible scholars were sunk in prayer together with the crowd, and swaying, they mumbled psalms and the "Shema Israel" (the most important prayer in Judaism; it is said at the time of death): "Hear O Israel: the Lord our God, the Lord is One." From time to time a shofar sounded —there were no speeches.

The counterdemonstration, at which none of the leaders of the most important parties made an appearance—probably for fear of alienating constituencies so close to the elections—seemed like an open-air event with refreshments and music. Thirty- and forty-year-olds from liberal Tel Aviv, but also from Jerusalem, had gathered because they felt that the Orthodox made too many demands on their secular state and neglected their civic duties like military service and spent their life in Bible study at the expense of the state. One speech after the other was delivered against "Khomeinism," against "religious tyranny," against attacks on democracy, and against the Court's interference in religious matters.

The cause of dissatisfaction in ultra-Orthodox circles was a series of "anti-Semitic" decisions of the Supreme Court and other courts that made them feel invaded in the way they lived their religion. These were questions such as the above-mentioned opening of a large shopping center on the Sabbath and the obligation of local religious councils to accept non-Orthodox Jews as members. Another example of such a matter was the registration of all those who had converted to Judaism (whether living in Israel or abroad) as "Jews" in the civil registry, irrespective of whether the conversion was carried out under supervision of the Conservative or the Reform movement. Another cause of the demonstration was the fine received by the chairman of the local religious councils in Jerusalem because he had ignored the decision of the Court that these councils would henceforth have to admit non-Orthodox Jews as members. This was also true for the detention imposed on three ultra-Orthodox men charged with molesting two Swiss Christian women who had settled in Mea Shearim and were carrying out missionary work, according to the ultra-Orthodox.

In the discussions in the press there was a question of verbal violence against the Supreme Court that was, among other things, accused by the Orthodox side of being "worse for the Jews than the Holocaust." A few days after the demonstration, Ovadia Yossef called all the judges of the Supreme Court "devils and desecrators of the Sabbath" who "caused all the misery in the world." Yossef said that "the judges did not believe in the Torah" and that this was an insurmountable problem: "They don't even know how to read a holy book—a seven-year-old child from our community knows the Torah better. They call themselves the High Court, but they don't even measure up to the name Lower Court."

The organizer of the demonstration, Menachem Porush, an eighty-three-year-old rabbi from Jerusalem, announced that he was fed up with the "anti-religious incitement." He had nothing against the democratic secular Supreme Court as such, but he felt that this body in which the Orthodoxy is not represented "may not make decisions about subjects that relate to religion. That should happen in the Knesset where we are represented." However, it appears that in practice the Israeli representatives send this kind of problematic subject on to the Court out of fear of losing the support of the Orthodox.

The secular journalist and historian Tom Segev, author of *The Seventh Million*, a book that is controversial in Israel, and *One Palestine Complete*, published in 2000 and which deals with the British Mandate, found the ultra-Orthodox demonstration impressive. According to him, the secularists' fear that the demonstration would get out of hand indicates their ignorance about the feelings of their religious compatriots: "The secularists are not able to organize a demonstration that reflects their feelings so clearly. I saw 250,000 Orthodox Jews who fear the dismantling of the Jewish state and the undermining of the Status Quo. The only thing that I admire about Ben Gurion, who I think was a real dictator, is the establishment of the Status Quo with which he involved them in the secular country."

Segev says that "the relationship between the secularists and the Orthodox is not symmetrical and the nonreligious will have to learn to live with certain discomforts that result from the presence of the ultra-Orthodox." Segev doesn't argue for approval of undemocratic demands, but he thinks that the nonreligious should be more understanding of a community that has felt threatened for decades and has fought for its own interests, until the establishment of Shas. According to Segev, many secularists forget that there are certain things that the ultra-Orthodox can't live with. He admires Teddy Kollek, the former mayor of Jerusalem, for the way he handled the culture war:

> Kollek was aware that he was governing a madhouse, and he had a number of ultra-Orthodox "advisors" in Mea Shearim whom he visited late at night to ask about their needs and their grievances.

For example, it became clear to him that the proposed construction
of a stadium near a religious neighborhood was encountering
insurmountable objections. Therefore he looked for another loca-
tion. Just like Ben Gurion he defined the need of the religious community as a general need. Therefore he built *mikvaot* [ritual baths],
just like he built schools, hospitals, and roads.

According to Segev, the Orthodox feel uncomfortable in the
Promised Land where most workers are left-wing and secular, and
they consider the media and the Court, which are hostile to them, as
"anti-Semitic bastions."

A month later, in March 1999, this was proved to be the case
when the political leader of Shas, the Moroccan Jew Machlouf Aryeh
Deri (1959 Meknes) was sentenced to four years of prison because of
fraud. This conviction affirmed once again the religious contradictions that exist in Israel and also emphasized the ethnic polarization.
The reaction of many Shas supporters who gathered in front of the
court in Jerusalem on the day of the sentencing was: "Deri is innocent"; "He remains our king"; and "The godless Ashkenazi anti-
Jewish court is trying to destroy our fast-growing political movement." The sentence offended them, some even cried, but above all
it affirmed their opinion that the state of Israel and the court still discriminate against Sephardic Jews. Many Orthodox and traditional
Sephardic Jews—among them politicians—plastered the windows
of their cars and their homes with life-size posters of Deri that read
"Deri is innocent." The election campaign continued, and it seemed
that the sentence was strengthening the unity of the Sephardic Jews.
Deri, who was discovered in his yeshiva by Yossef and became minister of the interior at the age of twenty-nine, had led Shas since 1984
and he would remain its leader despite everything, even if he had to
step down. The sums of money that he had diverted to the yeshivas
and to other educational institutes were not considered fraud by
many Shas supporters, but rather as fulfillment of a mitzvah, a religious commandment.

In *J'accuse*, a sensational videotape made especially for the occasion, Deri accused the secular Ashkenazi establishment of having
intended to convict him from the very beginning. He calls his conviction "Ashkenazi demagoguery." While a police inspector tells
how he got on Deri's trail, the following words appear on the screen:
"The purpose: to bring down Deri." Then Deri looks calmly into the

camera and says: "The only public processes have been the ones against Demjanyuk, Eichmann and Deri. They have humiliated me by accusing me of fraud in front of the whole world."

When it is clear that this carefully constructed video is slowly working toward a climax, Deri says: "There is a group in this country that thinks that this country belongs to them. We, the Sephardic Jews came to Israel with our Jewish heritage, with our pride, with our rabbis, with the Jewish family, and with the respect for our fathers and mothers. We came here as Jews. But the Ashkenazi want to establish a secular state where the Torah, Judaism, and Sabbath rest are forbidden." While Deri is speaking these words, Shulamit Aloni and Yossi Sarid, the ultra-secular Meretz members, appear on the screen. In May of 1999 these events resulted in a seven-seat gain for Shas, which won a total of seventeen seats, and in the appearance in the Knesset of the extremist secular party Shinui (Change) of the lawyer and journalist Tommy Lapid (1932). The latter had played on the feelings of hatred and disdain of the secularists toward the Orthodox; with his election slogan "Stop the *Haredim*" and his promise of keeping the *haredim* out of the government he gained six seats. In ultra-Orthodox circles this secularist from Hungary who didn't join Shinui until two months before the elections is called "the fascist Tommy LaPen." A non-Orthodox Jew who placed an ad in *Ha'aretz* a few days before the election compared Lapid's comment "a government without *Haredim*" to "die Nazi-Regierung Judenfrei," and his assertion that the *haredim* "are the source of all problems" was compared to "Die Juden sind unser Unglück," common remarks in Nazi Germany.

During a television debate with Minister of the Interior Eli Suissa of Shas, who felt threatened by Lapid's wishes, Lapid asked if Suissa wanted "to send him to a concentration camp." To this Suissa answered: "You've already been in one, but obviously you haven't learned your lesson." But Lapid had been in the Budapest ghetto for the duration of the war and never was in a concentration camp. His secular opponents accused him of "fanning feelings of hate among Jews." However, Lapid continued calling himself "the doctor" and ultra-Orthodoxy "the disease."

Lapid says, "According to them it's a mitzvah not to serve in the army, and I refuse to accept that they determine who is a 'real, good or bad Jew.' We are their goyim. During the Holocaust we were all alone, and after the war I was convinced that Jews needed their own state and that there was a need for Jewish unity." The price that Lapid has had to pay for his electoral success is that during the election campaign and right after it he had to have two bodyguards (later reduced to one) and that he receives threatening letters almost daily. One of the letters that Lapid received at his home in Tel Aviv reads: "I regret that they didn't kill you in the Second World War."

In the summer of 1999, as if none of this had happened, Ehud Barak opted for a coalition (for reasons that will be discussed in the next chapter) with Shas and Meretz, the party that shares the opinions of Shinui about the ultra-Orthodoxy. Three months after the turmoil around the sentencing of Deri, his successor Eliyahu Ishai and Barak signed a coalition agreement that Yossi Sarid had already signed. During coalition negotiations Sarid had managed to extort the position of minister of education. In August 1999 Shas threatened to leave the coalition because of the "desecration of the Sabbath"—the transport of a turbine from Tel Aviv to Ashkelon on a Friday evening. Eventually it was Meretz that quit the government at the end of June 2000 when it was once again apparent that the parties held irreconcilable points of view about financing of the Shas educational system.

From that moment on Barak's government went downhill. Early in July three other parties, Shas among them, left the coalition because of dissatisfaction with territorial concessions that Barak had made to Yasir Arafat. Because of these defections Barak held seven ministerial posts and carried out negotiations alone at Camp David. On his return home Barak suggested starting a civil revolution. This would among other things include the drafting of a constitution, the introduction of civil marriage, and the abolition of the Ministry of Religious Affairs. But this last attempt to save his own skin was in vain. The public agitation about the course of the peace negotiations, the internal political instability, followed by the meanwhile notorious visit of Sharon to the Temple Mount in September 2000, resulted in unanimity about Barak's failure. Instead of "a brain" his epithet when he took office, he was now called "a hypocrite," "a one-man-act," and "arrogant."

Some rightist Orthodox saw the hand of God in these developments. He had come to their side, and leftist secular Israel, which had had complete faith in Arafat and Barak, was in a crisis. The developments that succeeded each other at a rapid pace resulted in Barak's stepping down and in the electoral victory of Ariel Sharon who, with twenty-six ministers, assembled the largest government in the history of Israel in February 2001. The negotiations took place during a time when violence increased, and there were reports of Jewish solidarity, which tends to be great in times of need. Nevertheless the internal tensions came to the surface during the "fight" over ministries that reminded many Israelis about the *Kulturkampf*. After all, the conflict with the Palestinians would not change the minds of the ultra-Orthodox, the Sephardic Jews, the Russian immigrants, or the secularists about such matters as the constitution. The *Kulturkampf* remains, even though it is mostly hidden from view because of all the attention on the threatened freedom of the state of Israel.

According to many Israelis, the coalition discussions carried out by Sharon, the demonstrations against the court in February 1999, the conviction of Deri in March 1999, and the victory of Shas in May 1999 show (this is a very simplified but illustrative picture of reality) that Israel has split into two peoples and two cultures: one is democratic and liberal while the other is antidemocratic and dogmatic, or leftist secular and rightist Orthodox. The latter group consists of ultra-Orthodox Jews of whom the Sephardic *haredim* are most disdained in the secular community. The great quantity of children produced by this group, the exemption from military service, and the threat created by Shas to the coalition cause anger and irritation in the secular community. Conversely, many ultra-Orthodox are angered by the Western lifestyle and the aggressive antireligious rhetoric of many secularists who show no interest in them and in their law. They also regret that "so many Jews have strayed from the path." However, they still consider the secularists as "one of them" and therefore sometimes try to bring them back to the religion of the Fathers.

Fifty-three years after the establishment of the state, a deep gap split the country in two, a gap that has become increasingly large in the last years and will increase even more in the future. However, there are Israelis who believe that the ultra-Orthodoxy will eventually be absorbed in the secular population. Menachem Friedman (1937 Palestine), a professor of sociology at Bar Ilan University in Ramat Gan, thinks that the ultra-Orthodoxy is digging its own grave: "They will have to find work elsewhere, certainly when the state no longer has money for them, and they will have to live in a nonreligious environment and spend less time with the Talmud. The religious way of life whereby large families have one breadwinner is impossible to keep up in a situation with rising prices." Friedman, who grew up as a Hasidic Jew, teaches at an originally Zionist university, wears a black yarmulke, and is presently working on a book about the relationship between *hilonim* (secular) and *haredim*. According to Friedman, the increased impoverishment has consequences for spirituality: "Look at the impoverished ultra-Orthodox Bnei Brak district. It's the poorest neighborhood in all of Israel, there is crushing unemployment and there is less time for religion. This crisis will soon come to a head."

"There won't be a revolution," says David Landau, who is the British editor of the English language edition of *Ha'aretz* and wears a black yarmulke. Landau, who in 1993 published the book *Piety and Power: The World of Jewish Fundamentalism*, asserts,

> Friedman's picture is based on falsehoods. The current situation in Israel doesn't prove his assertion at all. The contrary is the case: there are now all sorts of math, language and computer training courses for *haredim*. They won't assimilate with their secular Jewish compatriots, but instead will work and pray at the same time. The ultra-Orthodoxy is stubborn and proud and will never lose its religious fervor. In the end they will find a balance between practical modernity and their spiritual modernity.

In summary it can be said that the *Kulturkampf* (culture war) doesn't have a theological or philosophical character for most Israelis. In principle the struggle is about different ways of life that have political consequences. Many secular Israelis are not unhappy with their life in Israel, which, in many respects, has a Jewish character. Ultimately they do want to live in a Jewish state, but their requirements for its Jewishness are lower that those of the ultra-Orthodox. For the secularists it is important to live in a modern pluralistic state where the law of the state prevails and where all citizens are equal before that law. The true problem in Israel is perhaps to draw the line between the state with "some Jewish content" and the "absolutely modern state." This is because the secular Israelis are unwilling to give up either their Judaism or their modernity.

Ben Gurion probably thought that with the Status Quo he had found the fine line that could be maintained and could result in a livable situation because he assumed that the Orthodoxy would remain weak and marginal. But because of the break in a potentially strong secular camp (formed by the Labor Party and Likud), the takeover by Menachem Begin in 1977, and the break between the Sephardic and Ashkenazi Jews, the support of the *haredim* became crucial for one of the two blocks. This situation caused the *haredim* to be in a favorable position to protect their own interests. Besides, with the foundation of Shas in 1984, the ultra-Orthodox demographic weight increased because this party won many Jews for the Orthodoxy. The balance that Ben Gurion thought he had found was upset forever.

Recently many secular Israelis have come to feel that the *haredi* political demands are harmful for Zionist Israeli interests: *haredim* are antimodern and claim financial means that should be earmarked for strengthening the state as a modern state that needs to have an edge over its hostile Arab neighbors. Moreover, a growing part of the population is not willing to contribute to the strengthening of the state—or at least to its economic and material well-being—by doing military service. The secular Israelis hate these developments, especially since the *haredim* are anti-Zionist while the Zionists have sacrificed much for the state and still do so by fulfilling military service. This is why many secular Israelis feel that they should resist every form of Orthodoxy, especially on behalf of the state.

The ironic and also discouraging side of the problem is that the Orthodox form a very small part of the population (10–20 percent) but despite this their efforts to make Israel into a religious state can't be stopped. Only if Israel could form a broad-based government, supported by Ashkenazi and Sephardic secularists, and if this government would strive for national goals (primarily peace and security) that they could identify with, then the support of the *haredim* would no longer be needed. But the question remains, as mentioned earlier in this chapter, whether the secularist Israelis will ever be willing to go that far in order to eliminate the influence of the ultra-Orthodoxy in the government.

This question was answered in July 1999 when Ehud Barak, the leader of the Labor Party who had been elected prime minister in May of that year, announced to the Israeli public that he wanted to form a broad-based government consisting of Ashkenazi and Sephardic Orthodox, secularists, leftists and rightists, and Russians.

At least it could be said of that government that it was a true mirror of Israeli society. It is difficult to say whether or not the Knesset that was chosen in May 1999 is a real mirror of the general mood in the Israeli society of February 2001, yet this can rightfully be said of the election of Sharon as prime minister and the establishment of a government of National Unity. But no one knows how long this government will last and how Israel will develop in the coming half-century. However, it does seem certain that the *Kulturkampf* has not yet ended.

TWO

IS A JEWISH DEMOCRACY POSSIBLE?

"The stubborn survival of Orthodox Judaism irritates the secular Jews because it hampers the formation of the non-Jewish state of Israel."

—Yeshayahu Leibowitz

JEWISH DEMOCRACY IS THE GREATEST OF all paradoxes in the history of Israel. Can a state that has as its purpose the preservation of "Jewishness" be democratic at the same time? The secular majority feels that this is not possible and wants to separate religion and state. The problem with this is that most of these secularists still want a state with "Jewish character" of which religion would be only a part. They value the national anthem that is in Hebrew, the star of David in the flag, the Jewish holidays, the bris, the Orthodox wedding ceremony, and Saturday as the day off, but they feel that this "Jewishness" should absolutely not be imposed by the state.

According to the Orthodox, the "Jewish content" can only be given to the state through spiritual activity, and it is therefore necessary for the Torah to play a role in public life. Therefore they see it as their duty to keep God's law, the halakhah, alive. They can do this anywhere in the world, but the Jews could just as well have stayed in the diaspora if the Jewish state was to be like all others. Hence the Orthodox feel that as a minority they have to stand up for their rights to prevent secular Zionists from watering down Judaism. After all, without the religion not much is left of Jewish identity. According to more and more secularists, Judaism is a lifestyle that in its strictest form imposes limitations to the democratic character of the country. The ultra-Orthodox enjoy exemption from military service, they have their own educational system, and they want public institutions to keep kosher. According to the Orthodox, the laws of God are more important than the laws formulated by men, and therefore they don't want to be subject to the decisions of the High Court. To be sure, there are many secularists who are grateful to the Orthodox for the conservation of Jewish patrimony and are even willing to support its preservation with taxes, but they don't allow Orthodoxy to lay down the law for them.

Ben Gurion thought that he had found the line between Jewish traditionalism and Israeli modernity in 1948 in the form of the Status Quo. Many secularists consider this choice undemocratic, but does this mean that Orthodoxy itself had undemocratic intentions? Or should the state be called undemocratic? Perhaps Ben Gurion should never have made this agreement. If he had thought of the organization only as a democratic state, the Status Quo would probably not exist, but he would have alienated the ultra-Orthodox minority, which also has rights in a democratic state.

The majority of Jewish citizens still want to hold on to the definition of Israel as a Jewish state the way it was set down in the Declaration of Independence. The country has democratic public institutions, but at the same time it has laws that are intended to preserve its Jewish character. Some secularists want to abolish laws that apply specifically and exclusively to Jews, like the Law of Return. The development of the Jewish and democratic components of the state of Israel is no more than a logical consequence of the establishment of the state. The Orthodox will have to live with the fact that the role of Judaism in public life in Israel will always remain limited, and the secularists will have to accept the fact that the democratic qualities of Israel will never be fully developed. The question remains whether the Jewish state can and will continue to live with this built-in duality which, according to some, borders on schizophrenia.

It is remarkable that the ultra-Orthodox Jews as well as the ultra-secular Jews in Israel feel threatened and think that their country is not democratic. According to the ultrasecularists, the religious minority causes the erosion of democracy by using public funds to finance their yeshivas, ritual baths, synagogues, and educational system. They are becoming stronger in a state they don't accept and in which they don't fulfill their military service, and many secularists point out that without an army there is no state and therefore no people. The two political and ideological opposites in Israel's recent history are the ultra-Orthodox rabbi Avraham Ravitz and the humanist Shulamit Aloni. Ravitz is a Knesset member for the anti-Zionist party United Torah Judaism; Aloni is a prominent Meretz member who received the Israeli honor "Humanist of the Year" in 1996 and the Israel Lifetime Achievement prize in February 2000. The jury awarded her this prize for her contribution to "a morally just Israeli society" and added that Aloni always led the struggle for equality between different religious convictions in Israel.

Ravitz and Aloni were at each other's throats during the government of Prime Minister Yitzhak Rabin (1992–1996) in which Aloni was minister of education and culture. This tension occurred mainly during debates about civil marriage, alternative funerals, conversions—topical subjects in Israel that all deal with the "Jewish content" of the state and the interwovenness of religion and state. According to Ravitz, complete separation is impossible. He accepts the state out of practical considerations and believes in the "perfection of the Jewish democracy" as soon as the "irreligious Alonis" convert. Ravitz considers Aloni "intolerant" and "anti-Semitic" because she doesn't respect his way of life. Conversely Aloni finds Ravitz "intolerant" because he disapproves of the fact that she eats pork, she goes shopping on the Sabbath, and she allows her son to marry a goy. In Rabin's government she tried to save democracy in this "racist country." She hammered on the importance of a constitution and equal rights of all citizens who "in Israel have no choice but to be stuck with religion." She is satisfied with the ten seats of Meretz in the Fifteenth Knesset, but laments the increase of the number of seats held by Shas, the ultra-Orthodox Sephardic party that is also part of the government coalition.

At the end of 1998 Aloni celebrated her seventieth birthday, but she doesn't lack energy. In March 1999, together with the writer Amoz Oz, she created the "pro-Meretz group" in order to "build a society based on justice, something that only Meretz can do." She works for Meretz, has a radio program, and gives lectures about constitutional justice and human rights at Ben Gurion University in Beersheba and at the University of Tel Aviv. Aloni states,

> The greatest problem is that we don't know what concepts like sovereignty, democracy, and national state mean in practice. Israel is still living in a ghetto, and Ben Gurion has made the biggest mistake by not formulating a constitution but the Status Quo. Now we're living in an ethnocracy, and the Orthodox destroy the little democracy that we do have. I can't talk with a doctrinarian like Ravitz because certain things "simply are that way" for him.

Sitting in her fragrant garden, she lights one cigarette after the other while Handel's *Messiah* blasts from her living room. Her house, situated in a prosperous secular city to the north of Tel Aviv, breathes the atmosphere of a well-read and well-traveled person. Antique chairs, chests and tables, carpets, paintings, candlesticks, and lamps crowd the living room. On the wall hangs a photo of the 1994 handshake of Yitzhak Rabin, Yasir Arafat, and Shimon Peres.

Every question I ask her seems to be an unwelcome interruption of her stream of words about the lamentable situation in Israel: "Homosexuality and prostitution are taboo, Arabs are discriminated against, civil marriages are impossible, all funeral homes are Orthodox. All this is because of the religious minority which is disproportionately represented in the Knesset." Aloni is leftist in the European sense of the word, and that is too leftist for Israel. This means that she is convinced that the Jewish religion is a part of the pluralistic Jewish culture, and Israel—she emphasizes—must be a state for all citizens, for Jews as well as for Arabs. On the Israeli identity card it should say "Israeli" after "nationality" for every citizen, instead of "Jew" or "Moslem" or "Christian." In short, she feels that "Jew" should not be a nationality.

Aloni continues: "Here we have the liberty to silence one another. Nowhere is it written that we have freedom of expression because Israel doesn't even have a constitution! And with a party like Shas in the government the constitution won't even come. After all, we have the Status Quo." Aloni opens one of her books and shows a copy of the letter that Ben Gurion sent to Rabbi Levin in 1947 to prevent him from opposing the establishment of the Jewish state:

> The Status Quo was born as a letter that has no official status at all and that says nothing about the Sabbath or civil marriage. The Status Quo is something flexible that has become increasingly elaborate because religious parties have a tradition of causing government crises that they settle only in exchange for money or for a religious law that then all of a sudden becomes part of the Status Quo. This country is governed in a primitive manner. The winners of elections are always dependent on the ultra-Orthodox who use their growing power to get money and to impose their way of thinking on others. The secularists become intolerant because of the greed and the impatience of the Orthodox. This democracy is manipulative and must be educated in order to become a full-fledged democracy. We thought that all of this would change with Barak, but he too seems to need rabbis!

Aloni thinks that only a constitutional separation between religion and state can put a stop to the additional theocratization and development of an Ayatollah state in which

> racists like Ravitz govern. . . . They do everything to separate us from the rest of the world. They build walls around the past, and the community is organized like it was before the Enlightenment when the whole world was held together by the religious establishment. It's absurd that in lands where more religious people live, like in America or France, state and religion are separated whereas here the lines between the government and the rabbis are blurred. Here you must be Jewish to have full rights, just like Isabella and Ferdinand who dictated that everyone who wanted to be Spanish had to profess Catholicism.
>
> Besides, Orthodox Jews never worried about security, water, transportation, and other practical affairs. Now, in their own state they care only about their own well-being. They are greedy. They have no respect for dissenters, they are racist, they hate us. A whole community studies, young people register for the yeshiva in order to avoid military service, but in the end it means that they don't work. This system is sick! Right now every secular family supports one *haredi* family, but if things continue this way, it will be five in the future! They don't work, they use our tax money for their yeshiva studies and then say that that's Judaism.

"We are not doctors, plumbers, or army officers, but we do keep the Jewish identity pure," says Rabbi Avraham Ravitz who has meanwhile been named deputy minister of education by Sharon. He sits in an armchair in the sparsely furnished living room of his apartment in the ultra-Orthodox residential area Bayit v'Gan in Jerusalem. A large, ten-seat corner sofa, a coffee table, bookshelves, and a large table leave enough space for his fifty-two grandchildren to play, who sometimes visit all at the same time. Mrs. Avigayil Ravitz, mother of twelve children, all of whom except for one are "of course" married through a matchmaker, is putting the last touches on the Sabbath meal and answers the telephone for her husband. He is the embodiment of peace and quiet despite a rather wild appearance caused by his beard and his penetrating gaze. Since 1988 he has been a Knesset member for Degel haTorah (The Flag of the Torah) which together with the former diaspora party, Agudat Israel, constitutes United Torah Judaism, the only Ashkenazi ultra-Orthodox party, with five seats in the Knesset as of this writing.

"Israelis think that only soldiers and taxpayers support the state and that 'our boys' in the yeshiva freeload," says Ravitz. "But they are actually the ones who see to our survival. We won the Six-Day war because of them. Syria and Egypt attacked on Yom Kippur because we study His word insufficiently. I value soldiers who risk their lives, but in reality it's only a very small percentage that is in real danger. Granted, the yeshiva is safer, but *lernen* is no picnic as the *hilonim* think. Being a Jew is not easy, and the students sacrifice their careers and lead frugal lives for this." Against the objection that not everyone in the yeshiva is so dedicated, alluding to the *shababs* mentioned in the introduction and the large-scale fraud with Talmud students, Ravitz answers, "Every society has its 'frayed ends.'" He shrugs his shoulders and is silent.

Ravitz was born in 1934 in Tel Aviv where his father was the head of a rabbinic court. He studied at the Hebron Yeshiva in Jerusalem where he received all the knowledge he needed "to understand the world." He was a member of the Jewish underground movement Lechi, and he served in the Israeli Army during all the wars except the Sinai campaign in 1956. At that time he was in the United States as a missionary of Pe'elim, an organization that fights "anti-religious tyranny" according to Ravitz. At the end of the seventies, Ravitz held what was considered by the Orthodox the "highest spiritual authority," the function of yeshiva head. It was Ravitz's teacher Eliezer Menachem Shach (1898–2001), the head of the Lithuanian Ponovez yeshiva (a yeshiva where learning is done according to the Lithuanian system), in Bnei Brak who encouraged Ravitz in 1988 to become party leader of Degel, founded in 1988. Ravitz managed to capture two seats in the same year. (Many of the votes turned out to have been bought in Arab villages.) The most important reason for the establishment of Degel was resistance to the messianic activities of Aguda. Shach felt that Jews should not do anything to speed his coming. The rabbi has since died.

In 1992 Degel and Aguda united to become United Torah Judaism because that year the election threshold had been raised from 1 to 1.5 percent and had lessened the parties' chances for obtaining separate seats. Ravitz was received in the Knesset as a "new style" *haredi* politician because he might be more "worldly" compared to his religious colleagues like the rabbis of Aguda and of the National Religious Party. But his "new style" is misleading because he remains the representative of his archconservative spiritual leader, Rabbi Shach.

Before Ravitz's arrival, the secular public had become used to *haredi* politicians who spoke *haredi* language. In contrast Ravitz used words like "equal rights" and "human rights," and in 1996 he dreamed up the election slogan "We want to be different but equal." In 1999 he waged a campaign with the slogan "being Jewish in your own country" because he felt (and still feels) that the state considered him less important than the secular citizens. Ravitz wanted to foster understanding for his attitude to life, but he regrets that he still keeps hearing that he uses his power to get money. Ravitz sighs: "After all, we are fighting for school hours, classrooms, and cultural activities, and for everything we need to stay alive. We don't ask for more than what we are entitled to, just like the secularists—but just tell a roomful of secularist that we demand equal treatment. As one, the audience will shout that 'they will also have to fulfill their obligations and serve in the army.'"

Military service is a subject that in his eyes keeps dogging him wrongly. Ravitz assures us once again that the yeshiva boys ensure that the halakhah remains alive—an argument that is immensely irritating to many secularists and especially to the ultrasecular party Meretz. "I know that," says Ravitz. "The Minister of Education, Yossi Sarid of Meretz, thought that I would have more understanding for him, but we must first have the right to fulfill our divine obligations. Have I hindered the formation of the religious military unit? No, and I also agree with the last proposal that tries to urge these boys to fulfill four months of military service, to go on retraining exercise every year, and to learn a trade. We think it's fine for our boys to serve, but they shouldn't be forced to."

Ultra-Orthodox young men continue to study at the yeshiva until they are twenty-five in order to avoid military service (for which everyone is called until that age). A governmental commission has devised a solution for this social problem, which is the greatest source of irritation in the secular community. In the new situation, which started in April 2000 but which should be called "temporary," the age at which a yeshiva student has to decide whether to continue his studies or start work has been lowered to the age of twenty-three. If he chooses the latter and wants to learn a trade or start work, he is first obliged to serve in the army for four months and then go on retraining exercises once a year for the rest of his life. In secular and religious-Zionist circles the reaction to this new situation is negative because there is still no equality as regards the obligation to serve in the army. They conveniently omit the fact that 50 percent of the secular Israelis avoid military service.

Many *haredim* fear that their children will become disaffected in a secular army unit. According to Ravitz, who has two sons who served in the army, the new Orthodox military unit Nachal, which has existed since 1999, is a "marriage of convenience between our existence in the state of Israel and our spiritual life in *Eretz Yisrael*." He continues:

> Our spiritual country doesn't need a defense, for us the state is important only for garbage collection, administration, police, and, because of the situation, the army. For me the Torah is a proof of purchase—and it should be for every Jew—the moral right to live here. Jewish existence began here not fifty years but 3350 years ago. From a spiritual viewpoint we live in *Eretz Yisrael* that God promised us, and we have that black on white.

Ravitz taps on the *Tanakh* lying in front of him: "After all, it says 'To you I will give the land of Canaan as your allotted heritage' (Ps. 105:11), and in the years to come God will remember the covenant with Jacob and with the land [see Lev. 26:42].

The exemption from military service for yeshiva students, as it was established by Ben Gurion in 1948, has aroused much public resistance and even anger in the last few years. It has even become the most important reason for the break between the secularists and the ultra-Orthodox in Israeli society. The fact is that there is now a new reality. The number of students that qualified for exemption in Ben Gurion's time was not more than 400—a number that had doubled in 1975—while at the end of the nineties approximately 30,000 students were exempted. In 1977 Menachem Begin abolished the limitation on the number of exemptions that had always existed for yeshiva students. In that period the main reason for the justification of the exemption shifted. Before that time it was the memories of the yeshivas in Europe destroyed during the Holocaust and the resulting wish to avoid closing yeshivas in Israel. Slowly, the argument has come to be the more general desire to make it possible for religious students to continue their studies without interruption. Moreover, there were doubts about the usefulness of military service for yeshiva students because of the problems that they would encounter with the secular army leadership and the army leadership with them.

Ravitz is not embarrassed about trying to bring God's law to life in the state. This is his task, and the Jewish state will survive only if it is fulfilled. He doesn't shrink from calling his secular compatriots anti-Semites who are guilty of *k'fiah hilonit* (secular tyranny) that leads to ruin and lawlessness:

> At least *we* protect the Jewish state. El Al doesn't fly on the Sabbath [until 1982 El Al did fly, but at the urging of the Orthodox the Saturday flights were abolished], there is no public transportation on that day, the stores are closed, and most public institutions observe the rules of *kashrut*, but there is an existential danger for us: the Status Quo is being undermined and the secularists are getting the upper hand. With a million Arabs, a million non-Jews, and a secular majority we have to guard the Jewish content of this state. If we don't do this, it is uncertain that Israel can continue as an independent state in this region.

According to Ravitz, no one knows exactly what the Status Quo is. There is no document called "Status Quo," but there is a kind of unwritten agreement that the Status Quo will be maintained. Ravitz says that when the subject is brought up, there is "always the question which Status Quo: that of today, of several years ago, or of decades ago." Ravitz points out that a distinction must be made between de facto and de jure and admits that in these last years more laws have been accepted in favor of the Orthodox.

> Some agree with this, others don't. The country isn't organized the way I like either, but he who has the power calls the shots. During the last government, the left signed the Oslo accords and opened shopping centers on the Sabbath, and now we are trying to turn back these decisions. The secularists have to admit that Israeli society has in practical terms become freer for them. Yet the average citizen hates us because of k'fiah datit [religious tyranny].

According to Ravitz, peace is a worrisome aspect for the Jewish people, especially because the secularists can lose their thin layer of Jewish identity:

> The secularists have no problem signing a peace accord, the death sentence of the chosen people. Peace pulls us out of our historical joints; we will assimilate in the Middle East. The Arab elite will marry Jewish women. It's difficult enough to remain Jewish with neighbors who want to murder us and surround us with Um Kaltum* and Beethoven's Ninth. Peace means the death of Jewish education. Why would godless authorities that bargain away our country tell their children that we live here because God promised us this land? That last thing, that's Jewish education, but they teach their children that we have to give the Arabs their land back. But there is no question of giving back: we're willing to give up a part of our country only to prevent bloodshed. This halakhic principle to preserve life, pikuach nefesh, is a Jewish duty. However, it was wrong to support "Oslo" in order to give the Arabs a state.

Leafing through the Torah, Ravitz says,

> The Arabs bother us less than the mentality of the hilonim who, brainwashed by Meretz, have forgotten what it means to be Jewish. They no longer fear that God will scatter us among the nations. God doesn't even give the land to the Arabs when the Jews misbehave. In their commentaries on Leviticus 26, verse 32

---

*an Egyptian singer [translator]

["I will make the land desolate, so that your enemies who settle in it shall be appalled by it"], the old rabbis explained that a blessing was hidden in this curse because they prophesied after all that the land would not tolerate any other inhabitants as long as Israel was living in exile. The land remains ours. It also says in Leviticus that it is permitted to make non-Jews into slaves—and to pass these slaves on from father to son.

He looks up triumphantly as if he has just been declared right by his teacher, but then adds that we should not lose track of the difference between theory and practice.

According to Ravitz the Israeli democracy is in a strange position. "In schools, in kibbutzim, and on army bases, ultra-secularists," as he calls Aloni and Sarid,

are permitted to hold lectures about atheism and Darwinism, but I'm not welcome to tell what the ultra-Orthodox think. Ten years ago this was different, but leftist Israel saw that people became religious through my influence. [Ravitz was head of a yeshiva for secular Jews who had become religious.] In a democratic country everyone has the right to be wrong. It's sad that the majority in Israel thinks that I'm on the wrong track, but I want to have the opportunity to convince people that I'm right. We almost never have the opportunity to do so, and that's undemocratic. The same is true for the Supreme Court. They call us *Khomeinis*, but the Court that's supposed to be so democratic makes decisions against us about religious subjects such as the Sabbath rest, store closing times and the religious councils. Judges should be elected, and the Court should abstain from value judgments about religious subjects.

Ravitz and Aloni embody the Israeli paradox par excellence: Ravitz emphasizes the Jewish-religious aspect of his identity and Aloni, the democratic-liberal aspect of her identity. Ravitz's political decisions are inspired by the advice of his spiritual leader, and those of Aloni by humanistic and democratic principles and by legislation. In spite of this—and with this step Aloni's party confirms the paradox of the Jewish democracy—in 1999 Meretz took its seat in the coalition formed by Barak. This government resulted from a Knesset in which the ultra-Orthodox possessed not less than 22 of the 120 seats, of which the United Torah Judaism of Ravitz has 5 and the ultra-Orthodox Sephardic party Shas has 17. Meretz's step seemed all the more improbable because this party had for years worked hard for a constitution and wanted "a government without Shas" as long as Shas has been in existence.

The composition of the Fifteenth Knesset and the government coalition must be seen against the background of the *Kulturkampf*. After all, this Knesset was formed by at least fifteen parties, and out of the 120 Knesset members a total of thirty-one belong to the religious camp. Among them are twenty-two ultra-Orthodox who increased their representation by eight in comparison to the Fourteenth Knesset. The religious Zionists of the National Religious Party, which at the time held nine seats, won five. Their loss can probably be attributed to the National Union (an electoral alliance of ultrareligious Zionists formed in 1999) that obtained four seats. On the left-secular side of the "doves," Shinui (the previously mentioned new fundamentalist secular party) gained six seats, most likely primarily at the expense of Meretz. The Center Party (an electoral alliance formed at the end of 1998 by ex-Likud members whose purpose was to bring down Netanyahu) had six seats.

The twenty-six seats of One Israel (an electoral alliance of leftist secularists that included the Labor Party) and the two seats of the labor union party One People bring the total on this side to fifty, not counting the ten seats of the Arab parties. The rightist secularists of Likud, also called "hawks," won nineteen seats, those of Israel Our Home (a new Russian immigrant party that is more nationalistic than the traditional immigrant party, Israel ba'Aliyah) won four, and those of Israel ba'Aliyah won six seats. The Orthodox and the rightist secularists, together called "Jewish Israelis," usually form an alliance that enables them to get a total of sixty seats against fifty in the secular camp, the "Israeli Israelis." It is therefore a misconception that the latter won the Knesset elections of 1999 over the "Jewish Israelis"—Barak's victory made it seem that way—after all, Barak was at the head of a predominantly religious-right majority.

In May 1999, during the coalition negotiations, left-thinking Israel was faced with a government without United Torah Judaism, but especially without Shas. The day after his victory Barak, who is known in Israel as "the best little boy in the class" and "the man without compassion," was flooded with telephone calls and faxes from Meretz supporters who asked him "not to govern with Shas." However, Barak announced that he was going to be "the prime minister for everyone" and that he was going to "form a broad government in order to heal the religious split in the society." He strove to form a coalition with Shas and Meretz, both of whom he needed to mend the gap between secular and religious Jews on the one hand and Sephardic and Ashkenazi Jews on the other hand. Therefore Barak didn't want to throw in his lot with Likud, which had won nineteen seats but was paralyzed by internal divisions. Moreover Shas, although it aroused aversion in many Israelis, was milder than Likud with respect to the peace negotiations that Barak wanted to resume as soon as possible.

President Weizmann, who interfered in politics more often than one would generally expect from a president, made a visit to Meretz leader Yossi Sarid (1941) during the negotiations to convince him to form a coalition with Shas. As a condition for this, Sarid stipulated that he would in that case become minister of education and that Shas leader Aryeh Deri would have to step down. Deri would step down only on the condition that his party would get the Ministry of Religious Affairs and that Yossi Sarid could designate a deputy minister from the ranks of Shas. Barak needed both parties to get a majority, and he granted the wishes of both parties because Meretz could crush his intention to be a "prime minister for everyone."

This is how the two hostile parties, Shas and Meretz, joined the government coalition in July 1999. Now Barak still needed the support of the Ashkenazi ultra-Orthodox party of Rabbi Ravitz with whom he had been at odds for some time. The *haredim*, who feel affinity with the more "Jewish" Likud, had always been convinced that they would never throw their in lot with the Zionist Labor party unless Meretz would cease involvement with education, culture, and other affairs that are part of the formation of Jewish identity. But at that moment Meretz had already been promised the Ministry of Education. Because United Torah Judaism realized that Barak needed them, this party demanded, in exchange for becoming part of the government, that Barak abandon his plan to establish military service for the ultra-Orthodox. Earlier that year, while he was still in the opposition, Barak had made himself very unpopular with the United Torah Judaism with that plan. (As mentioned earlier, since January 1999 there exists a separate army unit for ultra-Orthodox whose participation is optional. Barak hopes that the *haredim* will now feel more involved with the state; in turn, the *haredim* hope that they will be able to come out of their financial malaise.) United Torah Judaism did not accept any ministry because its Council of Sages (the spiritual leaders of the party who are also its political leaders and are therefore responsible for all political decisions) had forbidden them to be part of a government with Meretz. According to United Torah Judaism, which supports the government "from outside," there is an advantage to this arrangement: the party can leave the coalition whenever it wishes without losing anything.

Ravitz regrets that Shas has no objections of principle to a coalition with Meretz. But at the same time he says that he can't blame Shas because "the Sephardic Jews never had to deal with an advancing secularism in their surroundings and never had to fight for the preservation of their Jewish identity like the Ashkenazi Jews in Europe. Therefore they can't recognize the danger of an ultrasecular party like Meretz that believes in the new Israeli Jew and an 'ordinary' state for all citizens." Ravitz does blame Shas for the way they won: "The Sephardic leaders try to shake off their inferiority complex by taking advantage of the feelings of non-believing traditional Sephardic Jews. As ultra-Orthodox leaders they post political victory by using cultural and socio-economic tricks in which belief plays a subordinate role. We can't offer our voters that kind of eroded Judaism; that would be immoral."

Meretz was disappointed that Barak, who was brought into politics by Yitzhak Rabin as supreme commander of the Israeli armies in 1995, didn't make use of the historic opportunity to form a government without the ultra-Orthodox. With his overwhelming victory (for Israeli politics) in 1999—56 percent of the votes against 44 percent for Netanyahu—he broke through the electoral balance that had existed between Likud and the Labor Party for the preceding twenty years. He could have formed a government—and that hadn't happened in twenty years—without the ultra-Orthodox because he had a choice among fifteen parties in the Knesset. Instead of that he chose, according to Meretz, a coalition with parties that wanted to preserve the "Jewish content" of the state through the Law of God.

The secularists in Meretz were particularly dissatisfied with Barak's government, in which Shas occupied four ministerial posts (Social Services, Infrastructure, Health Care, and Religious Affairs), a situation that made the introduction of the constitution—one of Meretz's most important goals—practically impossible. In order to complete the constitution, four Basic Laws were still needed (as mentioned in chapter 1, during the course of the years eleven Basic Laws have been passed). The legal establishment of freedom of expression and the freedom of assembly will not cause much resistance from religious Knesset members. However, the chance that the other two, the Basic Laws for individual rights and for freedom of religion, will be accepted is practically nil.

The fact that the subject of the constitution is not a high priority for every secular minister was evident from the almost matter-of-fact reaction of the minister of justice, Yossi Beilin of the Labor Party. He thought that it would be "worth while" to try and complete the constitution, but then added that "the government can always stop if the process threatens to turn into a civil war." Then minister of health, Shas member Shlomo Benizri, announced that he would vote against any Basic Law, "even if it contained the Ten Commandments." For Shas, United Torah Judaism, and for some religious Zionists it wasn't simply that these laws were unacceptable, but that the constitution itself was considered a danger to the only Jewish law, the halakhah. A constitution would impede further religious legislation.

Politically, Shas became an important factor in 1992 when it won ten seats and participated in the government of Yitzhak Rabin (1922–1995 Jerusalem). In this government Shas clashed in particular with Shulamit Aloni, who drove the Sephardic and Ashkenazi communities into the arms of Benjamin Netanyahu with her anti-religious rhetoric. For the Sephardic Jews, the extreme left of Meretz was a justification of the rightness of their own culture and religion that they feel are "better than Aloni's 'prostitution' and 'gay marriage.'" In the 1996 elections 95 percent of the strict Orthodox voted for Netanyahu out of fear of a government with the Labor Party and Meretz. In the following years, Netanyahu gave them the chance to extend the Shas educational system by naming a Shas minister of the interior and an Orthodox minister of education. The tension between Meretz and Shas (which had ten seats at the time as well) was less at the time.

Barak's government had a more difficult time with the ultrasecular Minister of Education Yossi Sarid and seventeen Shas seats. In its short existence this government went through two crises that were both created by the tension between Meretz and Shas. The third crisis started with the appointment of Sarid. At the request of Shas, Sarid appointed a deputy minister of education from the ranks of Shas but neglected to give him responsibility over Shas's education system *Ma'ayan haChinuch haTorani* (the source of Torah education). Instead, he reduced the budget and drew up the so-called *Ma'ayan* reform plan that included, among other things, the closing of a number of schools. The anger among the Shas population increased when Sarid announced that in his department "no independent system, would be created that would push money to *Ma'ayan* according to the needs, values, and norms defined by Shas." For Shas supporters this statement meant that the Ashkenazi establishment was again trying to discriminate against the Sephardic Jews. In this way Sarid created a focus for the words of Shas spiritual leader Ovadia Yossef that started the third crisis.

During one of the traditional weekly Saturday evening lessons that took place right before the Purim festival in 2000, Ovadia Yossef compared the minister of education (whom he supposedly cursed) to the biblical figure Haman, who persecuted the Jews in ancient Persia. Because of this Sarid was viewed with hostility by Yossef and therefore by the Sephardic community. To give a picture of the rhetoric and the choice of words of this spiritual leader, who is called *gedol hador* (genius of his generation) by many of his half-million admirers, I quote a fragment from the lesson that Yossef gave on March 18, 2000, in his yeshiva:

> God has made things difficult for us. He has saddled us with this Yossi Sarid, this Satan, may his name be blotted out [cf. Exod. 17:14]. And how can we control ourselves . . . how long can we still suffer under this wicked creature? God will wipe him out just as he wiped out Amalek. . . . Is Haman cursed? Yossi Sarid be cursed! Where is his common sense, what is he planning? Does he want Mahmud Darwish? [Sarid had proposed making the poems of the Palestinian poet Mahmud Darwish a fixed part of the educational program in elementary schools]. Is that his common sense? Doesn't it pain him that secular Jews don't know the Torah? That they don't know "Hear O Israel." No. It pains him that they don't know Mahmud Darwish. May God ruin his plans and give him his just deserts. Just as He showed us with Haman's death. He will be avenged in the same way as Haman. And when you say "cursed be Haman" after reading the Book of Esther, also say "cursed be Sarid."

The following day Yossef announced that he hadn't meant "to advocate using violence against Sarid because that is not the way of the Torah. Therefore I hereby declare in public . . . that it is forbidden to hurt someone, even if this person is hostile to us." But these words that were supposed to serve as an apology were unacceptable to Sarid. A week later Yossef announced that he had not meant to incite physical violence, but that Sarid is a "racist" who "despises the Torah." In this weekly lesson the rabbi compared Sarid to the Egyptian pharaoh (referring to Passover, which was approaching) who "would never have pursued a policy like Sarid." Yossef then added that he was not taking back what he had previously said about Sarid and concluded, "The Holy One, blessed be He, . . . knows how to treat those who desecrate the Torah."

During his efforts to resolve the government crisis resulting from this affair, Barak's principal concern was the worry about the crucial phase of peace negotiations that he was involved in with Hafez al-Assad, president of Syria. Therefore he wanted to oblige Shas's wishes, but Sarid made it very clear that he would leave the coalition if Barak gave in. Shas threatened to leave the coalition if their deputy minster of education, Meshulam Nahari, would not become responsible for *Ma'ayan* and if the changes in the reform plan set up by Sarid would not be modified. Because Barak had preferred Shas as coalition partner in order to make the peace process go as smoothly as possible, he tried once again to convince Meretz that a flexible position was desirable because of the peace talks. He emphasized that the present coalition was not only the one with which to "conclude the peace" but was also the one for "the day after the peace." Barak was very disappointed when Shas announced that it didn't want to be bound by support for the peace process; this destroyed Barak's hope to avert the crisis by Shas's "return" to the coalition in exchange for a concession to their demands. Sarid announced that "Meretz had already gone as far as it could" in accommodating Shas's wishes and that "the limit had been reached." According to Sarid, reconsideration of the agreements about *Ma'ayan* would entail the transfer of tens of millions of shekels to the accounts of the network; he also said that "wherever the money may come from, it's tax money that could be better spent elsewhere."

Meanwhile, Israeli Attorney-General, Eliyakim Rubinstein, had announced that it was necessary to start a police investigation of Rabbi Ovadia Yossef because of "instigation to violence." (At the request of the police, Rubinstein made this announcement a few days later than he had wanted because it was expected that the decision could cause clashes and demonstrations that might interfere with the visit of the pope.) According to Rubinstein, it wasn't important to check whether the rabbi, who "had exceeded all legitimate bounds of public criticism," had intended violence but rather how his audience, which applauded enthusiastically and shouted "Amen," would interpret his words. (An opinion poll among Shas supporters showed that 5 percent of them interpreted Yossef's words as permission to commit murder.) Rubinstein felt that the rabbi's position in society made his remarks even more complex: "Unfortunately shameless insults are the order of the day in Israel, but Yossef's remarks can unfortunately not be compared to the remarks that we are used to nowadays and about which no investigation needs to be done. The advice given us in the *Tanakh* 'Words spoken softly by a wise man are heard sooner' ['than those shouted by a ruler among fools' Eccl. 9:17] is unfortunately heeded by few."

The days that followed this decision were dominated by reactions to the affair. Shas minister Benizri called the decision "racist" since it was made only because the Sephardic public was involved. He added that similar remarks by Ashkenazi secularists like Yossi Sarid and Shulamit Aloni would not be treated in the same way. Shas leader and minister of employment and social affairs, Eli Ishai, declared that the decision of the attorney-general proved that in Israel freedom of expression is the "privilege of one group." Shas minister of religious affairs, Yitzhak Cohen, said that Sarid had the "filthiest mouth" in Israel but that he nevertheless "enjoys immunity. He is the last person who can teach what is moral to rabbi Ovadia Yossef, the glory of this generation." The leader of the Ashkenazi party, United Torah Judaism, announced that he, too, supported Ovadia.

Typical of the political behavior of Shas is the concentration on their own "state," which is why it makes no difference with which party it forms a coalition. The party leaders don't even intend to establish a state based on the halakhah, something that many Meretz supporters mistakenly fear. Their only goal is their own "anti-state," whereby religion is used as a means to define the enemy and to justify their demands. In this case Sarid is the enemy because he "doesn't know the Torah" and the money is needed "for Torah study." The concept of "common good" does not exist for this party, and this is why the party leaders have no difficulty making high demands that they stick to until they get their way or until a crisis breaks out. As a solution Shas usually receives money in exchange for its support in the area of foreign politics, which is not high on its agenda.

Typical for the political behavior of Meretz, which shows significant similarities to Shas, is the aggressive approach to the Orthodox in Israel. Meretz has a social component too: it is the party for secular Israelis who emphasize their Western liberal identity. The feeling of oppression that characterized the Shas supporters for years has now pervaded the ranks of Meretz. As "Westerners" they feel pushed into a corner by the Orthodox. The fight for their own Israeli liberal identity is carried out in consultation with their own spiritual leaders, Shulamit Aloni and the writer Amos Oz.

For some time people wondered if it was wise of Barak to have included Meretz as well as Shas in his coalition—Shas's participation in the government was the more controversial of the two. Supporters of Meretz and Shinui felt that Shas should be "left to wither" in the opposition. As a member of the opposition Shas would indeed have less money for its institutions and would therefore lose a good part of its voting public. On the other hand, support for Shas usually increases as the feeling of being neglected increases among its supporters. The proof that support for Shas grows in difficult times is shown by the previously mentioned verdict of party leader Aryeh Deri to four years of prison on the charge of fraud—Shas received 430,000 votes during the last campaign for the Knesset; the Labor Party received 900,000.

Slowly a new political atmosphere has developed in Israel in which not only the religious but also the moderately secular parties (this excludes Meretz) can vote down bills that are meant to guarantee individual freedoms. The Orthodox minority now has a full-fledged position in the political and social life of Israel. It is impossible to imagine politics without its particularism, and this has consequences for the political behavior of the secularists. At the end of January 1999 a Basic Law regarding freedom of religion proposed in the Knesset by Meretz was voted down by forty-three Knesset members against twenty-eight. Why did many Knesset members of the Labor Party beg off? For fear of losing the support of the Orthodox at a later time? Or is the doctrine of being the chosen people so deeply rooted in the Jewish consciousness that it lives on even among those who no longer share the religious convictions of their forbears?

There are numerous examples of this political opportunism of the secular politicians. One of them is the vote of a few Knesset members of the Labor Party in March of 1998 in favor of the acceptance of a law forbidding the import of pork, a choice that, according to the opponents, was meant to "appease the ultra-Orthodox." The proposal came from the Orthodox parties. Opponents in the Labor Party called party members who had voted for the proposal "ideologically weak," and they called the law a "non-kosher parliamentary slaughter of the interests of the majority of the Israeli population."

Secular politicians are dependent on religious politicians. The religious parties are used not only because the Orthodoxy preserves Jewish identity and gives the state its Jewish content, but also because they are "cheap" coalition partners. The fact is that the religious parties have demands only in the areas of religion, education, and culture, and in return for monetary support in those areas they support decisions about foreign politics and social policy almost blindly.

Negotiating with United Torah Judaism and with Shas can be called "bartering" because these parties, in contrast to the religious Zionists who accept the state, don't participate in politics for ideological reasons. The ultra-Orthodoxy wants to exchange its political support for money in order to preserve its community. With this they show a certain feeling of moral superiority, and they generally hold on to their absolute religious truths—this makes reaching compromises a difficult affair. However, in setting high financial demands the religious party leaders risk having to choose whether or not to give up a religious principle that would endanger their religious integrity in case their demands are not granted.

Because the secular and the religious politicians need one another, the commitment of the secularists in the functioning of the democracy can disappear temporarily when a certain political move—no matter how objectionable in itself—can be profitable for the politician involved or for his party. Such a maneuver can be a political pilgrimage to a spiritual leader or a visit to a chief rabbi during a Jewish holiday. As a consequence of such maneuvers, consistency is rare in Israeli politics: coalitions can change from one day to the next and alliances are formed and broken equally fast. Politicians of all parties participate in this kind of improper political practice. After all, in Israel yesterday's blunder pales in comparison to today's catastrophe.

This government culture has come about because since 1948 politicians have let their agenda be determined by the concept of "Security." The theoretical foundation of the sovereign Jewish democracy—and with it the possible flourishing of liberalism and universalism—has suffered because of this. The establishment of a Jewish state with a Jewish character, the presence of an Arab minority, and the Israeli-Arab conflict in the region have made Israel a country turned inward, a country that spiritually places emphasis on the past. "Surviving," which for many is connected to exclusivity, recalls biblical history and the Holocaust and is in Israel still the core of collective awareness.

Almost all politicians have been using ethnic and religious Jewish particularistic rhetoric. Politicians who governed the country in the early years discovered quickly that it was easier to mobilize the population by referring to the common tribal identity, as found in "closed" Jewish feelings and common religious sensitivities, than by emphasizing liberal or socialist sentiments. Particularism has become an important part of the Jewish state and of Judaism that in the course of history seems to have acquired a monopoly on exclusivity. Even Ben Gurion caused unrest when in his speeches he did not glorify the return of the people Israel to Palestine as a heroic deed for which many sacrifices had been made.

Former Prime Minister Benjamin Netanyahu gave striking examples of Zionist rhetoric, directed to the Jewish people. A good illustration was his reaction to the above-mentioned ultra-Orthodox demonstration of February 1999. Netanyahu said,

> In contrast to other countries, the essence of Judaism is a combination of religion and nationality. The Jewish people is proud of its roots from which the state of Israel draws its existential strength. Absolute separation of religion and state is impossible in Israel, although religious tyranny is unacceptable to the secular and secular coercion unacceptable to the religious. Only dialogue makes it possible to find practical solutions. For example, in recent years

restaurants and movie theaters in Jerusalem have been open on the Sabbath. In the same city certain streets in Orthodox districts have been closed the past few years. Only with patience and by tolerating those who disagree with us can we keep living in this country where nationality and religion are interwoven.

Another example was his speech to the General Assembly of the United Nations in September 1998, in response to the approaching proclamation of the Palestinian state. In it he called the bond of the Jewish people with the land of Israel "eternal" and the establishment of Israel a "historical necessity." According to Netanyahu, both religious and nonreligious Jews considered this as a "modern wonder and the embodiment of the vision of the Hebrew prophets." According to Netanyahu: "No other people has suffered as much, and we are all the sons and daughters of Abraham." He felt that it was "characteristic for the Jewish people to live in hope, the name of our national anthem." In conclusion he remarked that "in the Torah portion of this week there is a wish for peace that we, the Jewish people, spread from our eternal capital Jerusalem, the city of peace, over all neighboring countries."

"It remains difficult to explain why Israel calls itself democratic while 20 percent of the population are second-rank citizens. Israel as a Jewish country is primarily meant for the Jews, and the Arabs are therefore excluded. That is the heart of the problem." Professor of political science and Jewish philosophy Eliezer Don-Yehiya (1939) of Bar Ilan University knows exactly where the Jewish democracy is shaky, but he doesn't want to abandon the definition of Israel as a Jewish state. He touches the core of the Jewish paradox with his remark:

> Many Jews want to live in the only Jewish state in the world, but they also want it to be democratic. Well before 1948 the Orthodox demanded a future home that would be Jewish. The fact that there is no civil marriage is problematic. Israel is a Jewish state, and the Jewish wedding is rooted in the Jewish tradition. But our state will still be a state after the acceptance of civil marriage. The only question is whether mixed marriages, which will take place on a greater scale as a result of legally established civil marriage, will in the long run endanger the survival of the Jewish people and the Jewish state.

Don-Yehiya has written about this subject in the article "Religion, ethnicity and electoral reforms: Religious parties in the 1996 elections." In "Civil religion in Israel" and in *The Book and the Sword: The Nationalist Yeshivot and Political Radicalism in Israel* he writes about the role of religion in Israel. He treats the subject carefully, and many of his principal clauses are followed by "but," "subject to," "that depends on," or "I want to be careful." The unstable situation and the fragmented makeup of the population make firm pronouncements practically impossible and force him to put himself in the position of sociologist, theologian, anthropologist, and historian. The contact with *haredi* family members is useful for his work, just like his own religious Zionist background (Lithuanian) and the *haredi* education that he received. (Before the Six-Day War in 1967, when he went to school, there were no religious-Zionist schools.) On his head is a crocheted yarmulke that in his case indicates sympathies for the National Religious Party. He calls himself moderately Orthodox and feels that the Oslo accords are too pro-Palestinian, but he won't protest against the Palestinian state.

> We differ from the Western European democracies, not because our election system or our party system is different, but because our nationalism has an ethno-religious background instead of a geographic or political one. In the Netherlands a Dutch Jew has the Dutch nationality because citizenship and nationality are one and the same. But in Israel an Arab Israeli has the Arab nationality and the Jewish Israeli has the Jewish one while both of them have Israeli citizenship. Our country is unique because citizenship (Israeli) and nationality (Jewish, Arab, or Russian) don't coincide. As long as Israel is a Jewish state and as long as the Arabs are not Jews, this problem will remain. We most certainly have a problem that is difficult to solve, but the state is defined as a secular Jewish state and not as a religious state.

Even though this fact imposes limitations on the democracy, Don-Yehiya feels that Arabs don't need to be second-class citizens in the Jewish democracy:

> Our state would still be Jewish if they received more government funds, had the right to buy any piece of land that Jews can buy, and if military service was also compulsory for them so that they would be eligible for more jobs. [In Israel, most employers expect

candidates to have completed military service.] Hebrew will remain the first language, I'll still be able to sing the *Hatikvah* [the national anthem], organize a seder, go to the synagogue, and my grandchildren will still be circumcised. The problem is that many Arabs don't accept the Jewish character of the state, and moreover many Jews are afraid that in the future the Arabs will dominate numerically and will assume control.

The worry about "Security"—which has everything to do with the presence of the Arabs in Israel and dominates the Israeli political agenda—is great and anti-Arab sentiments are widespread. Membership in the most important Knesset committee for foreign affairs and defense was until recently reserved for Jews. But in August 1999 the first Arab, Hashem Mahameed, became a member. The rightist and Orthodox members of the committee ignore him because to them his presence is a "danger for Israel's security and for its spiritual health." After his appointment a cartoon appeared in the leftist paper *Ha'aretz* showing a confused army officer who shows plans for a military operation to an Arab in a kaffiyeh. Nevertheless Mahameed feels that his appointment is a step in the direction of ending the racist policy of excluding Arabs from certain committees. But, he added, "it remains difficult for me to feel Israeli in a country that is intended for the Jewish people."

A number of prominent members of the government tend to react rather nervously about the influence of Israeli Arabs on decision making. The former National Religious Party minister of education and housing during the government of Barak, Yitzhak Levy (1947), decided at the end of 1998 that Israeli Arabs should not participate in votes in the Knesset about the Oslo accords. He didn't mention why, but everyone knew that this was decided because of security considerations. At the end of 1998 the Likud candidate for mayor of the northern Israeli city of Karmi'el openly resisted the construction of an Arab district because "the Arabs take over the city and continue to reproduce. They want to build a mosque in my city, then a school, and soon they'll want to buy houses in order to take over whole districts." Prime Minister Netanyahu's remark in the Knesset in November 1998—right before the vote on the Wye accord—took the cake. He announced that "votes of anti-Zionist Knesset members are henceforth invalid in voting about foreign affairs and about subjects that concern security. Anti-Zionist votes are valid for economic issues."

The leader of the Arab National Party, Abdel-Wahab Darawshe, said that the prime minister "does not take into account 20 percent of the population with this racist remark," and that same month he gave Netanyahu a lesson in good citizenship in an article in *Ha'aretz*. In this article he wondered: "Are these remarks racist?" He answered this question as follows: "No, of course not, after all he didn't say Arabs, but everyone knew whom he meant. Everyone in Israel knows that the Arabs are the only ones who don't recognize the state of Israel and are therefore the only anti-Zionists left." The coalition leader of Likud at the time, Meir Shetreet, reacted as follows: "Jewish or Arab, all votes count." A Knesset member of the National Religious Party called Netanyahu's remarks "anti-democratic," and president Ezer Weizmann said, "Arabs are Israeli citizens and have the right to vote on all issues." Knesset member Azmi Bishara of the communist party Hadash wrote in May 1998 in the same paper that "Israel has to exchange Zionism, the Jewish fascism, for a state for all citizens. Zionism has the unhealthy shortcoming that religion and nationality overlap, something that exists nowhere else in the world." Then Bishara continues, also lashing out at secular Jews: "This fascism is a consequence of the power that the corrupt secular Jews give the Orthodox because they want the extremists to keep the flame of Judaism burning. Something that they themselves don't want to do."

Eliezer Don-Yehiya, who has studied the behavior of the religious political parties for years, admits that the unequal position of the Arabs in Israel is a shortcoming of Israeli democracy. According to him, their position will deteriorate as the power of Shas and United Torah Judaism is strengthened, and he believes that this is the case. First of all, he points out the importance of the change of the election system in 1996; this caused the parliament to be chosen first and after that, in separate elections, the prime minister. This change was intended to contain the influence of the small religious parties but has boosted them instead, according to Don-Yehiya. It turned out that in 1996 and 1999 people could first show their political support by voting for Netanyahu and then make their cultural-religious wishes known by voting for their own party. (The old election system has been put back in place since May 2001, and people expect that Shas in particular will lose the next election.)

A second very important reason for the victory of the "Jewish

Israelis" is, according to Don-Yehiya, the fear prevalent in religious circles that Israel is in the process of losing its "Jewishness." This fear of "dejudaization," which was expressed in the election of Netanyahu, has become a part of the collective awareness of the Jewish people and especially of the religious Ashkenazi. The attacks on the Orthodox by Meretz members like Shulamit Aloni during the government of Yitzhak Rabin (1992–1996) have strengthened this awareness. In religious circles Meretz is called a "party for hedonists who have embraced a dissipated Western lifestyle and have thrown Jewish traditions overboard." The so-called Meretz-factor—as Don-Yehiya labels the unanimous Orthodox choice (in 1996) of Netanyahu out of fear of a government with the Labor Party and Meretz—is striking because five years ago the rabbis were still hesitating between the Labor Party and Likud. The Meretz-factor has consolidated the political course of the strict Orthodox: in 1996 and 1999, 95 percent of the Orthodox voted for Netanyahu (a nonpracticing Jew and an adulterer to boot!).

A third reason for the victory is, according to Don-Yehiya, the concentration of the religious parties on their own constituencies. The end of the electoral excursions of the Orthodox parties during the late eighties and early nineties turned out to be "home," that is to say, in the districts and cities where Shas and United Torah Judaism voters live. During the election campaign of 1996, Ravitz even told Shas that he was "not interested in ethnic rivalries." The one-seat gain of his party in 1999 was the consequence of natural growth of the ultra-Orthodox Ashkenazi community and was probably due to a number of Orthodox of the West Bank who had sympathy for Meir Porush of United Torah Judaism who was minister of housing in Netanyahu's government. As indicated above, Shas's constituency can be clearly defined and does not need to be looked for in the United Torah Judaism community.

This concentration on their own constituencies is possible because religious Israel is very compartmentalized. Not only does the address or district reveal political affiliation but the clothing, the outward appearance, the accent, and the newspaper that people read reveal their political preference. In the Degel district where Ravitz lives Yiddish is sometimes spoken, just as in Mea Shearim and Bnei Brak. The Orthodox of all sorts of Zionist and anti-Zionist factions who rush through these streets are all identifiable by their appearance. The religious persuasion of the women can be identified by their wigs or headscarves. As if kashrut is supposed to differentiate Jews from Jews instead of Jews from non-Jews, in the supermarkets there are kosher chickens that are approved by different rabbis: legs approved by the influential rabbi Ovadia Yossef and breasts approved by a total of thirteen different rabbis. Besides, there are usually frozen homegrown chickens and turkeys with 113 different kashrut certificates.

The interwovenness of religion and state in Israel is perhaps best expressed in the role played in politics by the Sephardic and Ashkenazi rabbis, spiritual leaders, and the Kabalists. This development started in 1977 after the election victory of Menachem Begin, the Likud leader at the time, whose victory broke the hegemony of the Labor Party for the first time in twenty years. He brought the *haredim* to the center of power, and since that year the synagogue has been working hand in glove with the right. The need to serve their own community through politics started to develop among the *haredim*. Slowly but surely the Ashkenazi Jews came out of their anti-Zionist isolation, a development that has accelerated since the establishment of Shas in 1984, and they turned out to be politicians without losing sight of the essence of their lives, the strict observance of God's word. Before Begin took office they were already receiving politicians in their Talmud Seminary for laying on of hands or advice, but they were not active in politics. After Begin took office, community members or good students were pushed forward as party leaders and suddenly had to represent their ultra-Orthodox party as Knesset members after years of doing nothing but *lernen*. For an ex-yeshiva student or an ex-yeshiva head there was no reason to break off contact with his spiritual leader. On the contrary, as someone who knows the word of God, the latter can guide him in his political career better than anyone. This is how the Kabala was introduced in Israeli politics and how the religious undermined their own religious credibility, at least in the eyes of others.

Gradually the spiritual leaders developed as eminent party leaders and have let themselves in for the anger of the secularists. Aloni says, "They take Israel back to the Middle Ages. They take Israel back to the times when the Church with its corrupt cardinals was able to force popes and kings to their knees. It used to be that in

Israel rabbis were rabbis and politicians were politicians, but the wall between them came down when the parties started to interfere with religion, and vice versa."

According to Charles Liebman, professor of political science at Bar Ilan University in Tel Aviv, the spiritual leaders have dragged Judaism into a particularistic antidemocratic direction. In his article "Religion and Democracy in Israel," Liebman states:

> Through their limited training and their xenophobic tendencies they have in the past ten years gained a great influence in politics at the expense of moderate Jewish scholars like Yeshayahu Leibowitz. A great number of poorly educated Sephardic Jews who call themselves traditional are less petty in their observance of the halakhah but are very receptive to the anti-pluralistic opinions of the religious tradition that the rabbis present to them.

When visiting the Knesset, one meets them, the men with beards, many of whom are rabbis but by no means all of them. In black coats, a hat and/or a yarmulke on their heads, they sit on the benches, walk though the halls, or eat a meal in the restaurant. In general, the men in black represent United Torah Party or Shas, while most Shas supporters are dressed "normally" but do wear black yarmulkes. The National Religious Party members can be recognized by their crocheted yarmulke and their lack of side curls. The spiritual leaders, who are often head of a yeshiva or carry out other religious activities, usually stay home where they are visited by their "disciple-politicians."

The presence of Orthodox Jews in the government regularly creates tragicomic run-ins with secularists. One example of this is the discussion that took place in the Knesset in 1998 about posthumous circumcisions desired by the Orthodox. The opposition leader of Meretz and the minister of education, Yossi Sarid, said, "I wish to be the only one responsible for my sexual organs. Nowadays the Orthodox seem to want to control not only our lives but also our death." A Shas colleague then asked, "Why do you have objections to such a circumcision but not to posthumous operations to remove lungs or other organs?" Another example of such a clash was the debate in the Knesset about kosher potatoes when McDonald's wanted to open its first outlet in the Holy Land in 1994. Another example was the discussion in 1996 between Knesset member and minister of health, Shlomo Benizri (1961), and the Israeli cabaret performer Gil Kopatch. During a performance Kopatch mentioned that Noah skipped around in Paradise "in the nude" and that at the reception of Abraham and Sara on the occasion of Isaac's birth "the whole biblical jet-set, including Tapusina (an Israeli model)" was present. Kopatch, who during the program wore old-fashioned glasses with thick lenses (the kind that the Orthodox wear most of the time), had to come to the Knesset to explain his remarks about Noah, Abraham, and Sara.

A disconcerting example had to do with the approval of the budget by the Finance Committee in 1999. Rabbi Avraham Ravitz, who at that time was the head of the committee, reserved a billion shekel in the budget for the Ministry of Religious Affairs. When, after a few night sessions, Ravitz added that he wanted a favorable settlement for the inflation correction of the "salary" that yeshiva students receive from the state, the Knesset turned into a battlefield. Meretz member and Minister of Commerce and Industry Ran Cohen (1939) reacted: "You should be ashamed; you steal from the treasury and have you ever contributed anything to the state?" Ravitz responded, "Stop that anti-Semitism, you little anti-Semite. We the *haredim* are no longer letting ourselves be ridiculed in public. Are we your garbage can?" Ravitz then reminded his audience that he and two other members of the committee had fulfilled their military obligation. The chair of the Knesset at the time, Dan Tichon, asked the Knesset doctor to come because he feared that Ravitz was becoming unwell. Meanwhile, Elie Goldsmith of the Labor Party intervened in the discussion: "Don't call him an anti-Semite; I've had it with those accusations of anti-Semitism in the Knesset." Ravitz, who was being helped into a chair by the doctor and covered his face with a handkerchief, answered, "You with your blue eyes, are you better than I?" (Ravitz was referring to the "new Jew," the ideal of the Zionists: tall, blond, and blue-eyed.)

The participation of the Orthodox in politics has given a strange twist to democracy and party politics during the last two decades: when requested, rabbis pronounce blessings and make predictions through angels who seem to reveal themselves only to them. The Shas constituency is particularly easy to entice with amulets against the evil eye that can often be seen in offices and stores next to posters and photos of Yossef. Political leaders kiss the hands of spiritual leaders, usually in times of political need. In January 1999 the minister of transport who was originally from Kurdistan, Yitzhak Mordechai (1945), in his role as leader of the new Center party kissed the beard of Ovadia Yossef, the spiritual leader of Shas. Mordechai, whose only goal was to defeat Netanyahu in the elections, thought that by this maneuver he would be able win over Shas voters. After all, the Shas leaders excel in activities of a spiritual nature. In October 1998, shortly before the municipal elections, pictures of Ovadia Yossef together with the ancient Sephardic Kabalist Yitzhak Kedouri (Baghdad, year of birth unknown, probably 1896) adorned bottles of olive oil with the following text: "All political parties are the work of the devil, except Shas." The bottles were handed out in the streets to potential Shas voters who left their telephone numbers with the bottle distributor who called them once again with a campaign message right before the elections.

Rabbi Kedouri is a senile man who can barely walk and is flown around the country to say blessings at election campaigns or at other events. Even so, with a political pilgrimage to Kedouri right before the elections of 1996, Netanyahu was offered a great opportunity to consolidate his political power. Right before the blessing, the Kabalist announced that he had been able to get a copy of the Book of Psalms from which dangled a key and in which the names of angels were mentioned. During the blessing Rabbi Kedouri whispered the names, asked for the election winner, gave the book a twist and mumbled, "You win if the key falls to the right of the book when it stops swinging." In September 1997, perhaps as thanks, Netanyahu whispered in the rabbi's ear, "Leftist Israel has forgotten what it means to be Jewish." (He realized too late that there were journalists nearby.) In June 1998, when asked, the deeply religious Rabbi Yitzhak Eliyahu of the National Religious Party told Netanyahu that according to his calculations the latter would not remain prime minister if he carried through the pull-back from the West Bank.

It isn't only in secular Ashkenazi circles that the influence of the spiritual elite on the government is encountering opposition. At the end of September 1998, it was of all people David Levy (1931), the minister of foreign affairs originally from Morocco, who opened fire on Rabbi Kedouri, who had just returned from blessing the candidate for mayor of Beit Shean:

I've had had it with amulets and sorcery; the blessing of candidates is lunacy. Israelis are witnessing surrealistic scenes with rabbis who are permitted to do things that harm the religion and the unity of the Jewish people. Rabbi Kedouri is being exploited. Does this very old man even know where he lives and whom he blesses? Why do I have to point out a phenomenon that should alarm every Israeli? Why does nobody say anything?

The Orthodox rabbinate agreed with Levy. The rabbis called the use of rabbis who shouldn't intervene in politics "in bad taste and excessive." Ehud Barak, the leader of the Labor Party, who had asked rabbis for a blessing from time to time, then announced that "he would not consult them any more because political intervention of rabbis is unacceptable." In the middle of this storm (about him), Rabbi Kedouri let himself be taken to the office of Prime Minister Netanyahu in order to bless him for the new year. Netanyahu declared that he considered the Kabalist "smart and wise" and called the attack on the rabbis "amusing"—after all these rabbis have their own opinions, just like professors, poets, and writers. He said that he found it "interesting" that "people like Barak who constantly pursue rabbis without receiving the desired blessing" now suddenly reject the phenomenon. (At the end of January 2000, Shas, the United Torah Party, Likud, and the religious Zionists of the National Religious Party succeeded in voting down a bill that would forbid the distribution of amulets during election campaigns.)

The importance of this subject was emphasized a month later, in November 1998, during a special session in the Knesset about "rabbis in politics." The immediate cause was the publication of an ad about the Wye accord in the National Religious Party newspaper *Hatzofeh* a few days after the signing. In the ad, which was signed by 161 rabbis, National Religious Party members were urged to leave the coalition so that they would no longer be part of a government that "bargains its land away to foreigners." Municipal rabbis, who had actively resisted the Oslo accords in 1994, were officially forbidden from carrying out political activities in public. The question raised during the Knesset session was why a rabbi who is a civil servant and receives a salary from the state can make his opinions known with impunity while a local government official is forbidden to intervene in politics during municipal council elections.

This question has remained unanswered, but it is perhaps possible to find out when rabbis started to intervene in politics. Originally, a rabbi was someone with judicial and spiritual authority who studied and interpreted the halakhah. In the Torah his function is described (Deut. 17: 9, 11): "[you shall] . . . appear before the levitical priests, or the magistrate . . . and present your problem. When they have announced to you the verdict in the case . . . you must not deviate from the verdict that they announce to you either to the right or to the left." The Talmud says about this that one should obey the rabbis of one's own generation "even if they declare that right is left and left is right."

Prof. Eliezer Schweid of the Hebrew University of Jerusalem says, "The need to make a distinction between spiritual and political leaders is rooted in the aversion to political involvement by the ultra-Orthodox Ashkenazi community." He teaches Jewish philosophy and for years he studied the phenomena of *da'at Torah* (knowledge of the Torah) and *gedolei Torah* (literally, the great of the Torah).

> In the Haskalah and during the years before the establishment of the state of Israel, this involvement was considered blasphemous, but the Orthodox understood that they had to remain in touch with their surroundings. That is how the Council of Sages (*gedolei Torah*) was created; it had to see to it that religious laws were maintained. The political leaders were subordinate to the Sages and were expected to follow all their instructions. After all, the Sages had divine authority that enabled them to decide even about subjects they knew nothing about. They became a kind of Pope and received the status that goes with it. Actually, Rabbis Shach and Ovadia Yossef are also Popes. In Israel the structure of Judaism has become hierarchic and therefore more Christian. The game of the Sages was to give old answers to new questions which were raised at the time of the emancipation but also in the modern world. They say that the Orthodox community remained the way it was during the time of Abraham and Jacob and that nothing will change; after all, "*chadash asur min haTorah*" (change is forbidden according to the Torah). Meanwhile, the *gedolei Torah* made it possible for the ultra-Orthodox community to justify changes.
>
> This system was created by Agudat Israel and strengthened its position in Israel as the political involvement of the ultra-Orthodox increased. The Sephardic communities in Iraq, Iran, and North Africa didn't have such an institution because, unlike the Ashke-

nazi Jews in Europe, they were not confronted with the modern era. That is why in Israel they have taken over the Ashkenazi model, which has always been very problematic. It's becoming ever more clear, especially in the Sephardic community, that the distinctions between spiritual and political leaders have been blurred. Rabbi Ovadia Yossef, who long before the formation of Shas had the status of a Sage, has become a politician whose authority is based on his original religious authority. In practice it turns out to be difficult to maintain the separation between politics and religion. The Orthodox system in which a rabbi tries to cooperate with the political leader of his party is starting to show signs of deterioration. The two leaders are involved in a power struggle that is especially visible in the Sephardic community. The fact that cooperation between a political and a spiritual authority is impossible seems to be a fact because both leaders will in principle never be able to agree with each other.

Schweid concludes: "But they themselves don't understand that their system is about to collapse because their admission of failure means that they will have to change."

The interwovenness of religious, socioeconomic, and political problems has become a part of the Jewish reality in Israel. But it is difficult to find political solutions for street confrontations between secular and religious and neighborhood quarrels. Especially in Jerusalem Israelis are reminded of the "Jewish conflict." In hospitals in the capital, except for the Hadassah hospital, patients who listen to the radio on the Sabbath are reprimanded. Private telephone conversations are not allowed on the Sabbath. But for medical purposes doctors are able to have telephone conversations via a Sabbath telephone that is designed in such a way that using it doesn't desecrate the Sabbath. The secular inhabitants of Jerusalem prefer not to live in an apartment with a Sabbath elevator (an elevator that goes up and down all day long and stops at every floor so that the Orthodox can get in without pushing a button, which would be a desecration of the Sabbath). They feel that such an elevator attracts the Orthodox. Sooner or later many secularists living in Jerusalem move to another city.

It is also wise for a driver not to turn into Bar Ilan Street accidentally on a Saturday because he could be surprised by ultra-Orthodox children who stand ready to pelt the car with rocks. The conflict about the closure of this street on the Sabbath has recently spread to the secular Ethiopia Street, which borders HaNevi'im (prophets) Street in the ultra-Orthodox Mea Shearim district.

According to biblical scholars, these disorders are the result of the secularization that they resist with the Torah in hand. For decades politicians have been wrestling with the question of where to draw the line between modernity and tradition. For example, the Sabbath and circumcision are signs of the covenant between Yahweh and his people. But Jewish Israelis who in 1997 proposed abandoning circumcision were called anti-Semites. The Sabbath is the Jewish day of rest, and the Torah calls for the death of anyone who desecrates this day: "You shall keep the Sabbath, for it is holy . . . He who profanes it shall be put to death. . . . (Exod. 31:14, also 35:2). For strict and dogmatic Torah students, among whom there are always one or two who forget to separate doctrine from practice, arguments can always be found to attack advancing secularization. In Haifa at the end of 1997 some rabbis lodged a complaint against the play *Zushi Bar* that was performed by the lesbian theater group *Zoo Show* during a women's festival. The play was "perverted" and "heretical," and the Orthodox lodged a complaint—unsuccessfully —with the mayor.

According to Zvi Werblowsky, a Dutch Jewish cultural historian and emeritus professor of comparative religion at the Hebrew University in Jerusalem, such situations demand understanding rather than premature condemnation: "The Jews didn't return to Palestine to establish another pluralistic Utopia but to realize the fullness of Jewish life, to fulfill a Jewish destiny, in short: to create a Jewish state, whatever that may mean." The question remains whether the Jewish religion can be considered one of the most important components of the Jewish personality. The majority of secular Jews will deny this but cannot escape the observation that the whole culture of Judaism was religious until the nineteenth century. Until that time, being Jewish meant being religious, and in the diaspora a Jew could and still can renounce Judaism. This is not possible in Israel. If someone in Israel wants to leave Judaism but still wants to keep a Jewish identity, problems arise. In Orthodox circles it is unthinkable for a Jew to define his identity without being observant, because in their view religion is the only essential component of the Jewish personality. Moreover, in strict Orthodox circles the point is often raised that Judaism is not a religion but a law. The practical implications of this point of view can be dangerous according to Werblowsky:

> If Judaism is not a religion but a way of life (of course this is true for every religion in a certain sense), then certain rules of conduct can be imposed by law without people becoming guilty of religious tyranny. If the prohibition in Israel on raising pigs or stopping all public traffic on the Sabbath are cultural equivalents of traffic rules, then a society can go too far in restricting individual rights and liberties and at the same time insist that it upholds freedom of religion.

According to Prof. Aviezer Ravitzky, head of the department of Jewish philosophy of the Hebrew University in Jerusalem and who published *The Religious and the Secular: a Kulturkampf?* in the late 1990s, Israel resembles less and less the state of the stereotypical authentic Israeli to whom one could point in 1948. "Israel has become the arena of the struggle for the Jewish identity of the citizens and for the Jewish content of the state. More than ever the authorities are forced to look for compromises. We must accept that Sephardic, Ashkenazi, Russian, Israeli, Arab, religious, and nonreligious Israelis demand their place in Israeli society." According to Ravitzky, who covers his head with a black yarmulke and calls himself modern Orthodox and is a member of the Meimad political party, this unrest among people did not come like a thief in the night: "The foundation of the state carried this germ of trouble within itself."

Ravitzky explains:

> The Status Quo was a mere palliative. In 1948, the secularists and the Orthodox thought that the other side would not survive in the end: in Orthodox circles a secular Jew was called a contradiction in terms, and the secularists called Orthodoxy an anachronism. Ben Gurion counted on the Jewish people to "normalize" and on the future to overcome the past so that his new "anti-Diaspora Jews" would have their way.

According to Ravitzky, this "normalization" of the Jewish people that would, among other things, include the establishment of a democracy was an abnormal development for the Jews. They never had their own country, their own language, or political independence. What was normal for other peoples—their own territory, their

own language, and their own democratic government—became a
historical drama for the Jews. Normality turned out to be inextricably bound up with abnormality.

Ravitzky feels that instead of normalization, and apart from the
development of a strong ultra-Orthodox Sephardic movement, two
other important developments have taken place:

> First of all, the religious community has become halakhic. This
> means that its members have started to think more and more in
> black and white terms; the tones of gray that existed when the con-
> flict with the secular was less intense have disappeared. In addi-
> tion, the community thinks that it can apply the halakhah in fields
> that they never had anything to do with, such as medicine and
> especially in politics. The mirror image of this halakhization is the
> fact that everything in the secular community is brought before the
> law. This means that the High Court is supposed to solve every
> religious-cultural or political problem that involves the separation
> of religion and state: The "Who is a Jew" question, store closings
> on the Sabbath, closing Bar Ilan Street in Jerusalem on Saturday,
> the conversion question, and now the conflict between Meretz
> leader Yossi Sarid and Ovadia Yossef, the spiritual and political
> leader of Shas. All the dilemmas that the government should solve
> are being sent to the Court where the halakhah stands in opposi-
> tion to the secular legal system. The result is an increasing polar-
> ization because the root of the problem is not removed. The
> problem is that the society obliges the Court to solve these prob-
> lems because its own institutions are not suited to do so. And the
> politicians make no effort to find a way to handle the problem.

These observations raise the question whether the continuous
frictions between Shas and Meretz—or more generally those
between Jewish fundamentalism and Israeli liberalism—should be
settled by the judicial system or by Israeli politics. The supporters of
a judicial investigation of Yossef's statements say this is necessary
because politicians have failed to react. Moreover they think that
there is a need to have a judicial verdict to know if Yossef has
crossed the limits of the acceptable with his words. The questions
that they think should be central in the investigation regard the
reception of Yossef's words by his audience. Are they considered as
exceptional, or are they within the limits of acceptable "normal"
remarks uttered in a yeshiva? How is the expression "cursed be

Sarid" interpreted by his audience? Did someone conclude that Yossef would use violence against Sarid if they met on the street? Or did the listeners understand that the rabbi's intention was to make clear that Sarid would be punished by divine intervention?

The answers to these questions aren't that obvious in Israel. Members of Neturei Karta, for example, use the word *Nazi* in the same way as the secular use the word *disturbed* or *crazy*. Years ago the High Court sentenced a rabbi who in his book *The Laws Regarding the Killing of Gentiles* extolled the use of force. Two of the seven judges, who had both gone to Talmud Seminary, acquitted the rabbi because of the subtitle of the book: *For Study by Torah Sage Only*. They alone could understand that this book was meant only for internal halakhic discussion and not as a order to kill non-Jews.

Arik Carmon, director of the Israel Institute for Democracy, thinks that Rubinstein made an error by subjecting Yossef to a judicial investigation, because such an investigation widens the gap. Carmon, who says that he is a secularist, declares:

> The secular Jews are in the midst of a deep identity crisis. This crisis is brought about by the fact that the secular community itself doesn't know how to define itself in a positive way. It knows that it's not religious and that it doesn't obey the commandments. Because of this uncertainty, they are not able to absorb the terrible words that Yossef said about them and their politics without having recourse to the law. This is a sociopolitical matter in which the law should not play a role. The fact is that a judicial investigation is the continuation of the conflict. After all, the Court in Israel has a secular Ashkenazi identity and this only feeds the definition of the secular identity as not religious.

Moreover, Carmon feels that a police investigation would not achieve its objective and that it might even have an opposite effect. According to Carmon, Yossef's remarks are a symptom of the illness that is consuming Israeli society. He feels that Israel is a democracy in the formal sense but not in the intrinsic sense because the Israeli public "has not yet internalized democracy." This lack of "internalization," as he calls it, "is manifested in the different groups in Israeli society that don't accept that the other groups are also a legitimate part of that society. This is how the supporters of both Yossef and of Sarid feel."

According to Carmon, the solution to the *Kulturkampf*, the tension in Israel between the Jewish and the democratic forces, must be found in politics:

> The problem is that politics is silent as the grave. Ovadia Yossef has said what he said, and the whole political system was silent. Now everyone is hoping that the judicial system will solve the problem. This is a mistake. The legal system can't solve political or social problems. Moreover, the parliamentary system has made it even more difficult to find a solution. The combination of religious authority and political power is dangerous, in every country and in every age. In our case this combination has made a tragedy of Ovadia Yossef. The political power of Shas has turned a leader who was known for his moderate viewpoints and his tolerant attitude into an arrogant, haughty braggart. The power of Shas can in no small part be attributed to the change in our election system which caused the creation of a fragmented Knesset that is not able to deal with this sort of problem.
>
> Leaving this problem to judicial powers will not only not solve the problem, but it will destroy the courts themselves. It is clear that the police don't want to be involved with this affair for too long and that it will be sent back to the attorney-general. If the latter closes the investigation without a trial, then he will have achieved nothing at the end of the day. If he decides to litigate, every decision the court makes will harm the status of the legal system in the eyes of the ultra-secularists or in the eyes of the Orthodox. A conviction of Yossef will infuriate Shas, and his possible acquittal will make the secularists furious. We're not eager for that.

The essence of the domestic problem in Israel is the chasm between two groups that don't understand each other. Israeli society, and therefore its politics, consists of two parts: one part identifies itself with Meretz and Shinui, and the other part with Shas and the ultra-Orthodoxy. The secularists—but especially the extremist secularists of Meretz and Shinui—feel threatened, but they don't see that they can hurt the Orthodox with their attitude. Proof of this is an interview with Yishai Sarid, a lawyer and the son of Yossi Sarid. The interviewer asked Sarid if he didn't feel that his father should also offer his excuses. Sarid didn't understand the question because he had obviously never considered the possibility that the secularists didn't behave very well either in this conflict.

That same day Yossi Sarid appeared on television and asked the ultra-Orthodox to restrain themselves. Why didn't he ask this of his own constituency? After all, his followers, not Yossef's, are the ones who listen to him.

All this is not to justify Yossef's words but to indicate that the conflict is not one in which one party is right and the other wrong. Moreover, all attention is on the great villain Shas and the other ultra-Orthodox. But if the so-called Western intellectuals and liberals don't change their attitude toward the supporters of Shas, the conflict will never be solved. The secularists should try to understand the pain of the Shas supporters; the responsibility to get closer to each other lies with both parties. But the party that thinks that it is more adult, more intellectual, and wiser should be the first to extend its hand and show self-control and calm. Only then can this party ask the other to control itself.

Will the investigation of Rabbi Ovadia Yossef cause the tensions between the Jewish component and the democratic component to increase or to decrease? A process will decide in favor of one of the parties. But isn't this culture war an example of a struggle in which there should not be a question of an absolute winner or loser but of a draw? This concerns a deeply rooted sociopolitical conflict between Orthodox and non-Orthodox Jews, and why wouldn't politicians take the trouble to find a solution? Or is the somber answer that the different parties are developing along parallel lines that can by definition never intersect? These are essential questions that should be taken seriously because Shas, a growing political party with a significant social component, causes a double "total" culture war with its struggle; the Sephardic component involves the Ashkenazi Jews in the struggle, and the ultra-Orthodox component involves the secular Jews. Inversely, it can be asserted that these questions are of essential importance because Meretz, which has as social component the Western-secular sector with its antireligious rhetoric and political measures, can in the future see to it that the support of Shas will increase. This will in the end result in the same "total" *Kulturkampf*. There are similarities between both parties, but Israelis seem to forget those in their emotional reaction to Yossef's words. A no less important question in this regard is whether the extremist secular Jews could perhaps think twice instead of treating the Sephardic Jews as "unenlightened primitives," which only fuels the conflict. For this reason the above-mentioned questions are not only essential but also of existential importance to the Israeli democracy. All these unanswered questions confirm once again that Israeli society has to contend with the paradox mentioned earlier in this chapter, a paradox that has turned out to be unsolvable and unavoidable since the days of Herzl.

THREE

WHO IS A JEW?

the orthodox monopoly on judaism

"The Jew is a person whom others consider a Jew: that is the simple truth from which one should start. . . . Therefore the Jew is in a Jewish situation because he lives in the midst of a community that considers him Jewish. . . .

"Since a Jew cannot be defined by his race, should we define him by his religion or by a strictly Jewish national community?"

—Jean-Paul Sartre

"For you are a people consecrated to the Lord your God: of all the peoples on earth the Lord your God chose you to be His treasured people.

"Therefore, observe faithfully the Instruction—the laws and the rules—with which I charge you today."

Deuteronomy 7:6, 11.

WHEN TOMMY DORON WAS A SMALL boy in Hungary his parents taught him that God would punish everyone who did not believe in him. As the youngest member of a *haredi* family and as the pupil of a school that was connected to the ultra-Orthodox Aguda party, he accepted the lessons of his parents and his teachers. But after the Holocaust he turned his back on religion, and during the 1956 Hungarian revolution he fled via Austria to Israel where he settled in Kibbutz Lahav in the Negev. He married and had three children. At the end of October 1998 his twenty-one-year-old son Zohar died in Lebanon. As if this loss weren't tragic enough, the army leadership refused to arrange a military funeral for Zohar because Doron refused to have a rabbi present.

"I absolutely didn't want to hear the words 'merciful God' during the funeral," says Doron who uses a handkerchief to wipe away his tears from time to time. "What merciful God would take away my son, and why should I have to say 'the Lord has given, and the Lord has taken away' [Job 1:21] and accept death as the decision of a righteous Supreme Judge. After that I would still have to praise His great Name in all eternity," says Doron who knows the prayers quite well because of his ultra-Orthodox education.

> I can't even say the Shema: "Hear O Israel, Adonai is our God, Adonai is One! You shall love the Lord your God with all your heart with all your soul and with all your might" [Deut. 4:5,6]. At Passover I sing "I love the Lord" [Ps. 116:1] and "Praise the Lord, for He is good" [Ps. 118:1] because these are beautiful songs but not because I believe in God. A merciful God would not have taken my son from me, so why should a rabbi be at the grave of my son or at the grave of any other secular soldier? It would be better if he took care of Orthodox conscripts like the religious soldier who was in the jeep with my son when the landmine exploded.
>
> In the end we buried him with a secular ceremony in the cemetery of our kibbutz. Don't think that it wasn't a dignified funeral. Friends and acquaintances, women among them, spoke and we played his favorite music—something that would have been impossible during a religious ceremony. How would he have been buried if we lived in Tel Aviv where a way of burying that differs from the norm is not possible? The supreme commander of the Israeli army at the time, Shaul Mofaz, showed his sympathy with a visit to our home. He said that we should have called him, but who thinks of that under these circumstances? The good news is that because of Zohar's funeral the Israeli army decreed in April 1999 that all wishes of the family concerning the funeral of a soldier will henceforth be granted.

I'm fed up with those Orthodox who call themselves God's representatives on earth and in His name feel they can tell other Jews what they should believe and in which way. The Orthodox get more power every day, and they use it to impose their will on the secularists. They even plague the Reform and Conservative Jews who share their beliefs. Often they shout slogans about Jewish unity—which no longer exists anyway—as the reason we would have to change our lives. For example, my two daughters can't marry in Israel. They have Dutch boyfriends, one of whom converted into the Reform community. They other one stayed Christian. Marrying someone who was converted by a Reform rabbi or marrying a goy is impossible in Israel—so they had to marry in Holland.

Doron is not the only person in Israel who has discovered that the existence of the Israeli Jew, whether or not religious, is in some crucial aspects in the hands of the Orthodox Chief Rabbinate. In Israel the Orthodox movement has the exclusive right to Judaism. The Reform and the Conservatives are not recognized in their religious functions by the Chief Rabbinate or by the state. In the British era—when the Chief Rabbinate was created—it was taken for granted that Orthodox Judaism would become "the state religion"; after all there were practically no non-Orthodox Jews living in Palestine. Recently the Orthodoxy has been doing everything in its power to retain this exclusive right, and despite small shifts against them, they seem to be succeeding for the time being: Orthodox rabbis still conduct most funerals of Jews, although the first alternative funeral has now taken place in Beersheba. In addition they consecrate all Jewish marriages and officially perform all Jewish divorces; moreover they are the only ones who can administer "conversion examinations" even though the candidate may have more affinity for Reform or Conservative Judaism.

These movements within Judaism that have followers, particularly among the American Jews in Israel and in the United States, are called diaspora movements by the Orthodox, who think that the non-Orthodox movements practice a watered-down version of Judaism. Among themselves they often speak English mixed with Hebrew words that relate to Judaism. In the course of the years two problems have arisen in Israel, partially as a result of the increasingly obvious presence of the non-Orthodox movements. First, the

struggle between the secularists and the Orthodox, which has come
to be called the "civil war" in the Israeli press and which came to a
head during the demonstration described in the first chapter.
Second, there is a "religious war," the struggle among the Reform,
Conservative, and Orthodox Jews about the correct interpretation of
the word of God. The following joke illustrates the tensions that
exist in Israel among these Jews:

> An ordinary couple from a suburb wants a rabbi to say a *bracha*
> (Hebrew for blessing) over their just-bought Mercedes. They call
> the Orthodox rabbi and ask: "Rabbi, could you please come and
> say a bracha over our new Mercedes?"
> "How could I possibly do that?" he answers. "I don't know
> what a Mercedes is."
> The next day the couple calls a Conservative rabbi.
> "Rabbi, could you please come and say a *bracha* over our new
> Mercedes?"
> "Please forgive me," he answers. "I don't know if I can do that.
> To be on the safe side I think I'd better not do it."
> Finally the couple calls a Reform rabbi.
> "Rabbi, could you say a *bracha* over our new Mercedes?"
> "Of course I'll do that," the rabbi answers. "But what's a
> *bracha*?"

"That's a stupid joke," says Reform Rabbi Meir Azari who was born
in Israel, "because many Orthodox drive a Mercedes. They ask
money for such a *bracha*, and that's easier than casting doubt on the
usefulness of a *bracha*. We reconcile the Mercedes and the *bracha*, but
at a death I cannot get the words 'the Lord has given, and he has
taken away' across my lips. And how can I say such a thing to a
friend who has lost his son in Lebanon?" Azari has a soft voice and
expresses himself carefully. There is nothing particularly Jewish
about his clothing, in his bookcase there is a lot of English-language
literature, and at the entrance of his office there is a sticker that says,
"There are different ways to be Jewish."
    Rabbi Azari (1959) is a remarkable rabbi, or as he himself says,

> a new kind of rabbi. I represent not-corrupt, non-halakhic Judaism
> that is more involved with reality than with spirituality. For the nine
> thousand schoolchildren who visited our synagogue this past year,
> my appearance as rabbi without beard and without yarmulke is a

revelation—I wear them only during prayer and during study. My appearance is part of the revolution that is taking place at the present.

Since 1991 Azari has been the rabbi of Beit Daniel synagogue, which was founded ten years ago in Tel Aviv and is flourishing, according to him.

Azari is a socially active rabbi who is particularly concerned about the lot of non-Jewish Israeli citizens who cannot marry or be buried in Israel. "I see the task of the Reform movement to find a solution for the 'Russian question' and to make sure that the non-Jewish immigrant can integrate easier into Israeli society. We offer a 'rush conversion' which is Jewish but which doesn't expect the converted to take up the Orthodox way of life."

Beit Daniel has a cultural function too. There are concerts and lectures in Hebrew, Russian, and English for young and old, but also "religious" activities such as a course in Judaism for new immigrants and for retirees. Azari emphasizes the importance of education and mentions receiving nine thousand schoolchildren the past year: "In this way the children and the parents become familiar with Reform Judaism. Many secularists who visit our synagogue turn out to support us and are surprised that things are 'normal' here. Then I ask them, 'Did you expect Jesus to jump out of the Holy Ark?'"

Azari accepts female rabbis; women can wear a yarmulke and a prayer shawl and can pray in the same area as the men. (During the service in Beit Daniel almost every man and one or two women wear yarmulkes.) "Together with other rabbis I have officiated at four hundred marriages, and we served at three hundred bar and bat mitzvahs. Ten years ago there were only four or five."

According to Azari, who admits a flirtation with secularism, the success of the Reform movement proves that most Israelis are Reform Jews:

> The Orthodoxy has managed to keep this truth hidden successfully for the past fifty years. Our synagogue is a significant political power which no mayor can deny. Many Jews no longer say: "The synagogue where I don't pray is the Orthodox one," but instead "The synagogue where I sometimes attend a lecture is the Reform one." We can no longer be pushed aside. We will expand, not through the High Court or the Knesset, but through our activities.

Azari is also aware that many secularists want to be married by him because they hate the Orthodoxy and after their wedding never again show up in the synagogue.

> We are a non-halakhic movement, and that appeals to many secularists because they, just like I, live in a world of doubts. I don't know for sure if the world was created in six days. Genesis is an interesting story, but we Reform admit openly that we don't know exactly when the creation took place. And sometimes when you don't know the answer, it's nice to tell a myth. Question marks are absolutely forbidden in the Orthodoxy. I'm not interested in the question whether fossils exist and how old the world is, but according to the Reform the world is at least five thousand years old. According to the Orthodox view, if God created the world he could also have created fossils.

Azari comes from a Sephardic background, and even though this is unusual in the Reform movement, he says that many Sephardic Jews are Reform Jews: "Except that they don't know it and just like my parents they keep calling themselves *Masortim* [traditional] even though they have the same life style as we do. Except that egalitarianism has not yet penetrated, but on the Sabbath they go to the synagogue as well as to the soccer field."

Azari says that as rabbi he wants to break through the image that many Israelis have of a Reform rabbi. They think that he is an American Jew who knows nothing about Judaism. "But I do know a lot," says Azari and he lists his studies: Jewish history and political science at Haifa University, Mishna and Talmud at the Hebrew University, and theology and Jewish studies at several institutions in the United States—among which were Christian ones—and he received his *smicha* at the Reform Hebrew Union College.

> They accuse us of being a Diaspora movement, but we shouldn't fool ourselves: everything and everybody in Israel is an import. Avraham Ravitz is still living in Poland and Aryeh Deri and his party members in Morocco. My whole life revolves around God, just like theirs, but at least I admit that I live in modern times. Being an Israeli Jew means discharging one's military duty. What have they done? Kashrut control? Army rabbi? That's good for Judaism but not for the Jewish people as a whole.
>
> Ten years ago the official language of the Reform synagogue

was indeed English, and we barely talked about the Talmud, but that has changed. After all, I have to take care that secular Jews don't throw aside their "Jewish baggage." And I have to give Reform Judaism an Israeli look in order to bridge the gap between secular and Orthodox Jews. Two million Jews in Israel have thrown their Jewish heritage overboard. They want a bat mitzvah or a bar mitzvah and a huppah, but they hate Orthodox Jews.

We the Reform don't feel that Judaism is the deep secret of a small group, and we have no patience for "Jewish" hairsplitting. The Reform movement was established to make Judaism more accessible, but we are less liberal than our brothers in the United States. There they perform marriages in the presence of a rabbi and a Christian minister. Most Jews who attend a Reform synagogue see themselves as believers, while many who come to our synagogue define themselves as "secular." For them, the "Orthodox" are the Jews of Agudat, the National Religious Party, and Shas. Moreover, in America the paternal lineage is accepted. There they say: "We have many mixed marriages [53 percent], let's not make things difficult for ourselves. If one of the parents is Jewish and if the children are brought up as Jews, they get a bar mitzvah." We have resisted accepting patriarchal lineage for years, but we need to reevaluate this decision in light of the Russian immigration.

(Many immigrants from the former Soviet Union have a Jewish father and a non-Jewish mother and are therefore not Jewish according to the halakhah. For this issue, see chapter 4.)

To indicate that the secularists have a distorted image of the Reform, Azari tells about his lecture for a group of soldiers:

> They asked: "Can you say these *brachot*?" and "Do you know the meaning of the Jewish holidays?" and "Who has given you the right to change Judaism?" I'm not changing anything, and besides, we originated at the same time as the Orthodox. I know the halakhah, but I'm a non-halakhic Jew.
>
> For us the Torah is not divine. Every Jew can decide for himself which law he obeys and in which way, and that's the greatest difference of opinion between the Reform and the Orthodox who try to obey the so-called word of God to the absurd. I would not be able to live in a "*Shulchan Arukh* world." According to the *Shulchan Arukh* a Jew has to get up as powerfully as a lion and do all sorts of things.

But Azari says that he wants to be free:

Sometimes I feel like staying in bed for a while and then get up calmly. How can we be so sure that He wants us to get up like a lion and that we first put on the right shoe and then the left shoe when dressing? Reform Jews live with doubt, and that is both our strength and our weakness.

They say that it's difficult to be a good Orthodox Jew, but they push everything ahead, to the time of the Messiah. For us He is something or someone for whom we are all waiting in vain. He will never come, and I am satisfied with this eternal expectation. The prayers about his coming are not in the Reform Jewish siddur. It is more difficult to live with question marks as a Jew. They accuse us of doing only what suits us, but we are honest, and that's the only way in which a modern person can live. We don't turn against the Western world and science which outstrip even the Torah. For example, we're now discussing gay marriage among Reform rabbis; there is clearly a need for this in Israel. I'm very easy about it, perhaps because I've lived in California.

The Reform prayer book is also "modern." It is often bilingual and abridged, and in the diaspora it is combined with local practices such as the profession of faith inspired by Christianity. Passages about bringing offerings to the Temple have been left out, and the prayer for the restoration of the Temple—the third part of the *Amidah*, one of the most important prayers in Judaism—does not appear in the Reform-Jewish siddur. In Reform Jewish opinion, sacrifices are unnecessary in modern times and besides, the synagogue has replaced the Temple. The Reform movement has added the poem "*Shabbat HaMalkah*" (the Sabbath, the queen) by Chaim Bialik and poems by Lea Goldberg to the liturgy. Azari says they did this "to show that the beauty of welcoming the Sabbath can have a religious meaning even without the word of God." Jewish men who have difficulty with the morning prayer in which the man thanks God that he is not a woman, can join the Reform because that prayer has been adjusted as well. In one of the morning prayers "Blessed are You, our God, King of the Universe, for not having made me a gentile, . . . for not having made me a slave, . . . for not having made me a woman," the Reform leave off the words *woman, slave,* and *gentile.* Azari continues: "We thank God that He has created us in His image and that He has made us into a free people."

Despite everything, Azari still has something in common with the Orthodoxy: like his colleagues in Shas and Agudat Israel he uses his sectarian interests for political goals. The community of Tel Aviv supports many of the cultural activities, and in the local press Azari is reproached for "collaborating with the political establishment." But Azari, who in 1996 ran unsuccessfully as Meretz candidate for the Knesset, is pleased with this accusation: "This criticism is a sign that we as a Reform movement are visible. We now have nine child-care centers in Tel Aviv and we have opened activity centers in other places like Mevasseret Zion, Ramat HaSharon, Ra'anana, Nahariya, and Zichron Ya'akov."

But what is the real status of Reform Judaism in Israel? Why has Reform Judaism never taken root in Israel? Why were Reform Jews never part of the Zionist movement? Has the Reform movement always lacked good leaders? "Despite everything, the non-Orthodox will bring about a great change in the Israeli religious landscape," predicts professor Efraim Tavory of Bar Ilan University. He did his dissertation on the diaspora movements in Israel and wears a cro-cheted yarmulke. "They keep challenging the Orthodox establish-ment through the Court which will in the end decide in their favor."

The Orthodox Jewish community in Israel feels that the Reform have moved toward Christianity in their religious experience, and that the latter were intent on making all sorts of changes in Judaism. The Orthodox object, among other things, to men and women praying together and to Jews in the United States holding Sunday services that are embellished with guitar music and choral singing.

The Reform community in Israel feels neglected because it receives insufficient support. According to a recent survey of the Reform movement, 35 percent of Israeli Jews want to be married in a Reform ceremony. According to the non-Orthodox movements in Judaism, the Orthodox synagogue is no longer the synagogue that Jewish Israelis do not attend; that was true ten years ago. According to the above-mentioned study, today 34 percent of Jewish Israelis identify with Reform Judaism, and 36 percent would attend a Reform synagogue if there were one in the area. Forty-two percent think that men and women should be able to pray together, and 38 percent are against it. "As a movement we certainly are a success in Israel," says Rabbi Azari, "but we don't get the status that goes with it. We're not even allowed to conduct a service near the Wailing Wall which seems to have become an Orthodox synagogue."

✦✦✦

"We don't even try anymore to get approval for mixed services at the Wailing Wall," says Rabbi Ehud Bandel, the leader of the Conservative movement in Israel. "We took a step back, and now we're asking to reserve a section on the square in front of the wall, but that can't be done without the intervention of the Court. We hope to hold our services there one day." Bandel is in his office in the center of Jerusalem; in the bookcases are religious books and on the wall are photos in which he poses with spiritual leaders from home and abroad: Pope John Paul II, the Ashkenazi Chief Rabbi of Jerusalem, Israel Meir Lau, and Hindu and Buddhist spiritual leaders. There is no photo with the Sephardic Chief Rabbi Baksi-Doron because the latter refuses to talk with representatives of non-Orthodox movements who call themselves rabbi.

In 1988 Bandel was the first sabra named as rabbi by the Conservative Schechter Institute for Jewish studies (training for rabbi of the conservative Masorti movement). He was brought up as a secularist, was Orthodox for a number of years, and then moved over to Reform Judaism. At the Schechter Institute he finally found the balance between dedication to the Torah and life in the modern world.

"The Reform believe in a 'progressive revelation' which comes down to the fact that the Torah is the reflection of the will of God written down by people. Most conservatives, for whom the halakhah is binding, believe in a 'continuous revelation.' This means that leaders inspired by God still communicate with God," says Bandel as he opens a book to a page that illustrates schematically the differences between the movements within Conservative Judaism. The Conservative movement, which stands between the Orthodox and the Reform and has thirty thousand members in Israel, is divided into four categories: one is close to the Reform, one is close to the Orthodox, and two are in between. Bandel, who says he's somewhere in the middle, continues as follows: "The Conservatives who are closest to the Orthodox believe that God dictated His wishes on Mount Sinai. For the Conservatives who tend toward Reform Judaism, the Torah is written by human beings and is therefore not of divine origin." When asked who according to him has authority in Judaism, he points to a box on the page with the words "God's will." After all, Torah scholars are qualified to change the details of the law and to adapt them to the present social and economic circumstances.

Bandel admits that the Masorti movement is not homogeneous, and he is very proud to stand "somewhere in the middle" because that is the essence of Conservative Judaism:

> We are striving to find a balance between a life that is too liberal or too Orthodox. We preserve our tradition, but at the same time we go along with the times. This doesn't mean that we are neither *fleishig* nor *milchig*, or that we are *pareve*—as some call us. Instead, our belief is based on a dialectic tension between tradition and change. We believe in the interaction between the concepts "*Torah min ha'shamayim*" and "*Torah lo min ha'shamayim*" [literally, "the Torah from heaven" and "the Torah not from heaven"; with this expression religious Jews refer to the holiness and immutability of the Torah that Moses received from God in the Sinai]. We believe that the Torah and the law were given by God, but we don't believe, as most Orthodox groups do, that the details of the halakhah and all the answers to future questions were given to Moses in the Sinai. We continue to have encounters with God, and the results of these encounters are incorporated in the laws so that they continue to reflect God's new wishes and lines of thought.
>
> In the struggle against the Orthodoxy we are forced to work together with the Reform community in Israel, but we have great differences of opinion. Yet we will never repudiate the Reform as a legitimate movement within Judaism, as the Orthodox do with us. To start with, Jewish law has little meaning for the Reform movement. We take the halakhah seriously, although we realize that in modern times we can't just like that apply the mitzvot as God gave them to us. For example, what is the position of women? Of homosexuals? What is our opinion of euthanasia and the use of modern household equipment, hearing aids, and electric wheelchairs? To solve these problems we have a halakhah commission.

Bandel walks over to the bookcase and takes out a thick folder:

> Their decisions are in this book. The Reform don't know the *halakhic* question and answer system because for them the autonomy of the individual is more important. In our movement a commission of rabbis makes decisions about subjects that modern times raise in religious Jewish households. For example, this commission has decided that Conservative rabbis cannot celebrate

marriages of homosexual couples. If a Conservative rabbi who is a member of our rabbinical counsel does this, he receives a letter from the commission which states that he can no longer be a member. The same goes for rabbis who drive on the Sabbath.

"The Orthodox Sabbath means nothing to me," says Conservative Rabbi Tammi Colberg, who drives a car to the synagogue. For this reason she has had to refuse a job as rabbi of a Conservative synagogue:

> Being together, the prayers and the meal make this day special—not the ban on driving. The Sabbath embodies the notion of 'time.' That one day is intended for relaxation, for the *neshamah*. For many Orthodox, a Jew who desecrates the Sabbath in public must be treated like a goy and is therefore no longer a member of the Jewish community. Moderate Orthodox still count him as part of the ethnic Jewish community, but no longer as part of the religious Jewish community. It makes no difference to me. I turn on lights and I cook on the Sabbath, but I don't work and I do no household chores.

Colberg, who used to go to the Reform synagogue with her parents, was recently hired by a Reform community in Ra'anana. She studied Jewish philosophy at the Hebrew University and after that, because she wanted to know more about Judaism, she studied at the Conservative Schechter Institute; the curriculum of the Reform training for rabbi does not include any study of sources or halakhah. She sees it as her most important task to study the sources with the *kehillah*. "My new synagogue is not halakhic, but I still think that as non-Orthodox Jews we should know where we came from," says Colberg. She bears in mind that she should be careful when talking about halakhah in order to prevent members from thinking that they hired an Orthodox rabbi. But she is concerned:

> I worry about Jews who neglect their tradition. Many Reform Jews, and many Conservative Jews too, no longer know their 'Jewish baggage,' and some even call themselves secular. But even the Reform synagogue is a religious community. A rabbi is first of all a good teacher who gives the members something spiritual to hold onto, and in addition the rabbi has a pastoral function. The rabbi must know the halakhah, but the rabbi's most important function is not to decide whether something is allowed or not.

Colberg continues: "I may for example use the halakhah in a discussion about the use of cameras in the synagogue on the Sabbath, about adding or leaving out certain prayers, and about determining the time when the Sabbath ends." The first difficult discussion that Colberg has to direct is about leading the service while facing the public, as is customary in many Reform synagogues, or while facing the Holy Ark as is done by Orthodox rabbis. "The former rabbi stood facing the public, but I will explain, through the halakhah, why I don't want to do that. Besides, Reform Jews should get away from the stigma that they are Christians."

Colberg admits that it's becoming complicated to explain who she is:

> Will I call myself a Reform rabbi in a while? I don't think so, but ask me that again in a year or two. Usually I say first that I'm a rabbi—after that I call myself Conservative. But now that I'm working for a Reform synagogue, that may change. I could also be Reform-Conservative, or Conservative-Reform, or even Orthodox-Reform. I'm simply a Conservative rabbi in a Reform synagogue. By the way, my synagogue is very traditional, it's even a conservative Reform community, but it turns out to be too liberal for my husband who for the first time doesn't come with me. He is staying with the Conservative synagogue in Kfar Saba.

Playing with these words proves that Judaism is a culture in which religion is only a part. This works out quite well because if you tell children today that Judaism is a religion, they want nothing to do with it. Colberg says,

> This is the greatest tragedy in our country. The Jews know nothing about their own cultural heritage. They seem to be Hebrew-speaking goyim, and that was because of the need felt by the secular Zionists to develop a new nonreligious Jewish identity. Not only the Orthodox look at me surprised, but most secularists also frown when they hear that I'm a rabbi. At the school where I was teaching, people asked me how I could be a rabbi and an academic at the same time. Most Israelis don't understand anything about the Orthodoxy that they associate with Judaism. They think of religious tyranny and of men with beards.

Prof. Alice Shalvi from Jerusalem says:

Jewish analphabetism is the greatest catastrophe in our country. Ben Gurion's generation made a big mistake in the fifties by developing three different educational systems. Their basic assumption was: "If you want to learn something about Judaism, you go to a religious school." Secular public education eliminated many of the Jewish courses, and the result is Jewish ignorance. The growing interest of secular Jews in Jewish sources is an important development that can lead to a pluralistic Jewish society and an equal treatment of women.

Shalvi grew up in a British modern Orthodox milieu that was "in retrospect very egalitarian in spirit." Her rebellion during her younger years was mild although in the synagogue she felt very remote from the service, especially during the Jewish holidays. Her early rebellion led to her appointment as *hazzan* in the Jewish organization at Cambridge University.

The lack of equality between men and women finally led Shalvi to Conservative Judaism. It wasn't until 1975, when she became head of Pelech, an Orthodox girls high school in Jerusalem, that she became aware of the limitations that are imposed on women in Orthodox Judaism. Her ultimately successful attempts to introduce Gemara and Torah studies for girls as well as an (alternative) military service were met with opposition from the Orthodoxy, and the hiring of a female Gemara teacher made her life at Pelech difficult. She maintained contact with Orthodox feminists as well. When she participated in a dialogue with Palestinian women after the first *intifada*, the department of religious affairs of the Ministry of Education gave her a choice: stop these political activities or else Pelech would lose its designation as a religious school. With pain in her heart Shalvi resigned her function as school director.

Shalvi comments:

During the course of the years my aversion to the practices of the Orthodox establishment has increased, especially after I experienced from close up the obstinacy of the establishment in its treatment of *agunot*. This convinced me that the Orthodox rabbinate is failing to continue the old and very fundamental Jewish tradition of interpretation and reinterpretation of the halakhah in the light of changed social values and norms. In Israel and in the United States the Masorti movement has taken over this role, and through a halakhah commission it makes decisions about contemporary

problems concerning marriage, divorce, conversion, sexual preference, and the position of women in general.

Shalvi was especially helped in her spiritual search by her contacts with like-minded Jews in the United States:

In 1979 I was called up for the first time during a women's prayer
in an American Conservative synagogue. I realized that at the age
of fifty-three I experienced what every Jewish man can—and usually does—experience when he is thirteen years old at his bar
mitzvah. Because I couldn't find a good equivalent in Israel, I
showed up less and less frequently at the synagogue. It wasn't
until 1996, when a good friend was certified as rabbi by the
Masorti movement, that I started attending the Conservative synagogue. First I just wanted to give her moral support because her
appointment met with opposition from some of the male members
of the synagogue. Although I felt at first uncomfortable with the
"mixed seating"—after all it is difficult to break free from years of
limitations—I was soon sold because of the chance that I might be
called up and give a *drasha* during the service. In this synagogue I
was considered equal, just as in my daily "secular" life.

Shalvi is proud that Pelech, the Israeli pioneer for Talmud study
for women, has taken the lead in developing yeshiva-like institutes
for Orthodox women. Today there are many Orthodox women who
have so much knowledge of Judaism that they could have been
rabbis long ago if they had been men. In addition to male *niddah* (literally, "menstruating woman"; also, someone who advises about
the purity of the family) advisors, there now are female ones.
According to Shalvi the separation of men and women in religious
practices can no longer be justified in a modern society where the
borders between "typically" male and female status are becoming
increasingly blurred.

I consider myself no longer part of the Orthodox community that
gives Judaism a bad name with its rabbinate establishment that is
stuck in a rut, the increasing politicization of religion and religious
coercion.
    In order to retain the Jewish character of the state, there has to
be separation of religion and politics as well as the dismantlement
of the chief rabbinate which was a British invention. Judaism has

to be unlinked from the Orthodoxy. Many Orthodox still resist women who study Judaism, and they are unable to make the distinction between "practice" and "study." Political parties that strive for a theocratic state instead of a pluralistic-democratic one should not be allowed to exist. This striving is often associated with superstition and a primitive concept of "reward and punishment." After all, isn't it primitive to assert that a building collapses because of the "mixed dancing" in it? [Shalvi refers to the collapse of a building during a wedding on June 1, 2000] A number of years ago a train ran into a bus with children who were on a school trip. There were rabbis who dared to say that the children's parents didn't have a mezuzah on their doorposts.

It's not easy for Colberg, Shalvi, Azari, and Bandel to deal with the criticism from intolerant Jews—as Bandel calls them—who think they are God's representatives on earth. Bandel says,

> They call us heretics or half-Christians because we supposedly make Judaism easier by adapting the Torah to modern times. According to them the end result is assimilation with Christians. That's not true, and as former chairman and present member of the Board of Directors of the International Organization of Christians and Jews I know that the Divine Covenant of Conservative Jews doesn't resemble the New Testament. I want to build bridges: Christians and Jews, whether they're Orthodox, Reform, Conservative, or secularists, all of them are children of God. This thought should bring us to admire His creation. Conservative Jews are not Christians or atheists, and we don't practice a heretical form of traditional Judaism as the Orthodox think we do. In contrast to the Reform movement, we are a halakhic movement and belong to the chosen people. They should be forbidden to call us "Conservative criminals" and to call our services "blasphemous" or to assert that whoever extends their hand to us violates God's name.

Bandel points to a framed declaration from the Orthodox rabbinate that is hanging on a wall: "There it is, black on white."

The diaspora movements represent 80 percent of the 5.5 million American Jews (in the United States); in Israel only 0.5 percent of the 5.8 million Jews are Conservative or Reform. In total there are between forty and fifty thousand Conservative and Reform Jews in Israel (thirty thousand Conservatives and between ten and fifteen thousand Reform). Even though these numbers are small and these movements are not growing in Israel, they often draw the attention of the state to the fact that their rights are being violated on a large scale. It has been shown many times that the three movements don't leave one another alone and that they aren't able to exist easily alongside one another. Often the non-Orthodox movements join forces in order to let people converted inside Israel and abroad (frequently these are adopted children) register as "Jew" through the High Court. Or they try to lift the prohibition against non-Orthodox to take seats in the rabbinical councils. In November 1999, a heading on the third page of *Ha'aretz* read as follows: "Officer: 'Reform and Conservative harmed Jews more than Nazis.'" During a lecture, army officer Peretz Gamliel had observed that the non-Orthodox movements are guilty of the assimilation of eight million Jews. According to Gamliel, these movements have done more harm to the Jewish people than the National-Socialists who murdered more than six million Jews during the Holocaust. An army spokesperson apologized, but wasn't sure that Gamliel would be relieved of his duties.

Bandel feels that he is personally humiliated on a regular basis. For example, in August 1999 he was invited by the secular chair of the Knesset Committee for Finance to participate in the discussion about the renovation of the Wailing Wall. When he had the floor, seven *haredi* members of the committee left the room. "We don't speak with people who stick a knife in our back," said Moshe Gafni of the United Torah Party as he left the room. "They don't respect us, so there is no reason for us to remain seated," Knesset member Amnon Cohen of Shas agreed. Bandel gives details:

> Those who stayed continued the discussion, but not about financing the renovation. The ultra-secular Jew Yossi Paritsky of Shinui felt that after fifty years it was about time for non-Orthodox to get permission to pray at the Wailing Wall which, according to him, is a national monument. Meir Porush of United Torah Judaism kept insisting that the Wailing Wall falls under the authority of the Orthodox "Rabbi of the Wailing Wall" who wouldn't think of reserving a section for minority groups. He said that the wall belongs to everyone and that there is always a Yemenite minyan and farther down a Lithuanian one. According to him that was the beauty—that everyone prays together. He said that no group has ever asked to pray separately. According to him

the Reform and the Conservatives are responsible for the experiment in mixed praying that exists in America. When the storm died down, I simply said that we wanted a small corner for our services. I couldn't say more because I was shocked at what happened. They have no respect for us, and they couldn't muster the courtesy to listen. They screamed. In a normal tone of voice I said that we will consider praying on the square in front of the wall.

For Bandel another example of humiliation was his joining the rabbinical court of Jerusalem by a decision of the Court in November 1998. This court decides among other things about divorces and about "suitability for marriage" and has more than fifty million shekels that it divides among the Orthodox religious communities every year. Since 1984 this court had not replaced its members while the law states that this must happen every five years. Bandel continues:

This decision by the Court was therefore an important victory for the religious minority movements—if it weren't for the fact that in protest the Orthodox members didn't show up for the first meeting. I was the only one. Four times we scheduled a meeting, and four times I was the only one. To this day the court has not functioned.

Nevertheless Bandel speaks of a "small victory" because the entry of a Reform Jew into the religious council was refused early in 1998 with the words "Reform Jews are greater sinners than Jesus."

The Orthodoxy considers American Judaism—as they call Conservative and Reform Judaism—blasphemous. It might harm the Jewish soul and should behave differently in Israel from its counterpart in the United States. The ultra-Orthodox Knesset member Rabbi Avraham Ravitz openly calls Reform Jews "losers who come with money to Israel where they lay down the law as if Israel is a banana republic." According to him, accepting these movements is the same as asking the pope to recognize Protestantism. Shas minister Shlomo Benizri is willing to recognize them as "separate religions like Christianity, for example." Chief Rabbi Meir Israel Lau considers them the way to assimilation. "I want to survive, and the Reform and Conservative Jews who enter into mixed marriages don't worry about assimilation," says Lau, raising his voice from behind his desk in his large office in Jerusalem. He wears a black yarmulke, a long black coat, and his hat sits on his neat desk. On the wall hang three portraits of rabbis among which one is his father who died in Treblinka and one is his father-in-law. Assimilation is Rabbi Lau's great fear, and that's why he's eager to show a table of the results of a study done in 1997; its title is "The future of American Jewry. Will your grandchild be Jewish?" Rabbi Lau says that he isn't worried about the identity of his own grandchildren because they are growing up in a protected Orthodox environment. Besides, two of his three sons are already rabbis (Rabbi Lau has eight children and forty-two grandchildren). Lau is afraid that the American situation where secular, Reform, and Conservative Jews barely have Jewish grandchildren will eventually develop in Israel as well. "The results are alarming," says Lau.

> Even if there is a 100 percent margin of error, we won't survive. According to the present percentage of mixed marriages and the average number of children per family, the chances that young Jews will have Jewish grandchildren and great-grandchildren become increasingly smaller. Of course with the exception of the Orthodox Jews who have an average of 6.4 children and among whom only 3 percent of all marriages are mixed marriages. Among the Reform this percentage is fifty-three and among the secularists it is as much as seventy-two.

Rabbi Lau exclaims: "This way we won't survive! Besides, they have few children. The number of children decreases by 50 percent in the second generation while it increases by 300 percent in Orthodox families."

Lau continues:

> I'm not happy; in this respect I'm worried and disappointed in the state which was actually established as Noah's ark for the Jewish people. At the time the Jewish people had to try and survive crossing the stream; nowadays we have to fight the danger of assimilation. We have known physical danger, but we are now confronted with a spiritual danger. We will survive in Noah's ark! More than that, in the Declaration of Independence it says ten times *Medinat haYehudim* [Jewish state]. This means that the state is a Jewish home for the Jewish people that can assimilate in the Diaspora but not here.

He then adds that the notion of "pluralistic Judaism" which the non-Orthodox movements strive for does not appear in the Declaration of Independence.

Mixed marriage is taboo for many Orthodox; Reform rabbis officiate at such ceremonies, but most Conservative rabbis cannot. A study from 1990 showed that 52 percent of marriages that involve American Jews are mixed marriages. And the conclusion of the *Annual Survey of American Jewish Opinion*, published in September 2000, says, "The Jewish taboo against mixed marriage has collapsed." A small majority of those questioned said they wouldn't be hurt if their children married a gentile. According to this study, 50 percent of American Jews called it "racist" to be against Jewish-gentile marriages, and 80 percent declared that such marriages are unavoidable in an open society.

Conflicts between Orthodox and non-Orthodox believers occur everywhere in Israeli society. For example, in 1998 conservative "heretical" books were kept from an Orthodox book fair in Jerusalem called Judaism in Action. In 1998 the opening of the Reform child care center Gan Telem in a secular district in north Tel Aviv encountered opposition from the Orthodox because the building was located next to the orthodox synagogue Ahavat Achim (brotherly love). "It's as if a church opened next to a synagogue," and Shmuel Gefen, head of the department of Torah culture of the city of Tel Aviv and member of the National Religious Party. Dana Avidar, head of the education department of the Reform movement defended himself: "We Reform Jews tolerate other movements within Judaism, and what makes Orthodox children into better 'children of God' than our children? Please note that Tel Aviv is the only city in Israel that supports the activities of the Reform movement."

Because of their small numbers in Israel, the non-Orthodox often receive support in their struggle from their American coreligionists. For example, early in 1999 a group of non-Orthodox male and female rabbis landed at Ben Gurion Airport. They were offended by the remarks of the Orthodox Chief Rabbi Eliyahu Baksi-Doron. The latter had compared Reform Judaism to the National Socialists after the High Court had decided that non-Orthodox would henceforth be allowed to join the religious councils. At the end of January 1999, the English language edition of *Ha'aretz* opened with the condemnation by Baksi-Doron: "Holocaust pales next to Reform." In the article Baksi-Doron declared that he would be willing to talk with the Reform as Jews, but not as rabbis. Attending "mixed" meetings is forbidden according to Orthodox teachings. Baksi-Doron continued: "They aren't rabbis, they don't believe in God, they don't take the Torah seriously, and they put Judaism to shame. Through their spiritual holocaust we have lost thousands of Jews, just in Israel. The number of Jews is decreasing rapidly as the result of mixed marriages which the Reform movement allows. We must learn from the Holocaust and do everything to preserve the Jewish people."

After arriving in Israel, Americans generally first visit the Wailing Wall, the symbol of Jewish identity and the holiest place of prayer for observant Jews. Generally it's here that the confrontation with the ultra-Orthodox Jews takes place—the latter having been informed of the Americans' arrival via the media. This was the case on this particular occasion as well. Reform and Conservative men and women wearing yarmulkes and prayer shawls tried to pray and were being hindered by *haredim* who had also gathered there. "Nazis! You're from Germany. Go back to Germany," shouted the *haredim*—referring to the German origin of Reform Judaism. "They're biological Jews, nothing more!" shouted ultra-Orthodox Knesset member Avraham Leizerson of the United Torah Party. "Do you think putting on a yarmulke makes you Jewish?" an Orthodox Jew shouted in English. He added, "It's as if I would go to the Vatican in Rome wearing my prayer shawl. They would think I was crazy. Do you want to start a new religion? Good. But do it elsewhere and leave us alone in Jerusalem."

A June 1999 opinion poll showed that 36 percent of Israelis supported maintaining the Orthodox monopoly on Judaism and that 54 percent of Israelis support the non-Orthodox movements. Recently the latter group has been aided by a number of prominent Israeli intellectuals like A. B. Yehoshua, Amos Oz, David Grossman, and the former Meretz ministers Shulamit Aloni and Yair Tsaban. They joined one of the two movements and, with a declaration published in the newspapers, they urged the Israeli public to "free Judaism from the hands of the enemies of democracy. The only remedy against discrimination and persecution of the non-Orthodox movements is to take action and, as an emergency measure, become a member of one of the diaspora movements. Non-Orthodox Judaism is closer to the democratic Jewish public than to ultra-Orthodox Judaism. All of us are Conservative and Reform Jews as long as they are being persecuted and discriminated against."

For Yehoshua (1937), who has leftist views just like the other signers, signing the declaration is proof of a deeper connection to his being Jewish than before. He calls himself an atheist, but Jewish rituals like lighting Sabbath candles, fasting on Yom Kippur and going to the Reform synagogue on that day are part of his family life. On Rosh Hashanah he prays in the Sephardic synagogue in Haifa where he lives to recall his youth through the melodies.

> I value the Reform and the Conservative movements because of the humanistic approach, but I find the service too "embellished" and too un-Israeli, and their future is mainly in education. My support has to do with strengthening the middle area between secularism and Orthodoxy rather than with religious support of a minority movement. When the problem with the Palestinians is solved, Israeli identity and the identity of the state will become the most important subjects that will divide the citizens.

This action of these nonreligious right-minded people was grist for the mill of the ultra-Orthodox, which had already been doubting the sincerity of the religiousness of the non-Orthodox. Their reaction was that intellectuals join these movements in the same way that people can apply for a scouting trip, a hobby club, or a social club. The Orthodox reason that it looks as though the Reform and Conservative movements are not serious religious communities but are rather a kind of "culture club" with *Yiddishkeit*, a kind of "Judaism-light."

Meanwhile a development has taken place that is revolutionary at first glance and that should have offered a solution for this "religious war" that is about such matters as performing marriages, granting divorces, and administering conversion examinations. In February 1999 branches of a conversion institute were opened in three cities in Israel. In these institutes Conservative, Reform, and Orthodox rabbis train converts. This institute is the only place in Israel where potential converts can gather and choose among different approaches to Judaism. Yet the institute, which was established after many quarrels and long night meetings, seems more modern than it is. The Orthodox spiritual father of the institute is Jacob Ne'eman, a prominent lawyer and former minister of finance. The only independent minister in Netanyahu's government, he was chosen in 1996 because of his exceptional knowledge. Netanyahu appointed him to find a solution to the conversion problem. At the opening of the conversion institute Ne'eman declared,

> The definitive conversion remains an Orthodox ritual that can never be performed by Conservative or Reform rabbis. Religion has held us together for centuries, and that is why the "Who is a Jew?" question gets a halakhic response. We can only remain unified as Jews if we all accept that God is the Creator and that the Torah, which God revealed to us around four thousand years ago on Mount Sinai, cannot be altered. In a Jewish state, which is different from other states, the separation of state and religion is impossible.

Bandel says,

> The conversion institute is undemocratic because the final decision about the important "Who is a Jew?" question remains a privilege of the Orthodox. And that means that a Jew is only someone with a Jewish mother or someone who has converted to Judaism in the Orthodox way. We haven't made much progress with the institute. As a religious minority we've got a foot in the door with the Orthodoxy, and this is the start of recognition of a pluralistic Judaism. But the question remains whether the rabbinate will in the end let our converts pass the examination and will recognize them as Jews. Take for example a woman who believes in the principle of equality and wants to become a Jew but who cannot identify with the Orthodoxy. Or a non-Jewish woman who wants to marry a *Kohen*. [In the original religious Jewish hierarchy, a *Kohen* was a high priest, but for centuries it has also been a family name. According to Jewish law, Mr. Cohen is not allowed to marry a convert or a divorced woman, or (just like other Jews) a bastard] The Reform and Conservative movements would convert the woman, and the couple would be able to marry. We've already lost six million Jews and therefore we need them. In order to survive and to prevent the exodus from Judaism, the Ministry of Religious Affairs will also have to register Reform and Conservative converts as Jews.

There is something odd about the institute. It is a typically Israeli compromise that goes beyond the intended goal, the equal treatment of minority movements. Moreover its training, financed by the state, has actually become a sociocultural naturalization program that has to turn 400,000 non-Jewish Russian immigrants into Orthodox Jews in one year—on paper. Therefore the institute teaches Jewish rites and symbols, prayers, and kashrut, not in Hebrew, but mainly in Russian.

The director of the institute, Benjamin Ish-Shalom—who is modern-Orthodox—also thinks that conversion is a halakhic act. Therefore he doesn't agree with Yossi Beilin of the Labor Party who argues for secular conversion. In his book *The Death of an American Uncle*, which appeared in April 1999, Beilin advocates a national secular procedure to be carried out by someone who wants to join the Jewish people. Beilin writes, "The Jewish people is vanishing, and there are spouses in mixed marriages who are willing to join the Jewish people but are unwilling to undergo a religious conversion for this. Therefore we should have a national secular 'admission' in addition to a religious conversion."

However, Ish-Shalom, who used to be professor of Jewish philosophy at the Hebrew University in Jerusalem and is still vice-chancellor at Morasha, the institute for advanced Jewish studies in Jerusalem, is convinced that a religious conversion is the only way to become part of the Jewish people. Letting a Reform or a Conservative rabbi perform a conversion is unacceptable to him. The right to administer the conversion examination remains reserved for the chief rabbinate—an Orthodox institution that in recent years has become increasingly influenced by *haredi* rabbis.

The fear of the non-Orthodox that the Orthodox will decide after a year not to accept students who chose Reform or Conservative Judaism is well-founded. What will be the answer to the exam question: "Was the Torah given to the Jewish people on Mount Sinai?" Will it be: "Yes, according to the Orthodox; no, according to the Reform; and the Conservatives doubt it"?

According to Ish-Shalom, someone who wants to join the Jewish people must satisfy two conditions:

> He must show he has the will to join the Jewish people, and he must accept that the Torah comes from heaven and he must uphold tradition. If the candidate doesn't accept one of the conditions, he isn't

suited for the Jewish faith. After all, being Jewish means having a great responsibility. Many secularists don't observe the Torah, but we can't take away their Jewish identity. But if someone wants to join our community, he has to accept our rules. It isn't that difficult to accept a fundamental principle like kashrut, is it? Especially in the state of Israel where it is more difficult to eat non-kosher. And what's so difficult about a kosher household for someone who really wants to belong to us? For very little money he can have separate dishes for milk and meat, and it isn't so difficult to take care that you don't mix them up and that you don't eat milk products until three hours after eating meat. Is that so difficult for someone who really wants to become different from what he was?

And if he doesn't want to, no hard feelings. But if the candidate is serious, this is the meaning of being Jewish. Therefore, conversion means acceptance of our rules that keep the country Jewish. Otherwise he stays who he was. Becoming Jewish is more than just citizenship. This has nothing to do with racism. We accept black, yellow, and white people, and there isn't even a one-thousandth part of racism in our criteria. There are simply a number of rules. For example, someone who wants to become Swiss has to live at least fifteen years in Switzerland, in the same place.

The non-Orthodox movements are less strict, and the Reform movement in particular allows non-Jews to convert for social reasons. Many secularists feel that someone who expresses the wish to become Jewish, for whatever reason, should somehow be able to convert. However, the Orthodox think that the candidate should first be found "suitable" (by the Chief Rabbinate) for the Orthodoxy. They insist that the Jewish people is an exclusive people whose purity should be guarded. That means that not just everyone can join, and those who want to join have to do something for it: they have to study Jewish history, learn Jewish rituals and prayers, and may no longer adhere to another faith. This conviction could be heard in its purest form early in 1999 from the mouth of Chief Rabbi Lau during a conference about assimilation at Bar Ilan University: "The candidates should be ready to carry the burden of Judaism; being a Jew is not easy. How is it possible that everyone can just become Jewish while those who decide about it are themselves unwilling to carry that burden. Admitting Reform and Conservatives to rabbinical courts and giving them approval to carry out conversions is unacceptable because it promotes assimilation."

Elchanan Italie, born in Rotterdam in 1920, director of the conversion *ulpan* in Kibbutz Yavne from 1986 to 1998 and now a Torah teacher, agrees with Lau: "I want to be sure that the converts can bear the heavy psychological and practical burden of being a Jew. That's why this conversion *ulpan* first administers a 'suitability' exam." Italie, a slight man who wears glasses, a long beard, and a crocheted yarmulke, had a religious education and didn't become a Zionist until after the Second World War. Right before the state was declared he emigrated to Palestine where he settled in Yavne, a religious kibbutz. "The first conversation," he says from behind his desk in a small, plain office in the kibbutz,

> is meant to exclude people who want to start the *ulpan* for nonreligious reasons. Very rarely do I ask about the Holy Trinity, about Mary and the worship of saints or his ideas about Jesus, but if I notice that the candidate sees the Messiah in him, it's finished. The same goes for someone who believes in the Holy Trinity; after all, someone like that doesn't believe in one God. But it must be said that these questions are usually superfluous. It doesn't bother the Reform that someone wants to convert to Judaism in order to marry and not to become a practicing Jew. But how can someone become Catholic and deny the Holy Trinity?

Most conversions take longer than a year, but with Italie the course takes only half a year because he wants to "deliver" forty new Orthodox Jews every year—all circumcised and immersed in the ritual bath. He doesn't always succeed, because there are candidates who don't pass the first time. According to him, the presence of non-halakhic Jews is a big problem in Israel. Italie states, "Mixed marriage is a disaster for our people. The consequences of the 'Second Russian revolution' [the immigration flood of the nineties] are all too obvious: more non-halakhic marriages. But *my* forty new Jews who have to counterbalance these influences are ready to carry the complete burden of Judaism."

"I don't know if I'm strong enough to carry the weight of all Jewish dos and don'ts," says the only Dutchman in the class. He had an Orthodox Jewish grandfather and he would like to live in Israel.

> During the "testing" we all said that we were ready to carry the burden of the commandments with us for the rest of our lives, but

the *ulpan* has become a struggle with myself. I'm not allowed to ask the how and why of the commandments because they are divine, and I have to resist all sorts of temptations. The Torah teacher says that Orthodox Jews are not free and can't just do what they want, but that's a part of the beauty of Judaism. I don't know if I'll be able to keep up the Orthodox life, but I think that Reform and Conservative Judaism are not real Judaism, they seem too much like the church.

In the dining room where there are prayer books and newspapers, he reports that there is a strange atmosphere in the *ulpan*: "We don't know about one another, why we are here, and how 'good' and especially how 'kosher' the others' daily activities are. We see one another every day, in the evening we study together, and often we work together in the kibbutz for a part of the day, but no one says anything about the number of commandments that he really observes and about the reason for his conversion."

Many religious Jews like Italie, Lau, Bandel, and Ish-Shalom are afraid that the Jewish people will vanish. This is one of their greatest fears, and each one tries to combat it in his own way. For example, the rabbinate seldom lets a candidate fail the conversion exam. After all, the failed student will disappear into non-Orthodox circles or will remain a goy. Therefore it is always better according to the rabbis to add to the Jewish people a poorly prepared candidate who may not be converting for a religious reason. In any case his or her children will be Jewish and won't be bastards. Someone who has continued his studies until the end has already passed because the conversion process is not simple. Every student is assigned a host family that keeps an eye on him during his studies, invites the student for the Sabbath dinner, and informs the rabbinate about the progress and motivation of the candidate. The Jewish partner, who is officially not allowed to live with the convert, also has to take Jewish lessons. If halfway through the study it appears that the intentions of the convert aren't pure, the rabbinate can still decide to disqualify him.

In the "proselyte class" there is a taboo against asking the reason for conversion, just as in Israeli society in general people usually don't ask if someone has converted to Judaism. In this class, where Romanians and Filipinos (Israel's non-Jewish guest workers) together with Russians and others learn to be Jewish, there is a fear of being betrayed. Each one suspects that the other doesn't believe in the

Jewish God either but that the purpose of the conversion is to marry a Jew or to get legal status, but this is never articulated. The rabbi's home visits exacerbate the fear of being tattled on. It's better that the latter doesn't find out that a student is living with a partner, wears miniskirts, or has a supply of pork in the freezer. Married couples are advised to remarry after the conversion because the rabbinate doesn't recognize the marriage contracted before the conversion and because the children born from that marriage will be bastards.

It is the strict Orthodoxy in particular that sees as its task the preservation of the purity and unity of the Jewish people. The Orthodox would like to turn every non-Jew who has a relationship with a Jew into a halakhic Jew so that the children will be Jewish and will in theory be able to marry Jews. The Orthodox establishment has no qualms about asking this of non-Jews who want to start a family in Israel but aren't interested in any conversion. After all, anyone who wants to become American, Swiss, British, or French has to make an effort, is the thinking of the rabbinate. Many non-Jewish women who have a relationship with a Jewish man think that these troubles are worth it. In most cases they become Jewish in order to spare their children difficulties in the future. A non-Jewish citizen can live quite well in Israel, but in a Jewish state it is easiest to live with a halakhic Jewish identity. At least the children of a mother who was converted in an Orthodox way can get married, divorced, and buried without a hitch.

But why should non-Jewish citizens who want to marry a Jew have to convert to Judaism? Can't civil marriages, funerals, and divorces simply be permitted? Until now no government has succeeded in solving this problem because the proponents of legally establishing civil marriage are unable to come to agreement with the Orthodox parties for whom this idea is the greatest nightmare conceivable. For them the Jewish marriage is a religious duty, a mitzvah, which has as its most important purpose the begetting of halakhically Jewish children. And just because mixed marriages don't produce full Jews, this sort of marriage is in practice not recognized in Israel. According to the Orthodoxy, they lead to two new classes within the Jewish people who cannot marry halakhic Jews: bastards and non-halakhic Jews. The children from civil marriages are halakhically not Jewish if the mother is not Jewish, but in the eyes of the rabbinate the children are always bastards.

If the solemnization of mixed marriages is legalized in Israel, the question of who is a Jew will in the long run no longer be relevant, just as the question today of whether someone is Christian is irrelevant in many Western European countries. Then, despite the resistance of the Orthodox community, more and more non-Jews will be born in Israel. Many leftist nonreligious Jews will start to consider being Jewish increasingly unimportant and will more readily marry non-Jews and therefore produce non-Jewish children. This scenario is a terrifying picture for the Orthodox Jewish community where the same fear is prevalent about the legalization of Jews converted in a non-Orthodox manner. The consequences will be that there will be two kinds of Jew; after all, in the Orthodox view those Jews who are converted by non-Orthodox rabbis have not yet joined the Jewish people. They are still Christians or Muslims and are therefore not permitted to marry an Orthodox Jew, and the Orthodoxy does not recognize their children as Jews.

These fears and this way of halakhic reasoning are deeply rooted in the religious Jewish community. A classic example of this dates from 1953 when Zerah Wahrhaftig, the deputy minister of Religious Affairs and Knesset member of the Zionist party Mizrachi (precursor of the current National Religious Party) expounded on the Orthodox marriage and divorce laws that had just been accepted in the Knesset:

> The Jewish laws have to guarantee the unity of the Jewish people, certainly at this time when the Jewish people in Israel is trying to forge a national unity. On the other hand, establishing civil marriage by law will estrange the Orthodoxy from the state. It is true that the imposition of Orthodox marriage on non-believers smells of religious tyranny, but every state and many laws are coercive, and for the Orthodox only the Jewish people as a whole is important.

This opinion, which is shared by many Orthodox in present-day Israel, arouses resistance in a number of them. This was true for Alex Lubotsky, the former Knesset member for the now disbanded "Third Way" party, and for Knesset member Michael Melchior (of Danish origin and former chief rabbi of Norway) of the moderate Orthodox Meimad party. Together with their secular colleague Yossi Beilin of the Labor Party they tried to make pluralistic Judaism acceptable during the government of Prime Minister Netanyahu by finding alternatives for the strict halakhic reasoning of the Orthodox.

In the preface of the document, called the new Status Quo, that was presented to the Knesset in March 1998, Lubotsky, Melchior, and Beilin state: "Israel must become more Jewish and more democratic, and the time is ripe for a new pact between religion and state because Judaism belongs to the secularists too." Actually, this document shows the inner contradictions of the state of Israel on a small scale: Beilin, a secular Jew, has to take into account the religious feelings of the moderately religious settler Lubotsky and the moderate Orthodox rabbi Melchior is Jewish in yet another way. Finally there are the Orthodox and ultra-Orthodox Knesset members who have even different opinions about who is a real Jew and what Judaism means. They can thwart acceptance of the document in the Knesset if their demands aren't sufficiently accommodated.

"We tried to find a number of practical solutions to the serious internal problems that confront us," says Lubotsky during a conference about this subject that was attended by rabbis, secular, and religious Zionists. Lubotsky, a talented mathematician who at the age of twenty-nine was appointed professor at the Hebrew University in Jerusalem, was a Knesset member for a number of years, but in 1999 he became disillusioned and withdrew from politics. An important reason for his disillusionment was that the Center Party, which was established right before the elections of 1999, was unable to come to a compromise about the new Status Quo. Lubotsky, who lives in Efrat, a West Bank settlement, says,

> I became a candidate for this party because I thought that only this party, with politicians from all sorts of persuasions, would be able to solve the Jewish *Kulturkampf* [culture war]. I thought that this party would finally be able to mend all the rifts in Israeli society that keep getting larger and therefore increasingly worrisome.
>
> I was the one charged with solving this problem, and I suggested using the new Status Quo that I had already worked on with Melchior and Beilin. The party leaders rejected the proposal: one party member didn't want to close stores on the Sabbath, another was afraid of losing ultra-Orthodox votes if he supported opening theaters and stores, a third one didn't want to touch this subject with a ten-foot pole. Instead of offering the government a realistic "centrist" compromise, in the end all the work resulted in a typically Israeli mediocre, motley whole of beautiful slogans about the need for reaching a national consensus about the Status Quo. I left politics just in time. There is a reign of cultural mediocrity. All

achievements in this country are a result of Israeli *chutzpah*, the conviction that we have to be best in everything. With all respect for the politicians who are trying to solve our territorial problems—perhaps more recognition can be gained with that—I am disappointed that so few politicians are aware that it's time to solve the internal problems. I have long since abandoned the illusion that we will become a completely democratic, pluralistic state. For decades we have put off our internal problems and now we are trying to solve unsolvable problems. The relation between the Orthodox and the secularists is a big dilemma, and I have a hard time remaining optimistic. In Israel you're almost an idealist if you try to find a solution for our internal problems because our state can't become more democratic and pluralistic and at the same time preserve its Jewish character. These dilemmas—and I can say this with certainty—are the most difficult in the history of Israel. Everyone has a different solution for them, so that it doesn't look like the Jews will soon agree on the answers to these questions. Fortunately I had an academic career that I could fall back on—otherwise I might have stayed and would have humiliated myself as a politician.

Meanwhile, the proposal has been taken over by Meimad, and Lubotsky still feels very involved and this is why he is attending the two-day conference:

The Jewish character of the state is being eroded: the young people distance themselves more and more from Judaism and because of this Judaism will lose its central place in Israeli society. In the long run the state will become less Jewish while on the other hand democracy is breaking down because of all sorts of religious laws. For example, selling *hametz* during Passover is forbidden by law. I prefer not to see it in stores during that time, but religious legislation drives the Jews apart and harms the democratic and pluralistic character of the state of Israel. In the future the state should try and free itself from religious tyranny.

From time to time Lubotsky sighs as he admits that the situation is very complex:

Take the Sabbath rest, for example—this has always been a very controversial subject in the history of Israel. A government can fall because a turbine is moved over a freeway on a Friday evening! This problem touches the heart of the Jewish state. If we strive for a twenty-four-hour economy like the Western countries have—and Israel sees itself as a Western country—then we are as far as that is concerned a country like all others. The inconsistency is that many Israelis want to live in a Western country with a Jewish character! The Sabbath rest is one of the most important pillars of the Jewish tradition which should become "more Jewish" in Israel, according to me and according to the new Status Quo. Critics immediately raise the following question: "Do you call that democratic in a country where 20 percent of the population is not Jewish?" Many Jews think that it is and that every democracy has its own short-comings. I agree with our new Status Quo which says that we should stop production on the Sabbath and that all commercial activities should be stopped. Only cultural institutions should be allowed to open their doors to the public. As compensation for this inconvenience, individual communities should be allowed to organize public transportation according to their wishes.

As regards civil marriage, Lubotsky thinks that Israel as a modern Jewish state should offer every citizen the opportunity to marry and to buy a house. He argues:

The fact is that in Israel a large group of immigrants, most of whom come from the former Soviet Union, have Israeli citizenship but can't marry in Israel. Starting a family is after all one of the most important hallmarks of Judaism. Most Orthodox and ultra-Orthodox are against establishing civil marriage for these immigrants because they fear that secular (real) Jews will use the opportunity of contracting a civil marriage, which is also possible between a Jew and a non-Jew. According to the Orthodox opinion, the Jewish people will assimilate and will produce an increasing number of bastards. [And bastards can't be married by the rabbinate.] According to strict Orthodoxy "a bastard shall not enter into the assembly of the Lord" [Deut. 23:3], not even in the tenth generation. The fact is that bastards are children born to a woman whose husband is not her legal (halakhic) spouse. According to the halakhah, this woman is still married to her first husband. For them the ultra-Orthodoxy [haredism] approves a "religious-judicial solution" which is in fact another name for a process that in practice amounts to the same thing as a civil marriage.

As regards conversion, Lubotsky, who is known as a moderately Orthodox Jew, thinks that Israel, like every state in the world, has the right to determine who can and who can't be a citizen. The state should support the citizens in conversion, which should be efficient and accessible. But according to the new Status Quo and the leaders of the new conversion institute, conversion is a halakhic process, which therefore cannot be carried out by non-Orthodox. A situation in which the Ministry of the Interior can register someone as a Jew (i.e., someone of the Jewish nationality) while that same person is not recognized as a Jew by the Ministry of Religious Affairs is acceptable according to the new Status Quo.

Since March 1999 the next of kin of Israeli citizens have the choice between a civil and a Jewish funeral. (Before that time, a civil funeral could take place only in a number of kibbutzim and at a high price.) Lubotsky thinks this opportunity to choose is an improvement. But calling up ultra-Orthodox—especially ultra-Orthodox women—for military service is "unnecessary" according to the new Status Quo. Those who see the study of God's word as their duty should be exempted from military service—the above-mentioned drafters of the Status Quo even say that "study of the Torah is of great value to Israeli society." Just as the Israeli army doesn't need Bedouin girls who barely leave their tents, drafting girls who belong to ultra-Orthodox movements is also absurd according to the Status Quo. Lubotsky, Melchior, and Beilin do agree about the new army unit for ultra-Orthodox so that "these students won't have to be dishonest later when they are looking for a job."

For centuries the problems that in Israel have become so closely tied to the Status Quo remained hidden. Marriages, divorces, and funerals were undisputed halakhic acts, and the Sabbath was always a day of rest in the diaspora. In Palestine the violation of this day became for the first time in nineteen centuries a subject about which Jews differed among themselves. This was also true for the way in which Jewish marriages were to be performed and Jewish funerals had to be conducted, and for the definition of Jewish-Israeli identity. Yet the need to answer the "Who is a Jew" question was continuously postponed in the young state of Israel because innumerable problems that seemed more urgent at the moment monopolized the nation's attention. Besides, in 1948 a Jew was above all the "new Jew," the Israeli, the "anti-diaspora person" who tried to be secular on the basis of two thousand years of religious history.

New immigrants, but also the Arabs who lived in Palestine before the state of Israel was founded, could be registered according to the Law of Population Registration passed in 1949. The Ministry of Interior Affairs registered personal data such as ethnic origin (in Hebrew this was *le'um*, which literally means "nationality" and which in Israel means "Jewish," "Arabic," or "Russian," for example), religion, and citizenship. Every registered inhabitant of Israel received an identity card on which these data were filled in. After *le'um* it said "Jew" for Jews, or "Muslim" for Arabs. Those who considered themselves a Jew, whatever that might mean for a particular person, were considered Jewish by the majority of the Israelis at the time and were therefore registered as such.

When the problems with the Arab countries seemed to diminish, more attention was paid to domestic problems that had become more urgent because of the influx of new immigrants. The Law of Return became effective in 1950; it was to give expression to the raison d'être of the Jewish state: *kibutz galuyot* (literally, "bringing together the exiles"). This law was based on the principle that every Jew, wherever in the world he or she might live, was a potential citizen of the Jewish state. The law said that every Jew who expressed the desire to settle in Israel had the right to immigrate, unless the Minister of the Interior had reason to believe that the candidate was "against" the Jewish people or was a "threat" to the "public health" or "public safety" of the state. Upon arrival in Israel, new immigrants received the privileged status of *oleh* (new immigrant) to which certain rights were attached, and they were registered as citizens with Jewish (ethnic) origin (*le'um*). From 1952 on, through the Law of Nationality, Israeli citizenship was officially attached to this status, a privilege that was limited to Jews. Others could become Israeli citizens through naturalization. With the Law of Return the first step was taken to the official distinction that is today still made in Israel between "nationality" (Jewish, Arab, Druze, Samaritan, Russian) and "citizenship" (Israeli).

Yet at the registration of new immigrants there was uncertainty at the Ministry of the Interior about who was eligible for the status of *oleh*. In the Law of Return the term *Jew* was not defined; this meant that the status of someone with a Jewish father or someone who had a Jewish mother but had converted to another religion and wanted to live in Israel created problems. In 1958, the minister of the interior stated in a government directive that "everyone who declared he was Jewish would be registered as a Jew" and "if two parents declared that their child was Jewish, this declaration would be considered as though it were a legal declaration by the child itself."

The religious Zionists of the National Religious Party, who had the feeling that they were still losing terrain in religious respects, felt forced to leave the government, a grave step for a party that had since 1948 ruled without interruption in a coalition with the Labor Party. But the National Religious Party could not be part of a government that had made a decision not in accordance with the halakhah. The party pointed out that the registration method of the Ministry of the Interior, which used personal criteria, was going to result in practical problems. For example, someone with a Jewish father, who, on registering with the Ministry of the Interior, had said that he "felt Jewish" and was therefore registered as a Jew and had also obtained Israeli citizenship, would be able to study without problems, to serve in the army, and be able to act as a good patriot in all respects according to the National Religious Party. But if, as the child of a non-Jewish mother, he submitted an application for marriage to the Chief Rabbinate, the rabbis would come upon the non-Jewish mother during their investigation of the family and—according the National Religious Party's reasoning—the applicant would come to the painful conclusion that he had until that time mistakenly thought that he was Jewish. The Chief Rabbinate instructed the rabbinic courts, which among other things consecrate marriages, not to rely on the fact that someone who might be Jewish according to the identity card (i.e., according to the criteria of the Ministry of the Interior) would actually be Jewish. This confusion was actually caused by the fact that two different standards were used: the halakhic one that gave a clear description of the term *Jew* and the civil "personal" definition of the Ministry of the Interior.

During this cabinet crisis, a debate arose in Israel as well as in the diaspora about the registration of children from mixed marriages. A government commission chaired by Prime Minister Ben Gurion had as its task to survey the opinions of professors at home and abroad about this question and then to formulate government directives. The goal was that these directives "would be approved in Orthodox as well as in non-Orthodox circles." Moreover, the commission would have to take into account the special circumstances in Israel as a "center for the *kvutsa galuyot.*" Until the results were made known, no identity cards would be given to children from mixed marriages. This procedure was exceptional because the Chief Rabbinate was not consulted about a halakhic question and because the opinions of the non-Orthodox (who practically didn't exist in Israel at the time) were included in this study.

The great majority of the scholars—including the Conservatives and the Reform among them—was of the opinion that Jewish nationalism and the halakhah were inseparably bound together. Personal considerations were therefore irrelevant in defining Jewish identity. Those who would have preferred the secular definition of the term *Jew* (because they thought that the biological bond with the mother has in many cases less spiritual content and meaning than the motivation of someone who for personal reasons wants to take on the Jewish identity) felt that "the time was not yet ripe." The prevailing sentiment was that a confrontation between the Orthodox and the secularists should be avoided. In 1960 the cabinet crisis was solved by an adaptation of the directives of 1958 from which the subjective criterion was removed. Henceforth, only someone born to a Jewish mother and who did not adhere to another faith could be registered as a Jew.

A year later the Eichmann trial took place. This reminded many sabras (Jews born in Israel who consider themselves more ethnically Israeli than religiously Jewish) that they, too, had a Jewish identity and that their way of thinking was in large measure formed by centuries-old Jewish religious rites and symbols. Yet this realization, together with the 1960 directives, did not at all guarantee consensus regarding the answer to the "Who is a Jew" question. In 1962 Brother Daniel, a Polish monk who was Jewish by birth and who considered his being Jewish as his nationality, caused renewed turmoil. That year he requested the status of *oleh* from the High Court after the Ministry of the Interior had refused because he had converted to Christianity. Brother Daniel, who died in August 1998 in Haifa at the age of seventy-six and was buried in a Christian cemetery, was born as Oswald Rufeisen, a Polish Jew who was active in the Zionist youth movement. When the German-Russian war broke out in 1941, he managed to obtain a certificate that said that he was a Christian. When the Gestapo discovered his true identity, Rufeisen managed to escape and landed in a monastery where he converted to Christianity in 1942.

Years later, when he applied for a visa for Israel at the Israeli consulate in Warsaw, he formulated his request as follows: "I still belong to the Jewish people despite the fact that I accepted the Catholic faith in 1942. In 1945 I entered the Order of the Carmelites because this order has a monastery in Israel, the country I have longed for since my youth." He was granted the visa, and once in Israel his request for the status of *oleh* resulted in a court case of historic importance.

Rufeisen's lawyer assumed that the term *Jew* in the Law of Return was used according to the *halakhah*. He contended that someone who is born a Jew always remains a Jew "even if he sinned," and that is why, in accordance with the Law of Return, Brother Daniel had right to the status of *oleh*. But according to the attorney-general, a Jew who had converted to another faith was no longer a Jew. A Jew who converts to another faith is called a *meshumad* in Hebrew. According to this view a *meshumad* has made himself worthless in nationalist terms. And it was for this reason that the court rejected Rufeisen's petition. Besides, in Israeli terms he was a man without a nationality because he had also given up his Polish nationality. The only way he could obtain Israeli nationality (Jewish) and the citizenship (Israeli) linked to it was through naturalization.

One of the judges explained the decision as follows: "In this secular law, the term 'Jew' means what the man in the street understands it to mean, I emphasize: what the normal, ordinary Jew understands it to mean. The Law of Return is an Israeli law, and who knows the meaning of 'Jew' better than Israelis? A Jew who has converted to Christianity is no longer a Jew for most Israelis." Another judge agreed:

> Would a Jew who has become a Christian still feel at home with us, and what do our national sentiments mean for them? I don't doubt that Brother Daniel loves Israel, but his love comes from outside, and this is why he will never be part of the Jewish people. It is impossible for Jews to deny the legacy of the past. Every Jew is connected to historic Judaism in which his wishes are rooted, from which derive his customs and holidays, and whose great thinkers nourish his national pride.

For the first time in its history the young state of Israel pushed aside the halakhic definition and instead used the definition of *Jew* in "nationalistic" terms. The majority of Jewish Israelis considered this a favorable development, and the Orthodoxy was relieved, too, that the Law of Return would henceforth not be used to admit *meshumaddim*. However, the Orthodoxy was aware of the explosive character of this decision.

A second case that created controversy over the "Who is a Jew" question was the excitement in 1963 about the non-Jewish background of Dina Eitani from Nazareth. She was born to a Jewish father and a non-Jewish mother and after the Holocaust had come to Palestine in 1945. She was able to register as a Jew without any problems because she felt Jewish. She served in the Israeli army during the War of Independence and afterward, the Chief Rabbinate, which at the time did not yet conduct investigations of family trees, solemnized her marriage to an Israeli. In addition she managed to let her children become a part of the Jewish society without their non-Jewish origin becoming evident. When it did become evident—after a neighbor had informed an official at the local population registry about Eitani's non-Jewish mother—the National Religious Party suggested that Eitani surrender her passport, which she had obtained "under false pretenses." Of course that would definitely not happen; when she registered, right after the Second World War, the personal criterion was valid. The fact that her Jewish origin was linked to her father and not to her mother did not come up at that time. In all aspects Eitani led the life of an average Jewish woman in Israel, that is to say that she obeyed the commandments in a way that suited her. However, for the Orthodoxy it remained obvious that she could not call herself Jewish unless she had undergone a formal conversion. The Ministry of Religious Affairs even went so far as to state that Eitani had to chose between an Orthodox conversion or her departure from Israel. Months later it became known that Eitani and her children had formally converted to Judaism.

The last case, which took place in 1968, ultimately resulted in the definition of the term *Jew*. A Jewish officer in the Israeli navy, Benjamin Shalit, had married a Christian woman, Anne Giddes, in Scotland. The attention of the whole nation was focused on him when he demanded through the High Court that henceforth the identity card not be filled in with "Jew" after both "religion" and "nationality," as had been the case, but only after "nationality." This meant that he wanted "Jewish" to become a nationality that could be adopted by non-Jews—for example, his own children, who were not born to a Jewish mother but were circumcised and reared as Israeli children with the Jewish "nationality." His wife's identity card said "British" after "nationality" and "none" after "religion." Shalit's own card said "Jewish" after both, even though he considered himself an atheist.

Shalit's case was postponed because of the Six-Day War and therefore did not begin until 1968. The court realized that the decision could lead to a serious political crisis. The government instructed the solicitor general to defend the directives of 1960 (namely, that only someone who has a Jewish mother and who doesn't adhere to another faith is Jewish) because the Orthodox had announced that they would leave the government if these directives were declared invalid.

Foreign Orthodox rabbis had warned the Israeli government about a split within the Jewish people by anti-halakhic decisions. Shalit stated before the entire nine-member court that "equating religion with nationality in a sovereign state is unacceptable and in such a state everyone should be able to determine his own identity." The climax of his argument was reached when Shalit mentioned the name of an Arab terrorist, Kamal Imri, who had been sentenced by an Israeli court. Imri's mother was Jewish and his father was Arab. Shalit said, "Is Kamal Imri, a member of Al-Fatah [a Palestine resistance group, which is part of the Palestine Liberation Organization and founded by Yasir Arafat], allowed to call himself a Jew while we, I as sabra and my wife who considers herself a Jewish woman, are not allowed to register our children as Jews?" His comment about Russian Jews was equally disturbing: "What would happen if the Jews from Russia who consider themselves Jewish, but are born to non-Jewish mothers, come to Israel? In Russia national identity is registered according to the person's choice. Would these people then be told here that they are not Jewish?" (Years later, this turned out to be the case; see chapter 4). By a vote of five to four the court declared the 1960 directives invalid: Shalit's children obtained the Jewish nationality, and on their identity card "none" was entered after "religion" and "Jewish" after "nationality." This established for the first time that the word *Jewish* in Israel indicates nationality and not necessarily religion.

The decision didn't result in a law, however, and in the years that followed the Orthodox persisted in their demand that the halakhic definition of *Jew* be statutory. Finally in 1970, this ideolog-ical-theological struggle resulted in the formulation of a long-awaited law: henceforth a Jew was someone who was born to a Jewish mother or to someone who had converted to Judaism without having another religious conviction. The law was not retroactive, so the decision of the court in the Shalit case remained in force. The new law satisfied the National Religious Party as well as the Labor Party. The Orthodox gained because being Jewish was halakhically defined, although they would have preferred to add "in accordance with the halakhah" to the phrase about conversion in order to exclude those converted abroad by non-Orthodox rabbis. The gain of the Labor Party was in the possibility that the conver-sions carried out in the diaspora by Reform and Conservative rabbis would continue to be recognized in Israel. To date, those converted abroad by non-Orthodox rabbis can be registered in Israel as Israeli citizens of the Jewish faith. However, those converted in Israel by Reform or Conservative rabbis can't be registered as Jews. (In Feb-ruary 1999, the court refused such a request from a couple that had two adopted Christian children who had been converted by a Con-servative rabbi in Israel.)

After all these years, the "civil war" and the "religious war" have still not been resolved. Parliamentary votes about subjects linked to these wars (changing the Status Quo, drafting a constitution, the redefinition of the "Who is a Jew" question) can still cause govern-ment crises. These subjects are perhaps the most problematic in the history of Judaism—possibly because they confront the Jews with the complexity of their own psyche and with the reality in their country. For decades politicians have avoided these subjects and have beaten around the bush about them as much as possible. The latter is especially true of the "Who is a Jew" question, which today is euphemistically called the "conversion question."

However, since the government of Barak took office in the summer of 1999, Eli Ishai, the minister of employment of the Sephardic ultra-Orthodox party Shas, has made this a subject that can be discussed. On Saturdays he sometimes had his non-Jewish inspectors—mostly Druze, non-Jewish immigrants, or Israeli Arabs—visit open stores in large shopping centers to check whether the people working on Saturday were indeed goyim. According to

Israel's Work and Rest Law, *asur l'hatzig yehudim b' yomei chofesh* (literally, "it is forbidden to employ Jews on days off or on holidays; *yom chofesh*: "day off, vacation day"). Since the Sabbath is a day off, Jews are not allowed to work on that day and can be fined. Jewish shop owners and their Jewish employees flee as soon as the inspectors approach, and they leave the *goyim shel shabbat* (non-Jews who are employed especially to work on Saturdays) behind in their stores.

"We stand at the eve of a crucial struggle," says political scientist Asher Cohen of Bar Ilan University in Ramat Gan who, in September 2000, published his book *Israel and the Politics of Jewish Identity: The Secular-Religious Impasse.*

> The domestic problems are still in the shadow of the peace process and our relations with the Arab neighboring countries. But as soon as peace is in sight, the struggle for the character of the state— about the "Who is a Jew" question and about the Status Quo—will have to be fought. The first subject on the agenda will be the status of the Reform and the Conservatives, and the second will be the new, non-Jewish immigrants who together with the guest workers now number in the hundreds of thousands. In the end a solution will have to be found for the problem these non-Jews encounter when, for example, they want to marry a non-Jew,

says Cohen, who wears a crocheted yarmulke. "The Work and Rest Law is barely discussed, but the Minister of the Interior has officially the right to fine Jews who work on Saturdays—and there are many. One of my students showed me an ad from a Russian language newspaper that sums up the situation: 'A secular employer is looking for a non-Jewish Russian who can work on Saturdays, to stop the ultra-Orthodox Jew Ishai from sending a Druze inspector to prevent the violation of the Sabbath.'"

"Only the Supreme Court can democratize Israel," shouts Boaz Moav, one of the founders of Meretz and chair of the alternative funeral business Menucha Nechona (Just Peace). "Even leftist politicians don't dare to break through the Orthodox hegemony because all hell will break loose in the coalition." Moav teaches biology at the University of Tel Aviv and was for four years a Knesset member of the Ratz Party (the predecessor of Meretz). He doesn't make any attempt to disguise his dissatisfaction about the ideological and political atmosphere in Israel. The body of his motor scooter is covered with stickers that say, "I'm sick of religious coercion" and "I'm afraid of *haredim*." "Guess what's in this?" he says, while ostentatiously placing a large envelope with the names of two extreme leftist politicians on the table of a sidewalk café. "Two black yarmulkes for leftist gentlemen who are letting themselves be taken in by the Orthodox," explains Moav as he looks impatiently for the courier who is supposed to deliver the package at the Knesset. He is worried about the future of Israeli politicians who do the bidding of the Orthodox and allow strange things to happen. One of the odd things about which he is agitated is the funeral of the immigrant Grigory Pesahovic, age fifteen, a victim of the bombing in the Mahaneh Yehuda market in Jerusalem at the end of July 1997. Moav explains: "Because of his 'doubtful Jewish origins,' as it is called in Orthodox circles, the funeral was stopped and the body was put back into cold storage while waiting for the decision of the chief rabbinate that wanted to study his family tree once more. After four days the Ministry of Religious Affairs gave permission to bury him—but it had to be done behind a fence because it says in the Torah that Jews should not be buried next to non-Jews."

"A human being is a human being, and that's why we bury Jews as well as non-Jews," continues Moav. In the fifties he sympathized with the movement of the Canaanites, a movement that has been discontinued but that wanted to develop an Israeli culture for Israeli citizens and no Jewish culture for Jews. "The fact that Israelis who are born to a Christian mother and have only a Jewish father or grandfather have to lie behind a fence is a polite way of saying that they don't belong. That's discrimination! Only Nazis and the Orthodox are interested in the question of who is Jewish. The comparison is demagogic, but for the Orthodoxy the 'Who is a Jew' question is more important than the right to Israeli citizenship."

It isn't his own funeral that worries Moav, but a government that doesn't dare to tamper with the position of power of the Orthodoxy. Therefore a roundabout way must be taken in Israel in order to make it possible to have civil legislation in the areas of funerals, divorces, and marriages. "Patience is the secret," says Moav, who litigated tirelessly for more than ten years to get alternative funerals off the ground. He achieved his objective: in March of 1999 the first funeral directed by Menucha Nechona took place.

In March 1998, after lengthy bureaucratic and political intrigues in which Moav participated, the city of Tel Aviv legalized the opening of theaters, cafés, and restaurants on the Sabbath and on holidays. These places have been open for years on these days, but the new law caused some unrest among the population. "All I've done is adapt the law to reality," explained the former mayor of Tel Aviv, Ronni Milo. Moav continues: "I started with this twenty-three years ago, and not a single secular politician dared to adjust the law. Even Milo postponed adapting it for fear of losing his Orthodox constituency."

"The Court has to pull Israel literally inch by inch toward normality. Politicians are afraid to fall out of favor with the Orthodox coalition partners," shouts Moav, who seems to be permanently angry. "And that's why we have to litigate for years. Now that the ultra-Orthodox are also trying to get a hold over the Court, the judges may more often try to kick the ball back to the Knesset, which will make everything take even longer. During the government of Barak this situation won't change because it has become a part of the Israeli way of government."

In Israel resistance to religious coercion always goes through the court. Because the court's decisions often disturb the government's peace and quiet, the government often tries to prevent the court from intervening by finding a typically Israeli interim solution through a special commission. This state of affairs reflects the complexity of the Israeli political arena and the sensitivity of certain subjects. For example, in 1996 the Knesset had to end the monopoly of Orthodox funeral enterprises because of a decision by the court. After that it still took another two years before the first civil funeral could take place, because Yigal Bibi of the National Religious Party and minister of religious affairs at the time, obstructed things. Moav says, "He preferred to have alternative funerals in Orthodox cemeteries, but how can we continue to accept the fact that non-Jews are buried behind a fence?" Moav died in early 2002 and was buried in Beersheba by Menucha Nechona.

"What's the problem?" asks Chananya Shachor, the proprietor of the funeral company Kehilat Yerushalayim (municipality of Jerusalem). "We have a grave for every deceased," he says, indignant. "Menucha Nechona thinks that the Torah, as Moses received it from God, is pluralistic. They dispute the religious foundation of the state while we live here according to the halakhah, which forbids us to bury a non-Jew next to a Jew. In the *Shulchan Arukh* it says: 'Build a fence and bury outside the community the non-Jews and those who have been cast out.' We have a special relationship with God which is continued after death." Shachor, who wears a black yarmulke and lets the tzitzit dangle along his legs, takes a framed license from the Ministry of Religious Affairs from the wall. "It says here: Jews only," he says almost proudly as he points to it. "But I did bury Pesacovic. Baksi-Doron gave me permission after one day. That's quite fast, don't you think? But he couldn't lie next to a Jew. I wouldn't want to lie next to a Muslim or a Christian either. After all, we live separated from them, don't we?"

What used to be a small problem has developed into a sizeable problem since the immigration from the former Soviet Union in 1989 and the increasing number of non-Jews. Out of almost one million Russian immigrants, approximately 400,000 are halakhically non-Jewish. Shachor continues: "This question is new for us. I'm the third generation of my family in this business. My father and my grandfather never checked the Jewish background of the deceased. Now we have to because many of the Russian immigrants are not Jewish according to the law."

According to most non-Orthodox, it's especially the Russian immigrants who in the future will be able to free Israel from the Orthodox interference in the life of the citizens. Together with the guest workers they form a new group of non-Jews who in Israel suffer under the most unpopular interference of the synagogue in the life of the people, namely the fact that the state doesn't recognize civil marriage. Most of these people are therefore forced to book a "honeymoon" to Cyprus where the British established civil marriage in 1923. For a number of years it was only possible to marry in Nicosia, the capital of Cyprus, and the couples usually stayed for two days. Today marriages can be performed in various cities on Cyprus, and they are often combined with a vacation.

"The requests which dribbled in when I started in 1983, now come like a waterfall," says David Kenan, the director of the Tel Aviv travel agency King Tours, one of the five travel agencies that sell "honeymoons" to Cyprus for about 1,500 dollars; Kenan sells about sixty of these trips every month. At first 60 percent of Kenan's clientele consisted of couples who couldn't be married by the rabbinate, and 40 percent were couples that didn't want an Orthodox marriage. Today, 15 percent of the couples can't be married by the rabbinate, 60 percent want nothing to do with the rabbinate, and 25 percent of the customers are from the former Soviet Union. In 1974 the rabbinate performed 26,000 weddings, a number that decreased to 21,000 in 1991 while the population doubled during that period.

Liora Carmon and Uri Naveh from Tel Aviv were married on Cyprus in 1998. "It was *our* way, *our* wedding," says Carmon. "No friends of my father, no waiters, and even more important: our marriage is valid. We are registered as husband and wife at the Ministry of the Interior and we receive a mortgage for young marrieds, and all that without exchanging a word with the rabbinate!" Naveh and Carmon are halakhically Jewish and therefore could have been married by the rabbinate, but like many Israeli couples from nonreligious families they were not interested in an Orthodox wedding. Only a legal civil ceremony could have kept them from their Cypriot adventure. The couple, who booked their honeymoon with Kenan, discovered that another Israeli couple, who had also come for a wedding ceremony, was overnighting in the same hotel. They decided to be each other's witnesses and to photograph each other. "Actually it was amusing," says Carmon. "You arrive in a strange city, you go to the city hall where the mayor reads a few lines that you have to repeat. Then the mayor pushes a button after which Mendelssohn's *Wedding March* resounds from a tape recorder and you kiss each other. Next the mayor pushes 'rewind' and the next couple enters."

Twenty percent of the Israeli couples that choose a Cypriot wedding have a Reform wedding in Israel afterward. Iris Sinai and Yuval Shalev, both twenty-seven years old, belong to this category. Originally they wanted an Orthodox marriage ceremony because Shalev comes from an Orthodox family. They changed their mind during the first meeting with the rabbi when he asked questions about Sinai's illegitimate child and about her menstruation. "I have a completely nonreligious life," says Sinai, "and I don't want to listen to an unsolicited lecture about the purity of the family, and I'm not planning to lie about my menstruation to be able to get married." (Jewish law forbids a woman to marry when she is menstruating.) Because Shalev wanted a Jewish wedding, the couple chose a Reform wedding ceremony in Tel Aviv after their Cypriot marriage.

✦✦✦

"What, we no longer have to go to Cyprus?" was the headline of one of the Russian newspapers in May of 1998 after the Russian immigrant party Israel ba'Aliyah had proposed a law for civil marriage. Things aren't there by a long shot in Israel, but Roman Bronfman, who submitted the proposal, wanted this law to offer a solution for the non-Jewish immigrants who cannot marry in Israel. Bronfman wanted to adapt theory to reality with this law, but the consideration of this bill was slowed down during the government of Netanyahu and seems to have disappeared from the agenda during the government of Barak. He wanted to speed things up after the abolition in February 1996 of the so-called Paraguayan wedding by mail; this wedding possibility had existed since 1963 for couples who were not allowed to be married before a rabbi.

After finding out about this proposal, a number of secularists spoke of "a capitulation before the ultra-Orthodox." After all, the proposal concerned only non-Jews, and in this new situation Jews would still be required to marry before the rabbinate or to travel to Cyprus for a civil wedding. A Knesset member at the time, Dedi Zucker of Meretz, spoke of an "alarming proposal that will create a closed caste established by law." Raising objections to the proposal, Zucker continued: "For Machiavellian reasons the rabbinate could agree to the Bronfman law which will take away the pressure that is being exerted on the rabbinate to find a solution for performing marriages for non-Jews. It is in our interest that the rabbinate, because it can no longer handle the pressure, will finally accept civil marriage." Others argued that this law would create second-class citizens, and the Israeli Institute for Democracy compared the situation that would arise to the "caste system in India where the members of one caste are forbidden to marry members of another caste." Bronfman replied, "There is a grain of truth in this, but the Reform who assert this forget that there are second-class citizens in the present system, namely the non-Jewish and half-Jewish immigrants. Besides, if I don't want the ultra-Orthodox to impose their laws on me, then I can't agree to the secularists forcing their point of view on the ultra-Orthodox."

Expansion of the proposal is problematic because of the resistance to it by the Orthodox establishment. The Orthodox leaders of

United Torah Judaism said they had great difficulty with the proposal, which would create a precedent by offering full Jews the opportunity to wangle a civil marriage, and as a result, not two but perhaps twenty peoples would come into being. "If Meretz had proposed the law, I wouldn't even have taken the trouble to look at it," said a representative of United Torah Judaism. "Although Bronfman is just as secular as the members of Meretz, I suspect Meretz of intentions that are not consistent with the character of the Jewish people." Shortly afterward the Chief Rabbinate decided: "Civil marriage is permitted for completely non-Jewish couples. However, a civil wedding ceremony of a Jew to a Christian or a Muslim or of a Jewish couple that according to the halakhah is not allowed to marry in Israel, is out of the question."

However, the greatest difficulties occur at divorce, not at marriage. If a couple breaks up in a friendly manner, and if they are secular and don't want a religious confirmation of their divorce, they can go through life peacefully as divorced people. But if they want to change their civil status on their identity card, they need halakhic proof of divorce, a *get*, which they have to show to the rabbinic court that had originally performed their marriage. The greatest problems arise when the woman doesn't receive this proof. She will henceforth go through life as an *agunah* (literally "chained woman," a woman who doesn't receive a get from her husband). If she wants to remarry, this can be done on Cyprus (not before the rabbinate in Israel, which can allow her to divorce her husband only if she has a *get*). If this woman has children with her new husband without having been divorced by a rabbinic court, the children are considered bastards because the rabbinic courts don't accept the new marriage. According to Orthodox law, this woman is still married to her first husband and therefore her new children are a product of adultery and are considered bastards by the Orthodox.

It seems as if the parents, if they are secular, can ignore this illegitimacy in which they don't believe. But if these children want to become religious or, once they are grown, want their marriage to be performed by the rabbinate, they will discover that they don't qualify because of a decision made by their parents before they were born.

According to the general director of the rabbinic courts, Rabbi Eliahu Ben-Dahan, in the year 2000 the rabbinic courts tracked down thirty-six men in Israel and abroad who refused to give their wives a get. In January 2001 there were a total of fourteen *agunot* whose husbands could not be found. Six uncooperative men were imprisoned because they ignored court orders instructing them to give their wives a *get*. The attitude of different movements inside Judaism with respect to these uncooperative husbands varies greatly. In contrast to their liberal colleagues, most Orthodox rabbis resist the violation of the halakhic principle that a marriage can be ended only with the consent of the spouse. However, in the modern-Orthodox communities in the United States and in Israel there are advocates of involving courts in "freeing" the chained women.

"All problems about social status are a symptom of the dissatisfaction with our identity and with that of the state. Many Jews want to 'normalize' Jewish identity and make Israel into a normal country where the 'Who is a Jew' question no longer plays a role and where the non-Orthodox are equal to the Orthodox, but that's impossible," says Menachem Friedman, professor of sociology and anthropology at Bar Ilan University in Ramat Gan. In Israel he is the specialist in the area of the ultra-Orthodox, and he has written a number of books and articles about Israel's theological dilemmas. Friedman states:

> The wish to be different and special lies hidden deep in the nature of the Jew. The Bible, our liturgy, and large parts of our tradition and culture, which are imbued with the element of being chosen, stand in the way of our equality to the rest of the world. The sentence "You have chosen us" is one of the most important foundations of Jewish consciousness, and this sentence forms the psychological background of many religious-national activities. As long as we Jews don't acknowledge our equality within humanity as a whole, we can't insist on political equality of the Jewish people.

It surprises Friedman that many Israelis can't comprehend that the Jewish "abnormality" is the difference between the Jewish people and other peoples and that the culture war and the religious war are its consequences. He thinks that even nonbelieving Knesset members guarantee this "fundamental abnormality" by, for example, voting for a law that maintains Orthodoxy's exclusive right to convert, for a law that forbids the import of pork, or against the law for religious liberty. If Israel were a state for all citizens, the

"Who is a Jew" question would no longer be relevant, according to Friedman. In present-day Israel it is still relevant because a part of the population says the Jews are a people and another part says that the Jews are a religious community.

"This paradoxical situation started with the Zionists, who knew that religion had held us together for centuries but still thought that the state should become secular and wanted to secularize being Jewish. The Jewish state is in itself a contradiction in terms which is best expressed in the Orthodoxy that has become besmirched in nationalism," says Friedman, who is wearing an anti-Zionist yarmulke. "Being Jewish often means being patriotic. When Ehud Barak says that he is Jewish, he means 'I'm a good Israeli citizen' and not 'I'm a practicing Jew,' which is what Orthodox Jews mean by 'being Jewish.' When premier Netanyahu whispered in Rabbi Kedouri's ear that leftist Israel had forgotten what being Jewish means, he meant that leftist Jews are not good citizens."

Friedman sighs after almost every question because in Israel more problems are being generated than are being solved. He starts many of his sentences with "the problem is" and often uses the word *paradox*. He answers many questions with other questions or with the statement that "our people has been wrestling with that problem for centuries." Friedman continues:

> Israel is afraid of the dentist. In addition to the unanswered "Who is a Jew" question, there is the "Who is a rabbi" question, or rather the unsolved question of who is an accepted Jew. These are old dilemmas, and every Jew carries some of them within himself: Does nationality, race or religion make someone into a Jew, or only free choice? If nationality is the determining factor, are there also Christian and Islamic Jews? And if religion is the determining factor, which movement within Judaism determines being Jewish?

As regards this last problem, Friedman remarks,

> Reform and Conservative Jews are apostates in the opinion of the Orthodox, but also in the opinion of many nonreligious Jews who act like "absent" Orthodox because the synagogue they don't visit is still the Orthodox one of their grandfathers.
>
> The politicians have always stuck their heads in the sand as regards all these problems, but the immigrants—halakhically non-Jews, Romanians, Filipinos, and other Christians—make the "Who

is a Jew" question topical. There is increased pressure on the government and on the Orthodox establishment to give up their monopoly. However, Orthodox and traditional Jews fear that once civil marriages, alternative funerals, and conversions carried out by non-Orthodox are allowed, Israel will become a state for all citizens just like all other states in which Jewish identity will no longer play a role. Moreover, and this is much more alarming in Orthodox opinion, the presence of Jews in such a state will no longer be of importance.

No kind of medicine can combat the source of evil in a troubled land that has no clearly stated reality. Israel is so heterogeneous, all its problems are connected, and the distinction between cause and effect is unclear. We lack a "governing culture," politicians don't listen, know everything better, and will never agree. Moreover, many secular Israelis who don't know or don't want to know the complexity of their own psyche are incapable of accepting the limitations of a Jew in a Jewish state. They want capitalism without unemployment, socialism without leveling of salaries, and a car that's too expensive at a price that suits them [this example is typically Israeli according to Friedman] and the Israeli wants to be Orthodox without being observant. We want to have the luxury to be both, and our state is too young to know that solutions can't always be compromises like those of the conversion institute!

Raising his voice, the professor says, "That's the height of absurdity! Accepting the non-Orthodox is a religious duty because these people are Jews, but for this the Orthodox don't want to pay the price, namely full recognition of the non-Orthodox movements. The typically Israeli middle course is the result: they can be part of the Jewish people, but their conversion rituals are not recognized. The idea is that the Orthodoxy (and also the state which finances the institute) legitimizes their existence; they may join, but only under supervision of the Orthodoxy."

According to Friedman, the Israelis have to learn to live with the discomfort of the entanglement of religion and state. For him that's not just a religious problem but a deeply rooted social problem:

Judaism is a way of life that determines every action of daily life. At most we can try to hate less. The secularists will have to understand that Judaism in Israel, as opposed to in the diaspora, cannot be "privatized" and the Orthodox will have to understand that they are not the only legitimate Jews. For them the Jewish land, with Jewish institutions, where the Jewish people speaks Hebrew, and which is recognized throughout the word as a Jewish country is clearly not Jewish enough. They ignore the Jewish majority in Israel which thinks, on the contrary, that this country is too Jewish but still is aware of being Jewish without believing in God.

Friedman thinks that the secularists shouldn't forget that the Orthodox have already made many sacrifices for their life in the secular Holy Land. To be sure, they never adapted completely to modern times, but they have given up their ban on voting rights for women, adapted many parts of their original educational system, and the curriculum of the religious girls' education in 1999 cannot be compared with that of 1920. Moreover, recently a number of ultra-Orthodox have been serving in the new army unit created especially for them. Friedman feels that the flexibility of the *haredim* is underestimated. The problem is that they don't move forward with the same speed as the secularists.

Many difficulties await us. Religion has been on our political agenda for two hundred years, but our greatest problem is that we built a Jewish state in the Holy Land. Since then a Jew has had to know what it means to be Jewish and to be part of a Jewish nation. In exile Judaism was primarily halakhic, and religion was the only factor that preserved unity. Therefore, in view of our history—since tensions, conflicting interests, and paranoia are part of our heritage—we shouldn't be surprised that the state has become a social and political hotbed with religious-nationalist touches.

FOUR

THE RUSSIANS IN ISRAEL

is being israeli jewish enough?

"Israel likes immigration, not immigrants."
Israeli saying

W hen Irena Appelman lived in Leningrad (present-day St. Petersburg) she was a Jew, and now that she lives in Israel she's a Russian. According to Russian law her father made her Jewish, and according to Israeli law her mother made her Russian. Irena tells her story:

It wasn't until I was ten years old that my parents told me that I was Jewish, and from that moment on I was always on my guard and often said that I was Russian. After my marriage to a full Jew—a label for someone with two Jewish parents that I learned later in Israel—we tried to register as Soviet citizens with Russian nationality. In this way we hoped to spare our children difficulties in the future. But the authorities registered us as Jews. Instead of his own name Appelman, my husband often used my maiden name Smirnakov, which sounds more Russian than Jewish.

To liberate us from a state that wanted to determine our identity we left for Israel, but the same thing happens here. I'm a goy here; the state wants "real" Jews and would prefer that the non-Jewish Russians are converted by the Orthodox rabbinate. When I saw religious people walking around for the first time, I thought I was in a museum. I knew that in Israel "Jewishness" was determined only by the mother. But I never suspected that being halakhically Jewish dominates life here—and the Sochnut [the Jewish Agency] that helped us with immigration never told us about this. And please note that it's in the Jewish state, where I thought that I'd be at home, that I have the Russian nationality! It's difficult to be a Jew in Russia, but being a Russian in Israel is much more difficult. My husband is a full Jew and therefore has the Jewish nationality while he's just as Jewish as I: he doesn't pray, he doesn't celebrate Passover, he doesn't go to the synagogue, and he isn't circumcised. I'm probably more Jewish than he because I'd like to be more involved with Jewish tradition, like celebrating Passover, Sukkoth, and Chanukah traditionally, and I'd also like to do more about the Sabbath. But it doesn't interest him at all. He always says: "Being Israeli is Jewish enough for me."

This situation is confusing for our two children. Alexander, the youngest, who is seven, put on a yarmulke the other day and asked his father why he doesn't wear a yarmulke and why we don't celebrate Passover. He feels completely at home here. Last summer when we arrived at Ben Gurion Airport after a vacation in St. Petersburg, he said: "*Baruch haShem, anachnu ba'bayit*" (Thank God, we are home). I haven't told him yet that according to Israeli law he isn't Jewish at all, that he isn't circumcised like all his Jewish classmates, and that he's growing up without a nationality. Sometimes Israel resembles the Soviet system in miniature: there are Russians, Moroccans, Romanians, Filipinos, Ethiopians, Yemenites, but everyone has to be Jewish. I have the Russian nationality because my mother isn't Jewish, and that's why I seem to be worth less here than my husband. Yet I feel above the "Who is a Jew" discussion, and I don't want to convert. I don't care whether someone is Dutch, French, Russian, Israeli, Jewish, or not Jewish. I thought I'd be able to live here just as a human being, and not as "Jew," "Russian," "Ukrainian," or "Caucasian." When filling out applications and during conversations in stores and on the street, I am constantly reminded that I don't have a Jewish mother and that my children will therefore not be able to marry in Israel.

Irena is a pianist, but today she earns a living by housecleaning. In 1989 she came to Israel with her children and her husband, an independent contractor, after Mikhail Gorbachev's reforms provided the opportunity to leave the country. They settled in the desert city Ashdod where, since the large immigration flood from the Soviet Union, people say that "Hebrew is also spoken"; these days more than half of the 110,000 inhabitants are Russian. The Russians, who abandoned the Zionist practice of hebraizing their names, largely determine the character of this city and of other cities like Beersheba and Kiryat Gat. Beersheba is in the Negev desert and one-quarter (41,000) of its population is Russian; the southern Israeli city Kiryat Gat has a total population of 50,000, of which 14,500 are Russians. In Sderot in Upper Nazareth and in the developing city Ma'alot 50 percent of the population is Russian, in Or Akiva 40 percent, and in Karmi'el 30 percent of the population is Russian. Russian-language newspapers and weeklies fill the newspaper stands, posters and announcements in shop windows are in Russian, the barbers cut hair the way they do in Moscow, Russian products fill the store shelves, and in the past few years the number of stores with bacon slices and other pork specialties in their windows has increased. The plumber is no longer called the *installator* but the *santechnik*, and older Russians sit and reminisce on the benches in the parks and in the shopping centers. Another example—two-thirds of the orchestra members of the Tizmoret Andalusit (Andalusian Orchestra) that plays only Sephardic religious music are Russian immigrants. Despite these familiar things in her direct environment, Irena says she doesn't feel at home in Israel, where she is always treated as a non-Jew or as a Christian.

Before coming to Israel, Irena had no definite opinion about the country that, for her, was simply a place on the Mediterranean with a better climate than Kiev. As is the case for many Russians, she came to Israel primarily for economic reasons and not for ideological or religious considerations. They are not interested in conversion, which is for them something like joining the Communist Party in the former Soviet Union—it increases their chances for a better life and a better job. In their eyes, a conversion is recognition of the power of the Jewish establishment that will make their life as a Jew easier.

It is striking that after more than a century Theodor Herzl's ideas still seem to be largely applicable to the Russian Jews in Israel.

In 1897, during the first Zionist Congress in Basel, Herzl praised the Russians:

> And then appeared before us a Russian Judaism whose strength we had not even suspected. All these professors, doctors, lawyers, industrialists, and businessmen are certainly no less educated than we. Most of them master three languages, and that they are competent in their field shows by the mere fact of their success in a country where that isn't easy for Jews. They still have the solidarity that Western European Jews have lost, and they are imbued with a Jewish-national feeling without a trace of national narrow-mindedness and intolerance. They are not tortured by the thought of assimilation . . . and yet they are ghetto-Jews. Their aspect made us understand where our forefathers derived the strength to stand by their beliefs even in the bitterest circumstances.

However, the crucial difference is that many Jews who settle in Israel today don't do so out of love of Zion. No less important is the fact that many of them, like Irena, are halakhically not Jewish. According to the minister of religious affairs, Irena is a goy and therefore doesn't belong in Israel. But the minister of the interior must admit her because of the civil Law of Return. Originally this law pertained only to someone born to a Jewish mother or who converted to Judaism. But since 1971 this law is also valid for the spouse of a Jew, the spouse of a child or a grandchild of a Jew, and for the descendants of a Jew. The change in the law that expanded the right of "return" to people who were not Jewish was meant to prevent families from breaking up, but it created a loophole in the law. Masses of people who were halakhically not Jewish could enter the country without too many problems. In 1998, 43.5 percent of these immigrants were not Jewish according to the halakhah—the Christian Ethiopian Jews, for example. And 27 percent of the 54,600 immigrants from the former Soviet Union were not Jewish, even according to the Law of Return. In 1999, 51.1 percent of immigrants from the former Soviet Union were not Jewish.

The right-wing religious political parties in particular worry about the consequences of the approximately 400,000 non-Jews among the one million Russian immigrants who now live in Israel. "They split the Jewish people, they contribute to the assimilation of the Jews, and they endanger the Jewishness of the state," say some who think that these people should convert to Judaism in the Orthodox way. The ultra-Orthodox minister of the interior under Netanyahu, Eliyahu Suissa of Shas, and the minister of the interior under Sharon, Eli Ishai, both hold this point of view. The former thought he would be able to put an end to the increasing flood of non-Jews by changing the Law of Return. He wanted only halakhic Jews to be able to immigrate in the future, but he didn't succeed with this plan. After all, a great number of non-halakhic Jews from the former Soviet Union entered Israel. Before Suissa took office, non-Jewish spouses of Jews were allowed to become Israeli citizens, even if they immigrated without their Jewish spouses. Suissa wanted these non-Jews to be accompanied by their Jewish spouse upon immigration. He felt that a non-Jewish spouse who came alone, even for just one day, forfeited his or her right to citizenship. He also limited the conditions under which non-Jewish immigrants could take along their parents or their children. Many non-Jews and half-Jews who managed to enter Israel and marry Jews then had to wait a long time for their citizenship. Many were sent back by Suissa, and many are still waiting for a permanent residence permit to which they are entitled, according to the Law of Return. Suissa defended his standpoint as follows: "Today you let them in as tourists, and tomorrow you have to answer all sorts of questions that they raise, and before you know it you've helped them to obtain a permanent residence permit. In this way criminals and terrorists come into the country."

Suissa's policy has left deep marks on the Ministry of the Interior. An example of this is the deportation in 1992 of a Russian boy, Jan Zhuchakov, who wanted to live with his non-Jewish mother in Israel. His parents divorced in 1989, and his mother remarried a Jew who wanted to emigrate to Israel. The biological father didn't allow Jan to go with them. In 1991, when the biological father developed a serious illness, he was no longer able to take care of Jan. He sent Jan to his ex-wife in Israel. There Jan's request for citizenship was refused despite the fact that his mother announced that she wanted to convert to Judaism together with him and that they had already been accepted in a conversion course in Haifa. In 2001 no decision had yet been made in this case.

Another example of the consequences of this policy was described in an article in *Ha'aretz* at the end of June 1999. The headline read, "Locked up, a deportee can't prove she's Jewish." The "deportee" is fifty-six-year-old Galina Dozotzva, whose Jewishness was doubted by Suissa's ministry. Dozotzva said she could prove it with a photo of her mother's gravestone in Tajikistan on which there is a Star of David. But at the time Suissa said that her documents had been forged and that he was therefore keeping her in detention. Dozotzva, who has no police record, has been sent back twice to Russia and once to Uzbekistan. The Ministry of the Interior contends that Dozotzva, who has a son, a daughter, and a six-year-old grandson who live in Israel, keeps coming back to make her temporary stay in Israel permanent.

Natan Sharansky is the best-known dissident from the former Soviet Union; he was picked up from Ben Gurion Airport by Shimon Peres himself and later became a minister (for the first time) in Netanyahu's government. When he was minister of the interior under Barak, Sharansky agreed deep in his heart with his predecessor's policy, but he could not say this in public. Sharansky's inner conflict became clear when, right after taking office, he said, "I won't be a green light unto the nations." This comment should not be surprising because it is known that Sharansky is traditional and that as minister of the interior he wanted to do whatever possible to ensure that Israel would remain a Jewish state; in addition, his wife returned to Judaism. Yet he has to take his Russian constituency into account, and Sharansky is aware that the Russian voters have placed their hopes on him.

Sharansky has hired a lawyer who is supposed to study the deportation orders that date from Suissa's time. In 1998 there were three thousand people in Israel who received a notification of deportation; forty-two of them were married or were having an affair with new immigrants. Sharansky says, "Since 1996 people have been deported on a regular basis. Henceforth my lawyer will give a final verdict about this, and the civil servants in my department will in the future have to comply with his decision." Sharansky announced through the media: "No deporting foreign spouses." Furthermore, he ordered his ministry to comply with the May 1999 decision of the court, which stated that anyone who is married to an Israeli citizen has the right to a permanent residency permit after twenty-seven months. However, people in mixed marriages who want to extend their visa still encounter civil servants who work according to Suissa's methods, ignore the decision, and expel them from the country.

"Suissa actually wanted to deport Irena," says Shimion Rabinokov (1954) from Sa-nur, an artists' village on the West Bank. In 1990 he came on aliyah from Kishinev (Moldavia) with his parents, who didn't give him a Jewish education. And in 1994 he met his present wife, the painter Irena Rasdvortav from Tashkent. "Suissa, who was Minister of the Interior at the time, thought that we had a fictitious marriage. I don't know exactly what Sharansky thinks, but he can come by here." Shimion met Irena, who didn't know much about Judaism, in Sa-nur while she was on vacation and staying with Jewish friends from Tashkent who had immigrated years ago. Meanwhile Irena is attending a conversion *ulpan* in Shomron, an Orthodox settlement, and she has become familiar with the rules because they regularly spend the Sabbath with the religious host family to which she was assigned by the *ulpan*. Because Irena was still married when she met Shimion, she had to return to Tashkent to get a divorce. "In 1995 I invited her in a letter to come to Israel as my cousin. I know that's illegal, but otherwise she would never have been able to enter the country, and we would never have been able to marry," says Shimion in broken Hebrew with a heavy Russian accent. "In July 1996 she finally came to Israel, but we still could not marry because I still had to get a divorce. This took a rather long time because years ago I had married a non-Jewish woman in a civil marriage that cannot be dissolved in Israel."

In November 1997 Irena and Shimion were married in a civil ceremony on Cyprus, and right afterward they went to the Ministry of the Interior to ask for citizenship for Irena, to which she is entitled as the wife of an Israeli Jew. But Suissa decided that Irena should first let her wishes be known at the consulate in Tashkent. She didn't go because they were sure that they would never see each other again in Israel. Since then, they have spent all their money on lawyers. In the spring of 1999 the Supreme Court decided that the Ministry of the Interior has to give legal status to the non-Jewish spouse in seven mixed marriages. Rabinakov continues:

> After that decision nothing happened—until Sharansky took office. He decided to give women like Irena a legal status that is valid for four years. Every year she has to renew it at his ministry, and after four years Sharansky will decide whether or not she receives Israeli citizenship. It wasn't until October 1999 that she received her work permit. All these years that Irena lived in Israel

she didn't exist. She had no work permit and she wasn't insured. Sharansky is more lenient than Suissa, but he doesn't look after the interests of his Russian constituency in the way he should according to them. This shows among other things in his fear that Israel will become a state for all citizens, but we are for that.

They aren't always interested in our problems and besides, the solution can take years. There is always something that distracts the attention: the Deri process, the scandals around Netanyahu, then the withdrawal from Lebanon, the peace talks with Syria, and another bomb attack somewhere. As regards that, we're not living in the right place on the West Bank. They're only interested in our life amidst the Palestinians.

Meanwhile Irena, whose Hebrew is not as good, only listens and picks up a folder in which all documents, letters, and newspaper articles that concern their affair are filed away in plastic. Shimion picks up an article that deals with the peace process: "Here everyone is only interested in politics. Journalists call often to talk about the Palestinians. Since the publication of this article I say that we have no problems here, that I don't want to give up any land, and that I vote Likud, but that during television or radio programs I only want to talk about our problem. When I say that, we're usually no longer interesting."

"Nationalistic humanism" is the way Yitzhak Razovsky, the founder of the Russian magazine *Kachestvo Gizhni* (the quality of life), describes Israeli politics that are aimed at preserving the Jewish people. According to him this is the greatest threat to Israel. In an editorial commentary in the first edition of his paper that appeared in May of 1999, Razovsky describes how the Eastern European international Zionists in Israel have become strongly nationalistic. Razovsky writes, "They haven't forgotten the humanist approach to the state and fellow human beings, but the fellow human being had better not be an Arab or a non-Jew. Anti-Semitic tactics are being used here, for example, the genetic tests that some Russian immigrants have to undergo in order to establish their Jewishness."

The number of non-Jews that emigrated to Israel increased every year during the nineties. Thirty thousand of the fifty-three thousand new immigrants from the former Soviet Union in the first half of 1999 were not Jewish according to the halakhah. Among them are half-Jews (those who have a non-Jewish father), non-Jewish family members, grandchildren, and great-grandchildren. Non-Jewish family members, that is to say spouses of Jews and their family members, have the right to immigrate to Israel through the Law of Return. This law makes no distinction between the non-Jewish spouse and his or her family members: they all fall in the category of "non-Jewish family members." The category of grandchildren and great-grandchildren is a small group of several hundred immigrants a year who are only allowed to immigrate if they come with their parents. This group has increased in recent years.

The arrival of these large numbers of non-Jews (the largest number ever in one day was reached in August 1999 when one thousand new immigrants arrived from the former Soviet Union) has partly been made easier by the scheduled nonstop service between Moscow and Tel Aviv and the increased number of flights for aliyah on the Israeli airline El Al since 1990. However, all this was largely made possible by the previously mentioned 1971 change in the Law of Return. "To this day I don't understand how this change could at the time have taken place without opposition from the religious political parties," says the historian Mordecai Altschuler, who is director of the Center for Eastern European Studies at the Hebrew University of Jerusalem. Since 1968 he has studied Soviet Jewry, he speaks Russian, has ten books and a large number of articles to his name, and has often visited the former Soviet Union.

> I think that the atmosphere in Israel was euphoric in the early seventies. After the Six-Day War people thought that deliverance was near and that all Soviet Jews were halakhically Jewish, and at that time people in Israel didn't think that Jews would sometimes come to Israel for other than Zionist reasons. This law created a tragicomic situation. The fact is that the Jewish state now assimilates others while in the past Jews assimilated into other cultures. Many in the Soviet Union—and this became a general phenomenon—wanted to marry Jews to get away from there, and through the Law of Return become Israeli citizens. Every Russian knows the joke: "You don't marry a Jewish woman for love, but she's a good means of transport."

This joke is known to Jacob Storch, a Russian immigrant who came to Israel via Poland in 1968, after the Six-Day War. Most people who immigrated to Israel at that time still did so out of Zionist considerations. Storch has a simple explanation for the present situation, which according to him didn't arise just because of the adaptation of the above-mentioned law: "In Russia everything is for sale: a passport, a birth certificate, and even an atom bomb." He worked as a volunteer at the Zionist Forum, which originally was called the "Jewish Forum." That name, however, was abolished when it became evident that a large part of the immigrants were not Jewish. While he worked there, Storch dealt with many forged and sold documents, since the "Forum" is a coordinating body of twenty immigrant organizations that was founded in 1988 by a number of Russian immigrants to receive new immigrants. "Upon arrival we first look at the appearance: according to Russians it's impossible to hide Jewish looks," says Storch.

> After that we check the papers. The problem here is that the birth certificates and other documents that are supposed to prove the Jewish origin of the immigrant don't mean very much. As I said before, in the former Soviet Union you can change Jews into Russians and Russians into Jews if you have money. We can't solve that problem here, that's the task of the Sochnut. I know numerous halakhically non-Jewish Russians who are nevertheless registered as citizens with Jewish nationality. They know nothing about Judaism, but they can't be blamed for that because you had to be a Soviet citizen over there, and if you wanted to have your son circumcised it had to be done on the kitchen table so that no one would notice. Being Jewish was so difficult there that people left as soon as they had a chance. The experts say that Lenin had a little Jewish blood too. If that was true, he would have hidden it at the time, and if he were still alive, he would long ago have taken advantage of his Jewish roots and have come here.

"If that were true, he would have been able to get Israeli citizenship through the Law of Return and would have received food and shelter from the Distribution Commission," says Altschuler, not without irony. "Through the Jewish activities that they organize on Russian soil, the envoys of the Sochnut would no doubt have tried to convince him or his children to emigrate to Israel." Altschuler continues, "I'm saying this to clarify the Law of Return because Lenin's parents converted to Christianity before his birth, an action that makes immigration to Israel once and for all impossible, at least in theory. The nationalist Russian anti-Semite Vladimir Zhrinovski, who has a Jewish father, would be able to get a permit to emigrate to Israel. His father is Jewish, or as he describes it: 'My mother is a member of the great Russian people and my father is a lawyer.'"

According to Altschuler, an often-used method to leave the former Soviet Union is to search for possible Jewish roots in one's grandparents, and preferably the mother's parents. In recent years genealogical research has really taken off in the former Soviet Union. For Russians unable to find a Jewish grandparent, there is always the possibility of buying a document from one of the many agencies that have in recent years specialized in forging documents. A good quality birth certificate costs between $700 and $1,200 in central Russia, according to Altschuler, who checked this out on the spot. Prices are lower in the south and in Siberia. The cheapest birth certificate, costing between $300 and $400, can be obtained in the countries of central Asia and the Caucasus. A birth certificate that guarantees the status of halakhic Jew (therefore a certificate of a Jewish grandmother on the mother's side) always costs more than a birth certificate of a grandfather on the father's side. This trade has became a veritable market where supply and demand determine price. Prices start increasing at the approach of winter, the season when emigration reaches its peak.

Today, anyone who wants to leave the former Soviet Union can easily claim that one of his Jewish grandparents was registered as a "Russian" or a "Ukrainian," according to Altschuler. The grandchild says to the official of the population registry of the city or village where he or she is living that one of his grandparents was Jewish but that he or she had chosen to be registered as a member of another national group. The most passable assertion, which is impossible to refute, is that the original birth certificate, which would have proved the Jewish identity of the grandparent, was lost during the Second World War. In most cases the grandchildren receive a new birth certificate from the authorities. Every economic or political crisis increases this phenomenon, which still remains marginal according to Altschuler.

> The problem of mixed marriages is much bigger. But we shouldn't forget that the percentage of mixed marriages in the former Soviet Union is as high as in the United States. If American Jews wanted to come to Israel, we'd have the same problems. In the former Soviet Union and in America, the percentage is on an average

between 60 and 70 percent. It's always been high in Russia, even before the Second World War. The idea that mixed marriages are a result of oppression of the Jews is inaccurate. This is not the most important cause of their ignorance about Judaism nor about their coming to Israel. There is no oppression in America, but the percentage of mixed marriages is 65 percent there as well.

Altschuler knows that people in Israel prefer not to hear this. "The argument about oppression is propaganda of the West and of Zionist organizations. The percentage of mixed marriages was high in these countries even before the Holocaust. Whether the person you love is Jewish or not is much less important there. The Sochnut says that being Jewish was made impossible there, but that is mostly propaganda," repeats Altschuler, who has little use for the Sochnut.

"Every year we bring an average of 60,000 immigrants from the former Soviet Union to Israel," says Chaim Chesler the day after he was named financial director of the worldwide Sochnut organization. He is receiving congratulations on the telephone and during every phone conversation he shouts the Zionist slogan "*Am Yisrael chai*" (the people of Israel lives). Chesler (1949), son of a rabbi of Agudat Israel who emigrated in 1938 from Bialystok, Poland, to Palestine, studied for six years in a yeshiva in Bnei Brak. In 1976, after he had exchanged his black yarmulke for a crocheted one, he started to study psychology at Bar Ilan University in Ramat Gan (near Tel Aviv). After completing this study, he went to Ireland for the Zionist youth movement Bnei Akiva. Today he is secular and has been working for the Sochnut for ten years: first as *shaliach* (literally, "emissary," someone who is sent abroad for a specified time in order to support the local Jewish community), then for four years as head of one of the branches in Russia. Since 1999 he has been head of the "Soviet Jewry" division.

My approach is based on the Law of Return and not on the halakhah. Out of the approximately 900,000 to one million Jews in the former Soviet Union, two-thirds have the right to immigrate to Israel through this law. For everyone who was in danger as a Jew during the Second World War there is a place in Israel. This means that we work according to the Nuremberg laws [in 1935 Hitler signed laws that were approved during a meeting of the National Socialist Party that determined, among other things, that anyone who had at least one Jewish grandparent was a Jew]. We bring Judaism to full Jews who are living as goyim—they go to church like Christians because they never had a Jewish education. We also bring Judaism to potential Jews, that is to say to everyone in Russia who according to the Law of Return has the right to Israeli citizenship: grandchildren, spouses, and children.

Chesler shows a chart that illustrates that in 1998, out of the ten million potential Jews in the Commonwealth of Independent States (CIS), forty-six thousand emigrated. "What we do is actually the ingathering of the exiles who no longer know the difference between Jews and non-Jews."

According to the chart, sixty-seven thousand Jews emigrated to Israel out of the 975,000 who have the right to emigrate according to the Law of Return. (In 2000 a total of more than sixty thousand emigrated.) Chesler is proud of this number because it is an increase in comparison to the year before. Out of this number 51.1 percent are not Jewish, and it is estimated that eight out of every ten Israeli citizens can't marry in Israel. He is enthusiastic about his success: "One of the newcomers came from Tinda, a small town near the border with China. The *shaliach*, who had never heard of this place, went there and encountered a community with a Jewish mayor and two Jewish deputy mayors. The non-Jews in town call the city hall the "synagogue." There and in other places they met so many Jews who wanted to emigrate to Israel that we strengthened our presence in the former Soviet Union, but especially in Russia, and expanded the Hebrew language courses and the 'Israel-Experience' programs."

While he is talking, Chesler emphasizes that every Jew, no matter where in the world, young or old, should have access to his or her rich Jewish heritage and that these Jews should be able to make level-headed decisions about the place where they want to lead a Jewish life. According to him that place is still Israel, and he has to make sure that the Jews of the world don't ask what it means to be Jewish without having the opportunity to find the answers. Chesler says that to help these Jews find the answer, Sochnut has created the worldwide Israel Experience programs that offer young Jews "positive, Israel-oriented experiences."

According to historian Bernard Wasserstein, author of the book *Vanishing Diaspora*, there are "absurd figures" in circulation about the number of Jews in the former Soviet Union. In the article "The end of Russian Jewry," published in the *Jerusalem Post* early in 1999, he writes that "Jewish organizations, obviously looking for clients, publish strange numbers. One organization suggests that now, in 1998, between 1,293,000 and 1,852,000 Jews are living in the former Soviet Union. Another organization estimates 1,492,000+ (note the plus!)." Wasserstein states that "these estimates are based on nothing but wishful thinking." A reasonable estimate of the Jewish population of the former Soviet Union in 1999 is about 470,000, according to Wasserstein. And according to him there is no doubt that the number is decreasing: emigration, which stagnated during the mid-nineties, is increasing once again because of economic malaise and the fear of mounting anti-Semitism.

Wasserstein, who bases his statements on the research of renowned Jerusalem demographer Sergio della Pergola, found that in the 1980s, in the former Soviet Union, in sixty out of one hundred households where a Jew lived, there also lived a non-Jew (according to halakhic criteria). At the end of the nineties this was the case in eighty out of one hundred households. The ratio of death and birth rates among Jews has changed in favor of the former. According to Wasserstein this signifies not just a decline but a demographic collapse. These data seem to fall on deaf ears in the Sochnut, which keeps insisting that there are still one to two million Jews (depending on the definition of "Jew") in the former Soviet Union. The Sochnut *Schlichim* (plural of *shaliach*) travel to the region to find them and to spend the Jewish holidays or the Sabbath with them in the hope that they will decide to emigrate to Israel. When they arrive in Israel, they receive the so-called *sal klita* (literally, "absorption basket"). This *sal klita*, which has existed since the early nineties, meant that for a temporary period the Sochnut paid the rent of the house, provided for the necessities of life, and paid for health and child care. In addition, the immigrants were entitled to tax-free imports. After a year the financial help was decreased or stopped, depending on the circumstances. As of 1994 the system changed because lack of money made it impossible to offer all these advantages to the growing stream of immigrants. But the Sochnut continued to supply them with enough means to build a new life in Israel during one year.

However, the *shlichim* (plural of *shaliach*) of the Sochnut, who bring many Christians who are married to Jews to Israel, neglected to tell the potential immigrants that families with non-Jewish children would encounter difficulties in Israel. A Sochnut worker was reprimanded by his superiors when he pointed out to someone with a Jewish father that his personal status (marriage, divorce, and funeral) would be different in Israel from that of "real Jews." The superiors let him know that he was perhaps "unsuited for this job."

According to a *shaliach* who wants to remain anonymous, his work in the CIS is judged on the number of immigrants that he brings to Israel. He states,

> A strong decline in the number of immigrants from a certain city isn't just considered proof of the fact that no more Jews are living there, but rather as the unsuccessful efforts of the *shaliach*. There is pressure on everyone. The head of the delegation puts pressure on the district head who in turn does the same to bureau heads who put their subordinates under pressure. A *shaliach* who reports that there is no interest in emigration will soon find himself returning home in the same airplane that is taking immigrants to Israel. Even when there are no immigrants, the *shlichim* send faxes home with the message that there is great interest in immigration to Israel. After all, there's no one who can check that.

The fact that life in Israel is better in certain areas if you have a halakhic Jewish identity became evident in September 1999 when the candidacy of the halakhically non-Jewish Konstantin Umansky for the function of *shaliach* in the Ukraine turned out to be controversial. (It should be noted that Umansky came to Israel through the Sochnut). If the Sochnut gives Umansky the job, he would be the first non-Jewish *shaliach* sent out by Sochnut. Umansky, whose grandfather is Jewish, immigrated in 1991 through the Law of Return and has for the last five years worked for the Immigrant Students Administration, a division of the Sochnut and the Ministry of Integration. A year ago he became a candidate for the post in Dnjespropjetrovsk, one of the largest cities in the Ukraine, with a population of about 50,000 Jews. He underwent the complete selection procedure, including the course for *shlichim*, which usually precedes being sent out, without ever being asked if he had a Jewish mother. However, when the local rabbi in Dnjespropjetrovsk discovered that Umansky was not Jewish, he informed the Sochnut that he couldn't let him work in the community:

Since 1990 we have worked with the Sochnut and we've never told them whom they should send. We've had people with earrings, nose-rings, and piercings in all sorts of odd places with whom we've worked with complete confidence. But sending us a goy who isn't even planning to convert, that's impossible. After all, he's supposed to work with the Jewish community and bring them closer to Judaism. How can he do that if he isn't Jewish himself?

"I hadn't though that my candidacy would be a problem for the Sochnut," says Umansky who wants to take his non-Jewish girlfriend along if he gets the job. He has announced in the Israeli media that it will be "abundantly clear that his disqualification, if it should take place, would be based on racial grounds" and that he will therefore institute legal proceedings against the Sochnut: "After all, the Sochnut works on the basis of the Law of Return, which doesn't discriminate between halakhic Jews and those who have only one Jewish parent or grandparent. Since my stay in Israel I've been involved with immigrants and I feel that I can give them a lot. I love the Jewish tradition, and I don't think that Judaism is a biological question."

In spite of this, some Sochnut staff workers are opposed to his candidacy—one of whom, Eli Yitzchaki, is responsible for sending *shlichim* to the Ukraine. The president of the CIS division, Reform Rabbi Asher Hirsch, expressed his opposition as follows: "I don't think that the Sochnut should send people who cannot be a model for the Jewish people, like non-Jews and unmarried couples." Chaim Chesler adds that a *shaliach* should have a Jewish mother in order to prevent internal conflicts. Those within the Sochnut who support Umansky feel that as long as the Law of Return makes no distinction between halakhic Jews and children and grandchildren of Jews, the Sochnut should not make this distinction in selecting the *shlichim*. In their opinion only professional unsuitability can be a reason for not sending out a candidate. If the commission for *shlichim*, which will soon consider the case, decides to disqualify Umansky for professional reasons, it is, according to Umansky's supporters, because they want to avoid a fundamental decision within the Sochnut.

"The changed Law of Return, which was meant to catch a few exceptions, has become an automatic one-way trip to Israel for numerous non-Jews," says Chesler, who can no longer deny that the Sochnut has been importing a problem. "The law in its present form forces the state to open its doors to non-Jews. The problem is that something which years ago was a marginal phenomenon has now become an uncontrollable flood. This has serious consequences for the state of Israel. Immigrants who have a Jewish grandparent or whose great-grandparents were Jewish enter the country with their non-Jewish partners, and later the non-Jewish family of the partner comes to Israel. In theory the Law of Return doesn't apply to them, but the state grants them immigration rights for humanitarian reasons." Chesler concludes: "In practice it's impossible to refuse distant relatives who have no connection at all with the Jewish people."

If the immigrants were willing to convert, wouldn't it be more fair to inform the immigrants in Russia of this and make those who value conversion into Jews over there? This is a sensitive subject for Chesler, who has to try and get as many immigrants within Israel's borders as soon as possible. "Those who immigrate have so many problems that we risk their not coming if we explain the complex reality of Israel to them," says Chesler. "Moreover, most of them are quite happy with the prospect of Israeli citizenship and the *sal klita*, but it would indeed be better to discuss conversion in Russia and to carry it out over there, although no one is obliged to convert."

"No one has to, but everyone is invited to join the large Jewish family," says the head of the conversion institute, Prof. Benjamin Ish-Shalom, to a group of twenty young women. They're barely twenty years old, wear high heels and make-up, and are from Minsk, Moscow, St. Petersburg, and Siberia. Five months ago, escorted by the Sochnut, they came to Israel where, as participants in the program Children without Parents, they have been preparing themselves for their life in Israel. Every year this program brings a total of one thousand children to Israel—in August 1999, an additional two hundred. These children's parents, in many cases a Christian mother and a father who is an assimilated Jew, are worried about their children's future in Russia. This is why, after consulting with the Sochnut, they send them to Israel—often without any knowledge about Judaism. It is the intention of the Sochnut that the parents follow, but reality is often different. After their arrival these girls started almost immediately to learn Hebrew in the *ulpan* in Karmi'el, a city in northern Israel, where there is a conversion institute. They learn Zionist songs, study Judaism, and take field trips to important Jewish sights. During the first months in the Holy Land everything is made as pleasant as possible for these non-Jewish girls. After about five months, conversion is mentioned. How can these children, who have often just turned nineteen and grew up in Russia thinking that they were already Jewish, form an opinion about the proposal to convert? After such a short time it's impossible for them to understand the Israeli-Jewish reality. Under the influence of the Sochnut workers and the carefully chosen Jewish host families who do their best to create a Jewish family tie and the proper atmosphere, these girls have started to think that it is better for their future to become Jewish. Before they came to Israel, but especially before they came in touch with the Sochnut in Israel, they had no idea about Judaism, and many didn't know until they were ten years old that they had Jewish fathers and therefore were Jewish according to Russian law. Most likely none of them had ever thought about conversion.

Ish-Shalom and Dan Biron, the head of the Northern Israel Integration division of the Sochnut, feel that it is important for the future of the immigrants, the Jewish people, and the Jewish state that these young women become "part of the Jewish family." It seems that all the stops are pulled out to make them feel that they're part of things and that they're special. During a two-day excursion in 1999 for American staff members of the Sochnut in the Karmi'el reception center, the young women—all wearing Sochnut shirts—are the center of attention. This is where they have studied for the past few months and where they will probably start preparing for the conversion examination. Biron makes them the center of attention and is full of praise for the program: "I'm proud to say that twenty-two of the students have already been accepted at the Technion [Technical University of Haifa]. You can see that this program is an enormous success. We teach Hebrew, mathematics, and *Yiddishkeit*, the Jewish identity that they were deprived of for generations."

Then Biron starts talking about conversion, a subject that people in Israel don't talk about easily. That's why conversion is often called "taking in the immigrants as brothers" or "spiritual and cultural integration," but the speaker will never say that "half-Jews are turned into full Jews." After all, the new institute brings together everyone who through the Law of Return has the right to be there but is not yet halakhically Jewish. There was good reason that little publicity was given by the press at the opening of the institute, for the subject is sensitive and a discussion about it inevitably reminds people of the "Who is a Jew" question. But because they are among themselves in Karmi'el today, Biron feels unconstrained and says, "Many of you are not Jewish according to the halakhah, and we are here in order to correct your Jewish status so that the rest of your integration into Israeli society will go smoothly."

Ish-Shalom also addresses the young women in less euphemistic terms than usual. He doesn't mince words today, and the tension increases palpably during his introductory remarks about the conversion course. While the young women listen to him in breathless anticipation, Ish-Shalom addresses them: "It's sad but true—here you are Russians while in the former Soviet Union everyone saw you as Jews. You are citizens, you can study like anyone else, you have no problems in the army, and you can work like everyone else." "But we can't get married," interrupts nineteen-year-old Lena Koslovskaya. She is from Moscow and came to Israel to study communication and journalism and says that she had no idea how much effort she would have to make before she could finally start her studies. She can't ask her parents for advice because they are still in Moscow and they aren't planning to come to Israel, according to her. Ish-Shalom answers,

> That's exactly what we want to do—we want to prevent the situation where you couldn't get married, and we want your children to be Jewish and be able to have a bar mitzvah. But you have to do something for that; not everything is easy in life. Not everyone can become a Swiss or an American, for example. During this course you will learn the Jewish rites and symbols that you can obey strictly, but you can also choose to be less strict. A Jew doesn't have a number of abstract principles according to which he must live. I don't expect you to become *haredi*—I wouldn't consider that a success.
>
> The most important thing is to feel a bond as a people, despite the fact that we are Russian, Sephardic, Ashkenazi, or Ethiopian. We are here because we were here two thousand years ago too. We have much in common, and you will discover that. Abraham, the patriarch of the Hebrews, described himself as "the ultimate other." With this he meant that the whole world stood on one side of the Jordan and he stood at the other. Being Jewish wasn't easy then, and I'm afraid that it still isn't easy; the whole world is still standing on the other side. Becoming Jewish isn't easy either, but on the other hand we are an example to other peoples because of

our tremendous heritage and we have a moral responsibility on our shoulders. Being Jewish always meant rebelling, being different. You are now the pioneers: you are going to study in the first institute in the world where all the movements of the Jewish people are represented. You are taking on both a mission and a great responsibility.

While he writes two telephone numbers on the blackboard, Ish-Shalom concludes his statement: "We will walk hand in hand with you, we want you to succeed, and you can always call me."

Philip Meltzer is a Reform Jew, one of the U.S. representatives of the Sochnut who has an interest in the acceptance of the Reform and Conservative conversion of these young women. He makes the most of the opportunity to ask questions. "The conversion institute which you praise so highly still accepts no Reform and Conservative converts," he says to Ish-Shalom. Then he addresses the young women: "You are young women and will hopefully have large families, but you should realize that it isn't at all certain that the Orthodox rabbinate will accept you as Jews." The Americans in the room make approving sounds and make their doubts about the institute known. Ish-Shalom counters: "Conversion is and remains a halakhic act; therefore as long as the rabbinate converts students taught by Conservative and Reform rabbis, nothing is wrong. Rabbis are aware of the extent and the seriousness of the problem and I fully trust that the rabbinate will accept our students and will accept their conversion."

Today more and more people are saying that they want to change the Law of Return. The presence of hundreds of thousands of non-Jews in Israel brings the domestic tensions to the surface, a problem that is increasingly discussed in public. The minister of integration and diaspora affairs, Rabbi Michael Melchior, said in a speech in November 1999 that he expected a "dignified and respectful attitude" on the part of the Jewish Israeli population with respect to the minorities and no "hate campaign." He articulated the problem as follows:

> The problems in Israel with immigrants are different from those in Europe because our immigrants enter via the Law of Return as *olim chadashim*, originally a status for Jewish immigrants, but nowadays most immigrants are not Jewish. This results in a different sort of problem from the European one. I don't mean to say that immigra-

tion should stop or should continue, but we should face the problem and not act as if we're not aware of it. If we do that, we'll soon experience a social explosion here in which we will see expressions of hate that manifest themselves in some European countries as well.

During this speech Melchior didn't talk about the identity of the state of Israel, which is up for discussion because of the presence of the non-Jews. Many Russians who want to live in Israel but who are not interested in its Jewish identity contrast Israel as a Jewish state with a very different one, namely Israel as a state for all citizens. In order for this state to be created—many leftist Israelis and Israeli Arabs would like this—the Law of Return would first have to be abolished. What will the Sochnut do if after the rescission of the 1971 amendment (when the clause was added that would admit people with a Jewish grandfather into Israel) it appears that the number of potential immigrants will decline from almost a million to only six hundred thousand?

Few politicians seem to want to get burned on this subject. Yet politicians realize that the controversy that has arisen about the Law of Return can't be ignored much longer. Ehud Barak was rather irritated when the law was placed on the political agenda, and he announced that it was not to be "up for discussion or change." The ultra-Orthodox members of the Knesset fear that Israel will become a state for all citizens and want to undo the 1971 change of the Law of Return. At the end of 1998 the participants in a four-day conference of rabbinic courts appealed to the Sochnut to "stop bringing in non-Jews." They argued in favor of an Orthodox institution that would in the future check the Jewishness of immigrants. In this context the Ashkenazi chief rabbi of Israel, Israel Meir Lau, remarked that he didn't oppose bringing in non-Jews for humanitarian reasons but that he opposed, as he put it, "the counterfeiting of Jewish identity." According to him "Who is who" is the most important question in the Jewish state. "We have to answer this question in order to prevent importing assimilation which nowadays dominates most countries of Western Europe. Israel has to remain a Jewish state and that's why we have to check the Jewish background of immigrants."

In the Knesset, members of the United Torah Party and Shas are chiefly the ones who want to limit the right to emigrate to Israel to those born to a Jewish mother. In November 1999, during a meeting of the Knesset Commission for Immigration, Integration and Diaspora Affairs, Knesset member Shmuel Halpert of the United Torah Party said, " We are creating a fifth column in our midst and with this a security problem. There are negative elements among those people, like the spies among them. It is the fault of the Sochnut which encourages non-Jews in the former Soviet Union to emigrate to Israel through advertisements aimed at everyone who has a Jewish grandparent." Halpert announced that he had submitted a bill that would limit the right to immigration under the Law of Return to those who are born to a Jewish mother.

A commission member of Meretz said that Halpert, as a representative of people who don't serve in the army, doesn't have the right to accuse non-Jewish immigrants of espionage while these immigrants serve the state, sometimes with danger to their own lives. A Knesset member of the strongly antireligious party Shinui, who had been a "prisoner of Zion" (a Russian Jew who was imprisoned during the Soviet regime because of activities in preparation of emigration to Israel), announced that he hadn't fought all these years to come to Israel for people like Halpert. "Non-Jewish soldiers also defend Halpert and his fellow believers," he concluded. The minister of integration, Yuli Tamir, called Halpert's remarks racist, and the minister of the interior, Natan Sharansky, considered these remarks offensive and added that Russian Jews in the former Soviet Union were also called a fifth column.

Sharansky, who, as has been mentioned, is more Orthodox at home than in public, had to keep his constituency in mind. He would have liked to limit the law and abolish the clause that gives grandchildren the right to immigration. An article in *Ha'aretz* at the end of July 1999 had the following headline: "Let's not change the Law of Return." Sharansky spoke these words to the chairman of the Knesset Commission for Immigration, Integration, and Diaspora Affairs. The chairman of the Knesset Commission of the Interior, David Azoulai of Shas, had placed a discussion of the law on the agenda because he felt that the law was being misused by "hostile elements." Sharansky, who as minister of the interior played an important role in the discussion, said, "The change in the Law of Return which differentiates us from all other peoples will ultimately lead to the abolition of this law which will cause the problem of illegal immigrants to become greater. The state will have to interfere less in the lives of its citizens." The chair of the above-mentioned commission, Naomi Blumenthal of Likud, who would like to change the Law of Return, answered that "it depends how wide the country wants to open its doors to non-Jews. I had the feeling that only the *haredi* Knesset members wanted to keep the Jewish character of the state and that the secularists are unconcerned, but that isn't so."

Marina Solodkina, a Knesset member for Israel ba'Aliyah, thinks that the change in the law no longer makes any sense. "Friends, I always say to the members of the Knesset, all the Russians are already here. In two years there will be no one left who has the right to emigrate to Israel under the Law of Return." Her party for Russian immigrants was founded in June 1995, by Sharansky among others, and in 1996 it participated for the first time in elections—winning seven seats (just as in the 1999 elections). This party fears any change in the law for electoral reasons. Its leaders announced in 1995 and have repeatedly confirmed that the most important goal of the party is to "bring back" to Israel as many Jews as possible and to help them with integration once there, but not with Ben Gurion's method. The party doesn't have as its goal, as was Ben Gurion's, to change the immigrants into Israelis.

"That failed," says Solodkina,

> because immigrants can't forget their own culture. We're called "Russians" here, are considered uneducated, not Jewish enough, and we seem to live in a ghetto. But I wonder who is living in a ghetto, the Israelis or the Russians. Israel is a provincial country. Our newspapers [in Israel there are more than fifty Russian language newspapers: four dailies, eleven weeklies, five monthlies, and fifty local newspapers] reprint articles from Israeli newspapers, but in their newspapers no articles translated from Russian from our newspapers are printed. Our children speak Russian, Hebrew, English and they also learn Arabic. We see ourselves as Jews while they say that we're not Jewish enough. Who are they to judge that? For three generations we lived under a regime that persecuted the Jews, but we're still Jews, with or without religion. Judaism is a culture, and religion is a part of it. And if they love Jewish culture so much, why don't they speak Yiddish? We have a long list of questions for them about why they aren't as Jewish as they should be. For example they've broken the tradition of Yiddish and Ladino. They were unable to continue Jewish culture, but instead of that they wanted to create an artificial Israeli culture.

After fifty years no one knows what it means yet. The Russians are loyal to the state of Israel without forgetting their own culture.

Solodkina explains that the questions about Jewish identity are confusing to the Russians. In the former Soviet Union, children with a Jewish and a non-Jewish parent could choose their own nationality. Children with a Jewish father usually chose the Jewish nationality while in Israel they are goyim. "But what does being Jewish mean?" asks Solodkina. According to her, after a while many immigrants have the feeling that they're living in a topsy-turvy world. In the former Soviet Union they had to watch out for anti-Semites, and in Israel they are the anti-Semites. This and many other problems in the Russian community in Israel are caused by their slow integration into Israeli society. At the time, Solodkina discussed the problem with Minister Melchior. She proposed to him that the immigrants make a declaration of loyalty to the state of Israel and to the Jewish people as a condition for obtaining Israeli citizenship, just like the oath that immigrants have to take in the United States. She also told him that she hopes converting to Judaism will be easier in the future. Solodkina says, "We're a democratic country and Judaism is not a missionary religion. Those who take the oath understand what their responsibility is—those who are not interested in Judaism can choose to leave or to integrate into Israeli society through the army or the school system. They will become Israelis in a natural way."

Solodkina (1952) obtained her doctorate in economics at the University of Moscow and also studied social history. She arrived in Israel in 1991 and went, as she says herself, straight from the airplane to the Knesset. In 1996 she published the book *Civilization and Discomfort: Soviet Jews in Israel in the Nineties,* written in Russian. She calls herself traditional, goes to the synagogue on all Jewish holidays, tries not to work on Saturdays, and eats no pork. "But," she says, "in the Knesset I vote like someone who does eat it because Israel has to become a country for all citizens, and not only for Orthodox Jews." When she arrived in Israel, she had a passive knowledge of Hebrew because she was never able to speak it openly in the former Soviet Union and had to learn it illegally together with Sharansky, during private lessons in people's homes.

According to Solodkina, "only" 150,000 of the immigrants from the Soviet Union are *safek yehudim* (Hebrew for Jews with questionable Jewish roots).

They came into Israel through the Law of Return, that means in a legal way, and for me they're no problem at all. They're a problem for the *haredim* and the religious nationalists. They want to change the Law of Return because they're afraid of damage to the Jewishness of the state. I've grown up with democratic principles. A state based on civil laws must allow its citizens not to be religious.

The Israelis are not prepared to see us as one of them. You have to watch out for Israeli propaganda; we couldn't care less about Israeli prejudices. We have many intelligent people among us, and more than 60 percent have studied fifteen years, including high school. We want to be represented in politics, and we will be represented because we use the rules of the society in order to influence it. Israel lives in constant tension. Shulamit Aloni's words, Yossi Sarid's rhetoric, and Tommy Lapid's fanaticism bring the country closer to a civil war. It's our calling to make this land into a normal country, a cosmopolitan state for all citizens. We can't receive only Jews in these times. The non-Jews among us have practical problems for which political solutions will be found within the next ten years. In twenty-five years we will no longer have problems with non-Jews. In the end everyone will be Israeli in the state for the Jewish people where many minorities will be living. We Russians will remain in the minority, and the ultra-Orthodox community will check whether someone is really Jewish.

Civil marriage will be accepted, and *safek yehudim* will be buried in special areas of Orthodox cemeteries, just as is already happening in several places. They can be 100 percent Russian, and that's no problem at all for me. Only people in Israel who think in halakhic terms worry about this, but for me this sort of problem is out of date. In the beginning, when I was just living here, I also thought that it was a problem, but now I ignore it and propose to speak only in twenty-first century terms. Conversion is the same kind of problem. Conversions are for people who believe in God, and we don't believe in God. The 10 percent who want to convert can make an appointment with the rabbinate, but we will stay out of the religious conflict—let the American Jews do that. In the United States I recently asked Reform and Conservative Jews why they want recognition from the Israeli ultra-Orthodox. Did the Protestants ever ask the pope for recognition?

The new immigrants, who are usually proud of their Russian culture, consider the Israelis more Orthodox, or at any rate more Jewish than themselves. The Israelis had to study the Torah at school, and as children and adults they were able to celebrate the most important Jewish holidays, whereas for decades it has been difficult for Jews in the former Soviet Union to express their Jewishness. Most of the new immigrants, the "real" Jews as well as the goyim among them, have kept their Russian nationality. Instead of adapting to Israeli society and becoming Israelis, most secular and academically trained immigrants from the nineties have created their own world: a Russian-language state within a state. Many have jobs (although not always in their own field), have bought a house, and own a car.

Perhaps it is because of their relative success that many Russian families that emigrated to Israel in the nineties are not respected by the Israelis, the Israeli authorities, or by their Russian compatriots. In Rehovot in the beginning of 1998, a fourteen-year-old Russian immigrant was stabbed to death by a twenty-one-year-old soldier during a fight. Near the spot where it happened, a seventeen-year-old girl from Rehovot remarked, "These confrontations with 'Israelis' occur daily." She was born in Israel, and her parents emigrated from Russia twenty years ago. Yet she feels more at home with "Russians" than with "Israelis." "There is always tension between us. We are always 'the Russians,' we haven't given the country a culture, we are bastards, goyim, primitive, and unreliable. We are told to go back and take a DNA test because, as they say, we're 'not even Jews.'"

The poor relationship between the Russians and the Israelis came about when people found out that on their arrival the Russians were welcomed with the previously mentioned *sal klita*. At the time, the government of Yitzchak Shamir and Shimon Peres thought that they could receive the Russian immigrants just as they did the Ethiopians who lived in reception centers for a long period of time. Later the government was compelled to develop a separate integration plan to keep its grip on the Russian immigrants who were coming in larger numbers and, in addition, had a more independent attitude. Newcomers received shelter and money to follow a language course and to retrain.

The dissatisfaction with the Russian immigrants is greatest among the Jews of Moroccan origin, particularly the ones who immigrated to Israel in the fifties—straight from Morocco or via France —and, as the former Shas leader said recently, "were badly received while the Russians are brought in on a red carpet and receive a *sal klita*." During the campaign for the May 1999 election, this envy reached its climax in the struggle between Shas and Israel ba'Alyiah for the Ministry of the Interior. In a political ad Suissa reinforced the feelings of dissatisfaction about the Russians that are prevalent among the Shas supporters in Israel. In his message he called the immigrants "non-Jews," "pork-eaters," "churchgoers," and "call-girl suppliers." The ad continued:

> They're afraid that all the butchers who sell pork will be closed. [In Israel pork is sold in more than one thousand butcher shops; this number was reached after the large immigration of Russians in the nineties.] A Shas minister will close all the churches that the immigrants have opened, and he will bar the way to Christians who want to come to Israel to strengthen their communities. A Shas minister will also forbid money embezzlers, cheats, and escort girls to enter our country. Israel BeAlyiah is wondering who will set up the religious community and who will finance the *sal klita* and their mortgages if Israel closes the door to everyone who wants to immigrate. However, Shas welcomes with love every Jewish immigrant from the former Soviet Union.

The truth is that he expressed the smoldering feelings of displeasure harbored by many poor Sephardic Jews. The spiritual leader of the Sephardic Jews, Ovadia Yossef, piled it on in one of his speeches during the election campaign: "They want the Ministry of the Interior and they shout that it should not remain in the hands of Shas because they don't want this country to remain Jewish. They want to bring all the goyim from Russia here, and they give them houses, not regular houses but palaces."

Natan Sharansky pointed out that these statements weren't just made by an actor but by an important politician. At Sharansky's request Suissa offered his apologies during a news conference. "We will do everything to reunite the Jewish people" were the words used by Sharansky to accept the apology. The reaction of the Russian press to these events showed that the trust between these two population groups had sunk to a serious low: "Ministry of the Interior: *Shas Kontrol? Nyet! Nash Kontrol*" (In the hands of Shas? No! In our hands).

Tension can increase tremendously because in general Israelis don't hide their feelings. "My parents hate you," says a Moroccan tailor in his shop in Herzliya to a seamstress, the only halakhic Jew of the three Russian seamstresses working for him. The tailor, who came from Morocco to Israel in the fifties, continues, "The state made a big mistake by wanting to take them all in and to treat them as poor souls."

"We're not poor souls at all," answers the seamstress, "it was definitely a mistake of my mother to come here: she doesn't feel comfortable here, she doesn't want to learn Hebrew, and she has no roots here. I like it here."

The tailor continues: "Six Russian families live in my parents' apartment building. In the beginning we gave them clothing and food, and we offered our help. One day one of them was at the door and asked if my parents would park *their* car. They had been given the car, but they had probably never bought a driver's license. Did you see that program?" He is referring to a popular Israeli television program at the end of 1998 about a Russian family who were filmed from the moment of their arrival in Israel. "First they buy all sorts of documents in Russia, and then in Israel they receive a car, a house, and money that they may spend as they choose." When the seamstress is gone, he says, "They're not integrated here. For example there is a good Israeli bakery across the street, but they take the bus to go to a Russian baker."

The kosher Algerian butcher, Alfredo Benarush from Ashdod, doesn't hide his displeasure either. He thinks that the Russians make the Jewish state too democratic. "My neighbors sell pork," says Benarush, who immigrated via France to Israel in 1966 and has fastened a crocheted yarmulke on his balding head. Photos of Rabbi Kedouri and Ovadia Yossef and hands against the evil eye hang on the wall. "When I opened my store here twenty years ago, pork wasn't sold anywhere, and nowadays you can buy it in fifty-eight stores in Ashdod. That's a result of democracy. It was better during Begin's time. At least he was really Jewish, like Shamir. They understood that a Jewish country can't be democratic. I don't know if my neighbors are Jewish, but there are many Christians here." Benarush asks his son, who will soon take over the store, "Do you think that they're Jewish?" The son shrugs his shoulders. Benarush continues: "They're most likely Christians. It's difficult because in France we were also allowed to sell what we wanted to, so the Russians should have that freedom as well. Still it's better to sell pork in a certain part of the city, the way it's now being done in Ashkelon."

"They say that we're goyim because we eat pork," says his blonde, plump Russian neighbor Yivgenia, who worked in a butcher shop in Russia. "My neighbor with the yarmulke thinks that I'm a goy because I eat pork, but who gives him the right to decide what I eat? Does he speak in the name of God? In Israel, at the end of the twentieth century, they have by law forbidden the sale of pork because pork seems to be a symbol of disgust for the Jewish people," says Yivgenia, who has a Jewish father and therefore has the Russian nationality in Israel. Her colleague Dina agrees with her: "For Jews, and also for non-believing Jews, salami symbolizes 'persecution' and 'Christianity.' That's what the judge of the district court said last week when he prohibited the import of pork. The prohibition on the sales only varies depending on the municipality. In Ashkelon ham can be sold only in a certain area of the city. Recently our colleagues there were fined." Yivgenia continues: "Our Orthodox neighbor is happy about that. He is Sephardic, and we Russians feel that they have helped to kill the Western character of Israel with their rabbi Kedouri who treats water with his healing powers. But that's not what it's about."

Dina says,

> Ninety percent of this neighborhood is Russian. If my store were in a Orthodox neighborhood, I would understand that I would offend the observant Jews with my pork in the shop window. But this situation is too crazy for words: in Russia they watch what comes out of our mouths, and in a democratic country they look at what we put in our mouths. Besides, they all say that they don't eat pork, but I'll tell you the truth. I sometimes have Orthodox in my store who buy ham. They've put their yarmulkes in their pants' pockets, they pay, walk a few streets away where they eat the ham, and put their yarmulkes back on. That's how hypocritical they are.

A public expression of this kind of hard feelings is not unusual in Israel. Sitting in a bus in Ashdod, on the way to one of the Russian districts, a middle-aged Russian woman who immigrated to Israel in the seventies tells why she doesn't like "the Russians" in Israel. She considers herself Israeli and not one of "the Russians." In the minibus there are at least five Russians who would have understood her—if they spoke Hebrew.

They say that they felt more Jewish there than they do here, but before they immigrated they didn't even know how to say "Yom Kippur," they'd never heard of Chanukah, and now they can hardly explain the meaning of Passover to their children. Many Russians of the 'last gulf' left for Israel not to practice their religion in the Holy Land or to live in Jewish surroundings, but because the situation in Russia was bad. Russian Jewish patriotism is almost nonexistent. I say "almost" for we came here because we wanted to live in *Ha'aretz*, while they let the Jewish people assimilate with other peoples. More than twenty years ago we had the choice between Canada, the United States, and France, but we came here because we didn't want our children to marry Russians or non-Jews. And now we have the same problem here because many of them aren't even Jewish. Really, they're totally uninterested in Judaism. They don't feel any connection to the country, the men aren't circumcised, couples haven't had a Jewish marriage ceremony, and the boys don't have a bar mitzvah. If they're not Jewish but are married to a Jew, they often don't want to convert.

The fact that many new immigrants aren't Jewish arouses mistrust not only among people on the street but also in official authorities like the rabbinate. This is also true for the Orthodox rabbis who perform Jewish marriages. Since the Russian immigration they have been checking documents more carefully. Lea Weiss (thirty-four years old) and Edward Feldman (thirty years old) wanted an Orthodox marriage ceremony. Weiss, a nurse from Siberia, immigrated to Israel in 1991, and Feldman, a computer scientist from Tashkent, came the same year. "We're Jews," says Feldman simply. But first they have to prove this to the rabbinate. Both of their identity cards say that they are Jewish, but five months after submitting their request to marry to the rabbinate they still had no notification that their marriage could take place. "They tell us everything in stages," says Weiss. "First they wanted our birth certificates, then those of our parents, and after that I had to come with my mother who lives here too. Finally, I had to go with her and with all my family documents to the Ministry of the Interior." Weiss remembers that "he looked only at the photos. 'One can see that you're Jewish,' he said to my mother, but to Edward he said that it would be 'very difficult to prove that his mother was Jewish.' After five months we felt that they had humiliated us sufficiently." When the rabbinate finally called Weiss and Feldman because they had passed all the tests, the couple was already on their way to Cyprus.

In order to improve the integration of Russian immigrants into Israeli society and to solve criminal behavior and the psychological problems that are the consequences of difficult adaptation, in 1994 the Ministry of Integration asked the Brookdale Institute in Jerusalem to do a study on immigrants. The ministry instructed the institute—and this is striking—not to ask about the Jewish identity of Russian immigrants. Now that the state of Israel is wondering how Jewish it should be and the "Who is a Jew" question is so important, Minister Yuli Edelstein did not allow this very question to be asked. He thinks that this question is "too sensitive," according to Sarit Ellenbogen, an anthropologist who assisted in the study. She shows the letter in question.

> No one would tell the truth in a face-to-face interview. A Jewish immigrant is afraid that he will have fewer rights if it becomes known that he isn't Jewish. According to the ministry, the purpose of the study is to help the Russians to get work faster by gathering information about their background. The first years we didn't take into account the differences among the various Russian subcultures in Israel. For the state it was important that the Jews came from Russia, but no one went deeply into the differences in the Russians in Israel from the Ukraine, from White Russia, from Central Russia, from Bukhara, Tajikistan, Chechnya, and the most European, intellectual ones from St. Petersburg and Moscow. Knowledge of the differences is important for a successful integration. But there remains a taboo on asking who among the Russians is Jewish.

"I asked this question in the seventies, but no one wanted to listen to me then," says Mordecai Altschuler, who is pessimistic about the possibility of solving the problems that the last immigration wave brought with it.

> At the time I literally warned scholars and politicians in a lecture that the immigration flood would in the future endanger the Jewish identity of our state. It was a fact that 70 percent of two hundred immigrants who immigrated from Leningrad and Moscow to Israel at that time were not Jewish. Jews from these cities were and still are the most assimilated, and mixed marriages were and still are contracted with the greatest ease. Besides, most Jews in the

former Soviet Union lived in and around these cities. Therefore my conclusion was obvious, but no one wanted to hear it at the time. The fact is that it was unseemly to say that the Russian Jews weren't Jews at all according to the halakhah. The only thing that people thought about at the time was that they were persecuted and oppressed, and because of that Israel wanted to save these Russian Jews. Nonsense! For the sake of convenience we forget that the Russians did not neglect the Jewish tradition because being Jewish was a shame—it was because many of them weren't interested at all in Judaism. Besides, it was unimaginable that immigrants would come to Israel in such numbers. And it was also unthinkable that if they did come, it would be for economic reasons, while it is now perfectly clear that almost every Russian emigrates for that reason. It's a fable that they choose to settle in Israel for ideological reasons. That's all talk and propaganda! Even in the seventies they came because conditions were bad there and not because they were Zionists.

Altschuler keeps emphasizing that he doesn't want to embellish the situation for the Israelis.

At the time we made a mistake by adding a grandfather clause, paragraph four of the law, to the Law of Return. Now the Sochnut legally brings Christian grandsons of Jewish grandfathers into the country and they go to church here. How can I have any reason for optimism?

We are now confronted with the greatest imaginable domestic problems that bring all inner contradictions of the Jewish state to the surface. It is difficult to point out our biggest problem because we have a thousand biggest problems. Yet I think that nowadays Israelis worry more than ever about the true identity of the state of Israel. This subject has become a real minefield in the past few years because of the immigration of great numbers of non-Jews from the former Soviet Union. We are all too aware that it can explode as soon as politicians or regular citizens set foot on it.

In November 1999 this became evident in Beit Shemesh, a city founded in 1950 by Moroccan Jews, about fifteen kilometers west of Jerusalem. The vice-mayor, Moshe Abutbul (whose parents became ultra-Orthodox), is of Moroccan origin and a member of Shas. He organized a demonstration against the increasing presence of Russian immigrants, saying that these days the city is "full of blond hair and blue eyes." This is a problem, he explained, because Christians—he meant the Russian immigrants—pollute the country with pork and prostitution. He expressed his fear about "blond youths who take the daughters of Israel" and the local youths who "marry the daughters of the goyim, who have blue eyes too." He even suggested that the Russians should go and live in separate cities where they would be able to sell as much pork as they wanted and would even be allowed to build a church. Abutbul said that they would be permitted to stay in Beit Shemesh but only on the condition that they would respect the Jewish character of the city. The brother of the former minister of health, David Benizri (of Shas) from Beit Shemesh, expressed similar sentiments in public: the immigrants from the former Soviet Union had supposedly brought in "diseases" and would "flood Beit Shemesh with horrors."

"Such a remark makes us face the facts and brings with it an avalanche of existential questions and discussions about the meaning of being Jewish, about who is a Jew, about the Law of Return, about conversions, and about how we will be able to solve the problem of the large numbers of non-Jewish Russians so that Israel remains a Jewish state," says Altschuler. He feels that the standpoint of the Orthodox part of the population in this discussion is clear: the immigrants who came to Israel without a Jewish mother would have to convert under the authority of the rabbinate. Otherwise they don't belong in the Jewish state because they incite to assimilation in the Jewish country, the one country in which this danger should not exist. According to Altschuler, the secularists in Israel have generally two opinions in this discussion about the Christian and half-Jewish immigrants.

> The first one comes down to the fact that the children of the immigrants—whether they be Jewish, half-Jewish, or Christians—will grow up like secular Israelis with the idea that Israel is their home. They will be absorbed in the Jewish culture, and I say "Jewish" because they won't be absorbed into the Arab culture. Those who will assimilate won't always convert to Judaism, they won't celebrate a traditional Passover, and the boys won't always be circumcised, but they will study Hebrew, will serve in the army, and in school they will study Jewish and Israeli history. This is also true for the Christian spouses of Jewish men who therefore have non-Jewish, Christian children. What makes things extra difficult is that these children will

later not be able to marry Jews and will be able to demand separate Russian schools through the immigrant parties. This desire has already been expressed in Russian-Christian circles because the parents want their children to have a Christian religious education, have the day off on Christian holidays, and be able to appear in public undisturbed when wearing a cross around their neck.

Altschuler, who originally believed in the first scenario, is becoming increasingly convinced that reality will resemble the second scenario as he talks with more Russians in Israel. "In Israel they are developing an ideology of 'Russianism.' They will see themselves primarily as Russians who don't participate in Israeli life in its cultural, spiritual and political respects. Therefore they won't assimilate but will continue to speak Russian and will continue to constitute a foreign element in the state. And half a million alien elements can no longer be neglected," says Altschuler, who admits that he will think it's "too bad" if one of his children marries a goy. "For them their home is still over there. This is evident from the number of Russian delis and Russian newspapers, for example. They look at Russian television and continue to speak Russian. This is particularly problematic because Russianism brings with it more domestic animosities and unrest."

"The fact is that Russians are racist," says Altschuler, who has visiteed the former Soviet Union often and has spoken to enough Russians to state with some certainty that racism was a part of Soviet society.

Black students who came to the former Soviet Union were poorly treated. In Moscow and in St. Petersburg, Caucasians and Georgians are called "crooks" and "Mafiosi." This rivalry continues here because it's a fact that there are criminals among the immigrants. In addition to these tensions, those between the Moroccan Jews and the immigrants from the former Soviet Union are also increasing, especially since the Moroccans resent the immigrants and the fact that many Christians profit from the *sal klita*, and in addition want to build churches and become priests. The Moroccans received nothing when they came to Israel in the fifties; on the contrary, they were badly treated.

The Israeli embassies in the various republics of the former Soviet Union are trying, according to Altschuler, to refuse permission to immigrate to Israel to those who declare that they are Christians. He emphasizes the word *trying* because these Christians—who often have a Jewish grandfather or are married to a Jew who isn't going to church yet but is most likely fully assimilated—have the right to immigrate to Israel according to the Law of Return. "This is actually the greatest problem. Christians have come here who frankly admit that they are happy to have a Jewish grandfather who, even though he's no longer alive, gives them entry into Israel through the Law of Return. This is the problem," exclaims Altschuler and emphasizes that he isn't talking about monkey-business but about a perfectly legal practice.

According to Altschuler, the presence of many non-Jewish Russian immigrants can in the end bring about the separation between religion and state. For those who have already come, a solution will have to be found, and the only solution according to Altschuler is for Israel to permit civil marriage. Establishing civil marriage by law will take another generation, according to him. The pressure on the rabbinate and on the government will become too great. The fact that one hundred people can't marry is a problem, but five hundred Israeli citizens who can't marry in their own country is untenable. Altschuler feels the problem is that the ultra-Orthodox fear that permitting civil marriage will also mean that many Jews will choose this marriage.

> This is the greatest fear of the rabbinate because in the future it will become increasingly difficult to check the background of a bride and groom who want to be married by the rabbinate. In many cases it will no longer be possible to check this. Another problem that will arise in the future is that a Russian immigrant of the second generation who may want to return to Judaism can't prove that he was born to a Jewish mother. It sounds abstract, but these are real worries within the Orthodox community in Israel which is also represented in the government.
>
> I myself can't identify with these particular worries. I think that we can remain a Jewish state if we have separate Islamic, Christian, Jewish, as well as civil courts to perform marriages. My problem is that the history of our country and our people consists of contradictions.

Altschuler sighs as he encounters unsolved second and third problems that result from the first problem. He repeats that solutions can't always be consistent and morally acceptable.

From opinion polls it appears that even the Labor Party doesn't always want to separate religion and state. No opinion poll is needed to find out that the Russian politicians, who are more conservative than the Russian immigrants (the Russian Jews and the non-Jewish Russian Israelis) whose interests they represent, are against it also. My worry—and here is my own conflict—is that I am for the separation of religion and state but at the same time I want to preserve the Jewish character of the state of Israel. It's precisely because we want to remain a Jewish state that we should try to prevent the flood of non-Jews and practicing Christians from increasing. This is why I think—and this is the inner conflict that many people in Israel contend with—that we should limit the right of entry of Christians with a Jewish grandfather. The present situation is paradoxical because the Jewish state takes in Christians through a law, the Law of Return, which is meant to offer Jews a homeland. This law—please note that it is a secular law—is racist. In order to belong to the Jewish people through this law, the immigrant has to give genetic proof. I don't want to sound racist, but the presence of too many non-Jews creates almost incalculable problems with our identity. I think that one generation is enough, and many Israelis think so too. Why should Christians with a Jewish grandfather have the right to Israeli citizenship through this law to which all kinds of financial advantages are attached? Of course they are permitted to live in Israel, but they can become naturalized as Russian Israelis through another process.

Altschuler admits that his solution is racist, but it originates from apprehension about domestic relations and, according to him, limiting the right of entry of non-Jews through the Law of Return is one step on the way to a solution. In this case the question is if the state can continue to act in a morally sound manner. According to Altschuler, not all problems in history can be solved in a morally acceptable manner. The majority of the Knesset members in the present government of Barak—no matter how secular they are— want Israel as a state to preserve something of its own Jewish religious tradition. In other words, they want Israel to remain a Jewish state. The difference between Russian Jews and Israeli Jews will continue to exist as long as the wish for Israel to continue to live as a Jewish state exists. Only time will tell whether or not this wish is an attainable ideal.

FIVE

CROSSING
THE LINE

new orthodox and new secular jews

"What is truth? An error that has become centuries-old. What is error? Truth, which lives only a minute."

—Baruch Spinoza

The first book that I read as a nonreligious Jew was *Crime and Punishment*. It was especially the title that appealed to me because for many years these two concepts controlled my life as an ultra-Orthodox Jew. We were taught that God who sees everything punishes every sin. We were afraid because as Orthodox Jews who have to obey 613 commands, we could make many mistakes. First I skipped a few prayers. Nothing happened. Then I smoked a cigarette on the Sabbath. I was afraid of God's punishment, so I held my hand in front of the cigarette so that He wouldn't see it. Nothing happened, not even when I didn't hide the cigarette with my hand. Then I telephoned on the Sabbath. Still nothing happened, but I didn't know exactly when He would punish. Of course it could still happen any time. I wasn't punished either for buying a television which I snuck into my house in Mea Shearim packed in the box of a microwave and which I then hid in a closet.

Then I knew: God doesn't exist. Otherwise I would already have heard from Him.

NOAM STARIK (1974) LEFT HIS PARENTS, his four brothers, and two sisters who lead the fundamentalist ultra-Orthodox, anti-Zionist existence of the Neturei Karta (Aramaic for guardians of the city) in 1994. At home he spoke Yiddish, lived in a simple home in Mea Shearim, dressed in a long striped coat and knickerbockers, and his name was Moishe. On his black yarmulke he wore, as he describes it, a "flying saucer" made of fur that he covered with plastic when it rained. He had long side curls that, according to tradition, hadn't been cut since his third birthday. On the Sabbath and during holidays he usually went through the streets of Mea Shearim in an off-white "festive outfit." When showing a photo, he almost makes fun of it. He studied in the strict Toldos Aharon yeshiva. To earn money, he translated two-hundred-year-old rabbinic manuscripts from old Hebrew into modern Hebrew. He was married at nineteen; the marriage was arranged as it was supposed to be, and he had seen his wife no more than ten minutes before the wedding.

At the time of our conversation, Starik is living in Tel Aviv. He wears jeans and a T-shirt, has short hair, and wears reflective sunglasses. He works as a doorman in an apartment complex and has passed the preliminary university exams, which are not easy in Israel. He is now studying history at the University of Tel Aviv. For Starik the most difficult part of the transition from an ethnocentric life to an egocentric life is rationalizing the moral principles of his youth. He takes as an example the command "You shall not kill."

> Why not? Now I say "because of moral considerations," but in the world of my parents people don't kill because God says so, just as you refrain from many things because He is supposed to have said so. You didn't look at other women because it is written "You shall not covet your neighbor's wife . . ." [Exod. 20:14 and Deut. 5:18] and you didn't cut your sideburns because it says "You shall not round off the side-growth on your head, or destroy the side-growth of your beard" [Lev. 19:27], and you wore the tzitzit because it says "look at it and recall all the commandments of the Lord and observe them . . ." [Num. 15:37–41].

"All my actions and reasoning had a divine source," continues Starik, who is sitting on a terrace in one of the most secular streets of Tel Aviv. Once in a while he lets slip a Yiddish word and orders "*wasser*" instead of "*mayim*." Yiddish was the language of communication in his yeshiva, except during the daily one-hour secular lessons, like the Hebrew lessons for example. Starik recounts:

> We called it the ordinary grocer's language. Sometimes a student who spoke Hebrew would be betrayed by a fellow-student and would get a beating. Punishment for this reason was a mitzvah. After all, speaking Hebrew was not permitted. Someone who laughed hard could also count on a beating, and that's still the case. No form of exuberance was appreciated. My father adhered to this mitzvah which he thought was pedagogically justified. I was constantly at war with his world and I received quite a few spankings as a result. I was constantly at loggerheads with the informants at the yeshiva. After all, their task is to inform the teachers about any infraction of the rules, like the use of Hebrew, laughing hard, coming late for prayers, using forbidden words, looking at girls—that sort of thing.

Until 1994 Starik lived only with divine truths. He knew that every city in Israel had a Herzl street, but he didn't know exactly why. Sexuality could be discussed only with the "guide to family life," whom parents send to every future married couple. This guide could tell Starik very little that was new because, as he said, he "already knew everything." Starik talks easily and is not embarrassed to discuss by name the feelings that didn't seem to exist during his youth. "In the beginning I didn't know what was meant by words like 'frustrated,' 'satisfied,' and 'love.' We never used these words, as if Orthodox people don't have these feelings. The word "girl" was taboo for yeshiva boys, and within our family the notions 'pleasure' or 'fun' were usually used with regard to the secularists who supposedly lived only 'for fun.' In contrast, the words 'pain' and 'happiness' did have meaning for us."

Starik was curious, and because he had guts he would sometimes buy a secular newspaper in another part of town. Later, when he lived together with his wife and had bought a television, he learned a lot, but at home with his parents any mention of secular subjects was sinful. The family and the yeshiva, together with the

Orthodox community, are of great influence on the education of the children of strict *haredim*, like the members of the Hasidic movements Gur, Satmer, and Neturei Karta to which his parents belong. The community shapes the way of thinking of every Orthodox child, who is entirely at home in Talmudic literature and in the Torah. In the strictly Orthodox community the Torah is the embodiment of God. Orthodox men and boys are trained—and they train daily—in reciting, and at a very young age every boy therefore knows an amazing number of complicated texts by heart. He considers as Torah all the prophets and scribes, an extensive complex of judicial and ethical literature and a generation of spiritual leaders, including such present-day rabbis as Menachem Eliezer Shach, Menachem Mendel Schneerson, and Ovadia Yossef, who have achieved not only spiritual but also worldly power.

The environment in which most of the new secularists have grown up has a rhythm different from that in other areas in Israel. Often men get up at the crack of dawn to go to the synagogue for the morning prayer. The streets usually remain quiet long after that time. Life doesn't really get going until after four o'clock in the afternoon. Particularly on Thursday afternoons, when the streets are jammed with women who are shopping and are in a rush because they have to prepare for the Sabbath. On Friday morning the last errands are done, and on Friday afternoon and the Sabbath the streets are deserted. Here and there are a few yeshiva boys who are bored or are perhaps discussing their religion or plans to leave it like Starik did. Now and then a group of boys rush to the yeshiva, and they won't return home until later to eat the evening meal. At twelve o'clock at night Mea Shearim can still be crowded with people.

Mea Shearim, the neighborhood where Starik grew up, breathes the atmosphere of a shtetl in seventeenth-century Poland. Yiddish is heard on the streets, but in the stores Hebrew is mainly spoken. There are no cafés, restaurants, or movie houses. It's difficult to find bathing suits and lingerie; generally they can be found in the back of the stores and are sold by men as well as by women. Stores selling wigs, grocery stores, furniture stores, greengrocers, clothing stores with fairly priced "modest" women's clothing, and stores selling household goods are present in abundance. The salespeople in these stores aren't only women but also men from the secular sector. Even though not all of the salespeople are religious, the sight of bare midriffs and arms and women dressed in pants is very unusual here. On the contrary, on the streets in Mea Shearim signs are posted that remind passers-by of the prescribed dress: "Keep your neighborhood holy. The Torah obliges every Jewish Daughter to dress modestly. . . . To pass through our neigbourhood immodestly dressed is forbidden."

The *haredi* adult male—and he is already considered as such at the age of eighteen, when he is usually married and sometimes even has a child—has an answer to practically every question. This makes life in the secular world difficult, especially right after leaving the religion, because nonbelievers usually have more questions than answers. By this time the young *haredi* has become used to referring to his father or the rabbi for their opinions about the political situation and many other subjects. The latter possesses special gifts for getting in touch with God, and moreover has *gelernt*. During the wedding of one of the twelve children of the ultra-Orthodox Knesset member Avraham Ravitz, one of the guests, a mother of seven, said,

> The secularists always say that we don't have opinions of our own because we always ask the rabbi everything. But I see it differently. Not everyone is able to form an opinion about all sorts of events and phenomena in society. Our husbands study and we work and keep the family going, and we don't have time to think about certain things. And why should we if there are others in our community, the *chachamim*, whose judgment we trust. In our community everyone has their own task.

Starik no longer trusts the judgment of the *chachamim*. Four years after his departure the relationship with his family remains difficult. His mother slips him money now and then, but he almost never speaks with his father. "Nowadays I represent for them the 'useless,' 'empty,' 'superficial modern life' where Western Zionist values and norms dominate. The Zionists—in their eyes I'm now a Zionist—have made Israel a country like 'all other nations.' At home and in the yeshiva I heard almost daily that Zionism equals collective assimilation. In Israel Independence Day is a day off, but for us it was a day of mourning. Wrapped in sackcloth, members of Neturei Karta demonstrated against the character of the Jewish state."

Starik remembers that on that day he once attended a lesson in the yeshiva entitled "Why we mourn during Independence Day."

They think that Israel is "sick," "weak," and "corrupt" because the country has abandoned the religious values intended especially for the chosen in exchange for the values of the goyim, which to them means Westerners. I was always told that Israel has to be "better" and that Israel as the chosen people is subject to different laws from the other peoples in the world. According to them the only purpose of a Jewish state should be to fulfill the commandments of the Torah, and they regret that the Jews—because of Zionism— have strayed so far from this path. My parents feel that I have taken this path too. I'm no longer worth anything in their eyes because I'm guilty of Jewish self-betrayal. In their eyes I'm assimilating into Zionist Israeli society, which is westernizing rapidly. According to them, the Jews are also on their way to becoming a people like other peoples.

My parents say that Jews are the chosen people and that they are an example for other peoples. What do they mean by chosen? In what way are we better? I've had enough of it. Maybe I'll want to become a Christian. My father doesn't understand my ideas or my new life. He saw the book *Crime and Punishment* in my briefcase and was surprised because of the title, actually for the same reason why it intrigued me. When he figured out that the story had never taken place, he asked why I was reading that book. Fiction doesn't exist for him, and he finds it incomprehensible that I recognize myself in Raskolnikov. "It would be better to mourn the destruction of the temple or the establishment of this state. And why do you no longer respect the Sabbath?" he often asks, just like my brothers. "Because I no longer believe in God," I say to my father; this is inconceivable to him. "But in that case what is the difference between you and a dog?" he then asks. It's a question I recognize because in the yeshiva we were taught that every Jew who doesn't work for God is an animal, and they don't want to have anything at all to do with goyim. I have a television, and therefore I tell him about Kosovo. "They're only goyim, why are you worrying about them? You'd be better off praying and fulfilling your task as a Jew. Why don't you do that anymore?" he says. Then I answer: "No matter how often I pray, it still doesn't help and you sin too." If you don't put on your tefillin once, or you skip a prayer once—and that does happen—then you've sinned and God doesn't listen. Being an observant Jew is impossible. God has burdened us with an impossible task.

Nevertheless Starik admits, like many who 'leave', that life in the *haredi* community offers social certainty and for many this means psychological peace. But for Starik the thirst for knowledge, and the urge to read and study were compelling. Besides, the social isolation that he experienced because of his doubts about God had become unbearable. When he was thirteen Starik went to the yeshiva where he studied from five o'clock in the morning until ten o'clock in the evening. In the early morning he would look through the wastepaper baskets for newspapers. "I was looking for photos of girls and I wanted to know what was happening around me," says Starik. In a matter-of-fact tone he reveals details about his own past and about his parents' and his community's ideas as if it were someone else's past. "When it became known that Netanyahu had lost, they announced that this was impossible because the rabbi had said that Netanyahu would win. Unbelievable, isn't it?" He seems to approach his family like an anthropologist. Sometimes it seems as if he is poking fun at his strict religious background.

> At the wedding of one of my brothers where I'd gone because my mother wanted me to, they looked at me as if I were a monkey. I was the only one without a yarmulke and side curls. Many former yeshiva friends wanted to talk with me and meet me somewhere else later. But we had nothing to say to one another. I'm afraid that I disturb the harmony in the community and in the family by talking with them about my life. I know that my departure has harmed the reputation of my family and that I have left them behind in incomprehension and despair. When I left my home, my father first thought I was crazy. Someone who makes such a decision can't be normal. When it appeared that I could manage and that I hadn't gone crazy, he thought that I'd left because I wanted to earn money, for materialistic reasons. But he doesn't want to accept the real reason, the fact that I don't believe in God.

Anything to do with women was taboo in his family, but not for Starik. After he had advised a friend what to do during his wedding night—and when the latter informed the head of the yeshiva about this advice—an order for expulsion was pronounced over Starik. (This is a centuries-old Ashkenazi custom for which the word *herem* is used.) No one was allowed to talk to him, and he was never allowed to leave the yeshiva by himself. Starik decided to change to another yeshiva. He continued to read newspapers with friends, and he started listening in secret to Hebrew music on tapes. Starik says, "We even read *Playboy*. In the morning the head of the yeshiva would make the rounds and with tears in his eyes he would collect the newspapers that we had thrown out. It went from bad to worse. Then I started telling jokes about God that my friends found hard to take. At that point I knew that I no longer believed, but I thought that everything would turn out all right. When my parents arranged a marriage for me, I thought that this would make my life settle down."

But the marriage didn't help. Now Starik had still another person from whom he had to hide his reading habits, his absences from the synagogue, and other sins.

> I can't say if I loved her. You loved only God. Love between two people was of no importance, only starting a Jewish family was important. The thought that I would have to live like that for years on end depressed me. I tried to make myself Orthodox, and I listened to tapes of organizations that try to make Jews religious again. But these tapes put me on the secular path. The interpretations of the preachers didn't convince me. I found the errors in the arguments right away—you can't even call it reasoning. Then my eye fell on a notice in the ultra-Orthodox paper *Ya'ated Ne'eman* about the Hillel organization.

He looked up the telephone number and called.

Hillel was founded in 1991 by an ex-*haredi*, Shai Horowitz. It receives the newly secular and tries to familiarize them with the secular world (Shai Horowitz himself has returned to the *haredi* milieu). Hillel doesn't have reception centers, but it finds host families (for example in a kibbutz) where the newly secular get time and receive help to be able to adjust. Approximately two hundred volunteers work for Hillel, among whom are a large number of newly secular like Starik. They help the newly secular with his departure, which has to be prepared in secret because his family will not have any understanding of his decision. In general, his family members and the head of his yeshiva interpret his choice of the Western world as a denial of his background and of the way of life of the community. In fact, his departure harms his family, who will have to account for this shame in the community. During the preparatory period the departing person usually skips more and more of his religious duties and focuses on the opportunities offered by the world that he will soon join.

With the help of the workers of Hillel he prepares himself for a new everyday language, and he learns about practices that were totally foreign to him until the moment of his departure. For the first time in his life he buys trousers that are not black, learns about handling money, renting an apartment, and educational opportunities. Often these newly secular look for books about life on a kibbutz because that's where they generally find lodging with a host family at first.

For Starik this period lasted one month. After that month, during which he didn't see his wife and read books about socialism, the Zionists, and kibbutzim, he wrote his wife telling her that he wouldn't return. He ordered a taxi in which he changed clothes. At the home of his host family in Kibbutz Nir Yitzhak he could get used to secular life. The first thing he did in the kibbutz was cut off his side curls. Especially in the beginning he was lonely in an unprecedented way. Forming friendships was a new phenomenon for him because in the Orthodox community of the yeshiva boys he had more quickly felt at ease. At the beginning he had this feeling of emptiness, especially on Sabbath and during the Jewish holidays.

In Israel, Starik—and all others who leave the religion—is called a *chozer bish'elah*, someone who has returned (*lachzor*: Hebrew for return) to the question (*sh'elah*), the doubt—that is to say secular life. Sometimes he is called a *ba'al t'shuvah*, which means literally "owner of the answer." In addition to those like Starik who exchange the ultra-Orthodox existence for the secular, there are also Orthodox who choose the secular life. Their number is higher than that of the ultra-Orthodox "immigrants" and it has increased the last few years, probably because the transition is less radical and seldom involves traumatic experiences. Ideologically, the transition from a religious Zionist to a secular existence requires less adjustment because the shift can take place gradually. After all, religious Zionists are fully integrated into secular Israeli life: they don't reject the state of Israel, they fulfill their military obligation, and they combine secular education with religious education. In addition, the appearance of the religious Zionists differs less from that of the secular: they wear a crocheted yarmulke, some wear their tzitzit visible, others not visible, and others don't wear them at all.

Every religious Zionist family, with an average of six children, has at least one child that has left the faith. Many religious Zionists live on the West Bank where parents try to prevent their children from hitching a ride to Jerusalem for fun in the evening after the quiet Sabbath. In the newspaper of the National Religious Party, Yona Goodman, the general secretary of the religious Zionist Bnei Akiva youth movement, wrote in May 1999 that "our youth is going astray and we have to try to keep them under God's wing." Evidently many parents have difficulty raising their children "as Jewish" as they themselves were raised. Although this phenomenon is no longer a shame, many couples are not willing to talk about it. Some parents seek help in discussion groups, therapy, and lectures. One of the causes of the ever-increasing departure of religious Zionist youths could be the concentration of the religious Zionist movement on the nationalist rather than the religious aspect. With the Oslo accords, the movement that wants to realize the dream of a greater Israel by the colonization of the West Bank of the Jordan as a way to make redemption real has landed in a spiritual and political crisis (see chapter 6).

"In order to limit the feeling of loneliness as much as possible, we try to lodge those 'leaving' as quickly as possible with a secular host family," says Anat Nevo, who works for Hillel. She has offices in Tel Aviv and Jerusalem and has telephone office hours in the evening. Nevo has been involved with the organization since the beginning, originally as translator of the secular language, but gradually more as a kind of guide. Nevo says, "Some don't know how they should behave in our world. Those 'leaving' are usually curious and enterprising, and they make an effort to get hold of books about secular Israel, but they have problems with bank accounts, applying for a telephone connection, looking over a rental agreement, and making contacts with girls."

According to her, the above-mentioned matters can be learned, but without help it takes a very long time, and the new secularist often loses heart. "We don't encourage them to leave. That wouldn't be moral, because the adjustment to a non-Orthodox world involves psychological problems that not everyone can handle. We are not an anti-*haredi* organization, and this is not a missionary operation as the *haredi* assert in their newspapers," says Nevo.

Their "previous life" offered support in exchange for the observance of strict rules and obedience to certain rules of conduct. The community demanded complete dependence of the members, each one of whom appreciates this individually. For many this certainty is spiritually and emotionally satisfying, but for independent thinkers who doubt these values there is no place. *Haredim* who doubt have to "live with lies" and are not allowed to express their thoughts. It's precisely those *haredim* whom we want to help with the emigration from their world to our free world.

The step from a protected environment, where everyone helps, to our more standoffish world is big. As a new secularist, the ex-*haredi* feels like an immigrant in his own country: he knows practically no one, he doesn't speak the language, and he isn't familiar with many institutions. Many of them don't dare to ask questions, their Hebrew is poor, or they are shy, and almost all of them are practically ignorant about anything not related to religion. That's why a host family is worth its weight in gold. Initially it's not the character or the background of the new secularist that makes adjustment to our world easier or more difficult. Those who don't want to go to a host family because they think that they will once again land in the kind of prison that their own family used to be will remain behind in their former world.

Nevo finds the work with the newly secular stimulating because according to her they are survivors who are courageous and original and have not yet been shaped by Western society.

In 1998, the first year about which the organization published numbers, the Hillel volunteers showed 107 believers the way in the secular world. From January until October 1999 this number was 237, an annual increase of 167 percent. Nevo says that one of the reasons for this increase is the access to the Internet, which makes it easier for the Orthodox to study the secular world and to come out of their isolation. Besides, Hillel has been better organized the last few years, and in 1999 Yossi Sarid, the Meretz minister of education at the time, promised financial support to Hillel. The organization never received this support because of the fall of the government. However, the government reserves more than 100 million shekels every year for organizations that try to put secular Jews on the religious track.

Hillel's methods are controversial. "Anat received me with cheese and sausage," says Yechezkel Frank, a Dutchman who is living in Israel and has become Orthodox again after a long period of doubt. "That shocked me because I had not yet turned my back completely on Orthodoxy. I think it's too bad that the Hillel workers don't know my national religious background. You can't receive someone who has been Orthodox all his life with cheese and sausage. Many Hillel workers are not knowledgeable enough about the world of the Orthodox and are insufficiently aware of the problems the person 'leaving' can face."

The anthropologist Sarid Barzilai, who wrote the dissertation *Chofshi v'Chared:. Sipuran shel haYotsim liShe'elah m'ha'Chevra ha'Charedit* (Free and Afraid: The story of those "leaving" the *haredi* community) has problems with Hillel as well. She used Hillel to track down informants, but she doesn't care for the organization: "Hillel has declared war on the ultra-Orthodox. They depict the *haredi* milieu as authoritarian, repressive, and violent. They hold out the prospect of a new life of freedom and happiness to the 'newly secular' without warning them that they will have difficulties. In most cases it does appear that those 'leaving' are headed for eternal unhappiness because of their decision. Despite the help from Hillel, they seldom find a balance between their old and their new life." Barzilai, who received her doctorate from the Hebrew University in Jerusalem, continues: "The rest of their lives often consist of eternally balancing between *t'shuvah* [repentance, return, answer] and *sh'elah* [literally, "question"; here: not believing].

"They are doomed to vacillate between their new and old worlds: the new one remains strange to them for a long time, and the old one considers them as traitors, or even worse, as animals. Their ultra-Orthodox background proves to be an incurable wound." Barzilai says that she has filled the role of psychiatrist for each of her informants, many of whom ended up becoming writers, philosophers, or artists. "They experience the change as a 'rebirth,' but none of them know who they are now. The secular world is disappointing because it doesn't offer any alternative to the well-defined Orthodox identity of their past, or to the community and to the family. They think that you can teach children a secular identity. Some ask for a secular *Shulchan Arukh*, that is to say, a book in which you can find answers to all questions."

Menachem Friedman, a professor of sociology at Bar Ilan University in Ramat Gan and a specialist in the ultra-Orthodox community, notes that the Orthodox exodus has been occurring on a large scale among Ashkenazi Jews since the *Haskalah*, the Jewish Enlightenment, around 1780. Friedman explains:

At that time the younger generation chose a secular life. Nowadays not every *haredi* family is affected by this "exodus," but it remains an important social threat. The percentage of people leaving remains low—the exact number is unknown because such a study is difficult to carry out—but not because the community has become more flexible and has started to accept other ways of life. The *haredi* world still doesn't tolerate different opinions. According to a well-known anecdote, a Jew says to his rabbi: "Rabbi, I have doubts, I no longer believe . . ." "Why do you worry?" answers the rabbi. "As long as you suffer because you don't believe, nothing is wrong. Go home, fulfill your duties, and it will pass." In these circles this is the accepted psychological method for dealing with doubts and uncertainties. The rabbi is actually saying: "It's a part of the process, don't fight it."

The *haredi* community makes every effort to prevent the "flight." Mental disorders occur frequently in this community—more than in the secular world—because many want to leave but don't have the courage and the means to do so and are doomed as nonbelievers to lead the life of believers. Many have a fatalistic outlook on their existence and are resigned to being part of a greater system. They fear the reaction of their family, of their acquaintances, but especially of God. Most don't want freedom; they're afraid of it.

The person "leaving" is often between sixteen and twenty years old and usually does not yet have a family, financial responsibilities, or obligations. He wants to extricate himself from the closed Orthodox world where his fellow students and family members seem to be satisfied with age-old answers. According to Friedman, a boy who is hindered by his family from gathering other than religious knowledge will become restless and rebellious.

At that age he is also sensitive to sexual urges and feels attracted by the "big" world. The size of the group of "doubters" who try to leave depends on the mores of a certain community. In a community where severe punishments are the norm, the "doubter" can give himself up and become reconciled with the community. He can also rebel, curse the community, and try to flee. Most remain in their familiar surroundings because of convenience and for fear of punishment.

At the present Friedman is working on, among other things, a book about the relations between the *haredim* and the *hilonim*. He continues:

> As an answer to the threat of the "exodus," the *haredi* community has created a world that is parallel to the modern world. One generation ago an ultra-Orthodox Jew ran the risk of being labeled a traitor if he left the shtetl. Nowadays the *haredim* have built small *haredi* islands in Israeli society and outside it. On these "islands" computer training, courses in English and medicine, and all kinds of trade take place. The ultra-Orthodox Jew can now travel and develop professionally without having to leave the *haredi* world or put it to shame, and even more importantly, he can do this without believing in God.

"I kept it up for five years," says Naftali Volacho (1973), who left his parents and his nineteen brothers and sisters in 1994 when he was twenty-one. He speaks about his family in a less matter-of-fact way than Noam Starik, and he still seems to hesitate. He misses his family and tries to stay in touch with them. Even after five years he says,

> I feel lonely here, and I don't know if I've made the right decision. Going back is impossible because I don't believe. I can't lead a life of lies. Noam is more anti-*haredi* than I, but he had a very rough time. He was beaten a lot. I had to be careful of the so-called snitches who could have told the rabbi that I had books by Dostoyevski in my locker, but I was beaten much less. It wouldn't have turned out well for me if the rabbi had found out. I was always asking questions in the yeshiva and of my friends. People could have figured out that I was doubting because these were questions that shouldn't be asked.

Naftali, a short, slender youth in beige pleated trousers and a black shirt, speaks Yiddish and Hebrew, and the bank where he works in Tel Aviv has given him the opportunity to follow a short course in English because he wants to go to the United States. Naftali explains his situation:

The problem in Israeli society is the hate. When I still walked around wearing side curls, a hat, and a black coat and would occasionally be in a secular street, I felt that I was hated and that the secularists looked at me as if I were crazy. But here in Tel Aviv they also think that I'm not normal when I tell about my past—so I don't talk about it anymore. My secular contemporaries are not interested in me. But I can't just erase the first twenty years of my life that I spent in Orthodox surroundings. There's no one here whom I can tell about this without feeling horrible. I love the Tanakh, and I read it often. Sometimes I feel guilty that I read it without believing.

It might have been better to stay in my familiar surroundings. Then I would have been spared the painful confrontations with the secularists, the risks, and the fears about adjustment in an unknown world.

Presently Naftali lives in Tel Aviv in a small attic room where the temperature sometimes reaches ninety-five degrees Fahrenheit in the summer.

The new world doesn't accept you, and without doubt it is psychologically easier to remain Orthodox. The Orthodox world is safe. At first I was afraid that I wanted to change my life because I wanted to be free materially and physically, but that wasn't the reason. I wouldn't have respected myself if that had been the case. I've done everything to remain in the well-organized, protected religious community of my parents because the secular world is psychologically more difficult, certainly for someone who is used to imposed discipline. I now know this from experience. I will always continue to float between Mea Shearim and Sheinkin [the most secular street in Tel Aviv].

My first doubts were about prayers. On Yom Kippur, for example, we recited an incomprehensible prayer by Yehuda Halevi from the twelfth century. When I began to doubt, I noticed that the rabbis taught us which questions a "good Jew" should ask. Those are the questions that have been asked for centuries and for which the rabbi always has a well-constructed answer. The other questions are "bad" and are not answered. Therefore it is not customary to ask questions to which there is no solid answer—i.e. one that was formulated centuries ago. When I noticed that my doubts remained, I submitted all my questions about "time" and "space," about Einstein and Darwin—concepts that are eternal according to me—to the rabbi. He gave me superficial answers—answers that rabbis usually give to *epikores*, as they call "doubters." These answers are somewhere in a book with the title *Answers for doubters* that rabbis study extensively during their training. I did everything I could to remain Orthodox, but I continued to doubt.

I respected the faith of my classmates, but I wanted to convince them that my doubts were legitimate. But how? I wanted to explain to them that everything they do and believe is based on an axiom. Those who have chosen to believe in it respect those who don't believe in it. But they hadn't chosen it: all these axioms are for them the norm with which they are born. That's why it didn't occur to them that a person can make his own choices. I can now determine my own rules, which today may be different from tomorrow. I didn't take off my yarmulke until I was ready for a secular life. I had already cut my side curls. From that moment on I could break the religious rules. I forced myself to eat pork and to desecrate the Sabbath, which is still difficult for me. I wanted to be afraid of nothing. With a yarmulke on, I would never turn on the radio on Saturday, or eat pork, or do other things that offend Orthodox Jews. That is called *chilul haShem*, the desecration of God's name. In my parents' eyes I am now a *goy she'dover Ivrit*, a Hebrew-speaking goy.

Yitzchak Ezrahi, a rabbi who taught Naftali, is the head of the Mir yeshiva. He lives in a Orthodox neighborhood of Jerusalem, not far from the yeshiva. "Are we more anti-Zionist than anti-Christian?" While he rolls a comfortable desk chair from his study, Ezrahi says, "Listen, for us these are two different dangers. The Christians wanted to put an end to our bodies, and the Zionists wanted to finish off our spirit, our soul." His wife, the daughter of a well-known rabbi, nods in agreement. She adds that she accepts the state, but not the way it is organized. "We do in fact speak Hebrew," she says, "and we voted for Bibi and Sharon. But others speak Yiddish and don't vote, and they can serve *baruch haShem* [the almighty] in the yeshiva because they receive money."

"It's a terrible shame that some Jews leave us," says Ezrahi and pauses briefly.

It's all because of the Zionists who deceived us. They lured us with the prospect of our own country, but we never knew that it would be at the expense of the Torah and of Judaism, which they changed.

That's why we build the character of our boys in the yeshiva. We teach them how to live as a *ben Torah* [a son of the Torah]. What must you do in this world, and what price must you pay to be a good Jew? Poverty is a price we pay for it. We live frugally and modestly. And we don't need anyone to force us into this way of life. It happens by itself, and it's striking that many of the students don't of their own accord want to waste time reading newspapers and novels, and that they don't want to watch television or eat pork. They want only Torah. The government should not force us to serve in the army; there they do sports, make secular music, and play games. Why? It's good for the morale, they say. For us only the Torah is good for the morale. We wage war with the truth when we study the Gemara in which there are many truths. When we *"lern,"* we get excited, for it isn't irrelevant. *"Lernen"* is to live.

Fortunately there is lots of Torah in Israel nowadays. And that's a good thing because without the Torah there would be no world at all, not even a secular one. In a flash we would return to the wilderness, to a state of *tohu va'vohu*, wasteland and emptiness. And that's a good thing because the Russians in Israel are a great problem. They are not religious, and many among them aren't even our Jewish brothers. In the end the Messiah will determine who is really Jewish, and then they won't make the grade. Until that time we must ensure that as many Jews as possible return [to the Orthodox faith].

Ezrahi gets up and takes a stack of pamphlets from a closet. While handing me some brochures, Ezrahi says, "These are for Jews who have strayed from the path and have forgotten that the Torah is the truth. In total 750,000 Jews have already returned to the tradition, the *ba'alei t'shuvah*. Shas has done good work because all these Jews have come to the conclusion that Shulamit Aloni, Yossi Sarid, Tommy Lapid, and the kibbutzim are wrong. The *ba'alei t'shuvah* are important for us, and these booklets can help them to return to us."

For this "return" to the faith to which Ezrahi is referring there is a Hebrew term, *lachzor b't'shuvah*, which means "to repent" or "to return." Someone who has returned is a new faithful and is called a *chozer b't'shuvah* or a *ba'al t'shuvah*, Hebrew for "master of repentance." According to a study carried out by *Ha'aretz*, about 5,500 Jews return to Orthodoxy every year. This seems to be a difficult process, and many *ba'alei t'shuvah* express it as follows: "In our godless past our soul was covered with mud and has to be cleansed." Many experience *t'shuvah* as "drastic," "difficult," or even as "a rebirth." Often the return takes place in special yeshivas for new faithful, and it occurs in two phases: the awareness of sin, the expression of regret, and the insight into errors committed. During the return the *ba'al t'shuvah* also pronounces the formal expression of confession of Moses Maimonides, the eleventh-century Spanish Jewish philosopher and halakhah expert: "Oh God, I have sinned, I have committed grave iniquities, I have broken your laws. I am sorry, and I am ashamed of my actions, and I shall never do it again."

At the beginning of their return most of the *ba'alei t'shuvah* temporarily turn their backs on the duties of their previous life. They study in yeshivas that were established especially for the newly religious and strive to be able to study in a "real" yeshiva. If a Jew hasn't learned the laws at home, he has to try to reach the level of a Jew who has had a Jewish education as quickly as possible. As soon as someone understands the arguments of the rabbis in the Gemara—usually after a year and a half—he is ready for a "real" yeshiva. The cultural background of the person, his character, and the political developments in Israel seem to play an important role in the decision to return. From the stories about the past of many newly religious, it appears that things didn't go well for them in their lives. First they undertook long journeys in search of happiness. During their search many read the works of the great philosophers about Christianity and Islam, and often they immersed themselves in the teachings of Zen Buddhism. After wanderings that could last for years, they came to the conclusion that their "home," their roots, Orthodox Judaism, could be the remedy for their structural unrest. Many experience the return as the attraction of the Jewish God who has called them and who speaks the truth. His Truth is the only truth. He has all the answers to their questions, and his mitzvot appear to give structure to their lives.

"The 'return' is closely linked to personality," says the psychiatrist Jair Carlos Bar-El. This secular Argentine Jew has a daughter who has returned to the faith. He works in Beit Neffesh Psychiatric Hospital in Kfar Shaul, a district of Jerusalem. This hospital admits people who suffer from the "Jerusalem syndrome" and other psychological disorders caused by religion.

The people who return are often emotional personalities who feel insecure and are unable to develop their own system of values. Often they feel that the life they are leading is "unreal" and "unsatisfactory" and conclude that "life revolves around God and not around secular knowledge." They haven't found anything to hold onto in modern life, where the family plays a lesser role than in the past. They are in a psychological crisis and think they can find a solution in religion. Some Jews use Judaism to survive.

This change usually has psychological causes rather than religious and cultural ones. By the way, the change to a pious life is the least pathological solution. Many become addicts, women become anorectics, some choose to spend time alone in the desert, or they take a trip to Thailand where they hope to find themselves. These options frequently have the same function as the "return," which most often takes place after one of the other methods has been tried.

There are three kinds of *ba'al t'shuvah*. The first group is formed by those "returning" from abroad and especially from the United States. In the sixties and seventies the first ones came to Israel to try their luck and not with the idea of becoming Orthodox. Rabbi Meir Schuster, who at that time "brought in many new Jews" for the *ba'al t'shuvah* yeshivas like the famous Or Sameach yeshiva, "found" many of them near the Wailing Wall, at the central bus station in Jerusalem, and at the Hebrew University. He would invite them for a lesson, which often became the turning point in their lives. Frequently they decided to exchange their secular existence for a religious life in a radical way. Especially at Or Sameach (founded in 1972) there was a coming and going of long-haired young men with backpacks and guitars. Today many of the *ba'alei t'shuvah* join Chabad, the international messianic movement, and settle in Safed.

The second group of *ba'alei t'shuvah* comes primarily from poorer districts of large cities in Israel and from new cities. In these places there live many Jews of African origin, children from traditional families, and Moroccan, Persian, Iraqi, Yemenite, and Kurdish immigrants who have voted for Shas since 1984. Their *t'shuvah* is in part a reaction to the Ashkenazi establishment of Israeli society. For a Sephardic Jew the *t'shuvah* is a religious answer to the secular and Western Israeli society. However, the return often flows from their need to breathe new life into the Sephardic Jewish tradition in Israel. In their yeshivas the Jews don't only confess their sins but they also point to the failure of the secular Western 'Ashkenazi' society as the source of their wanderings.

The third group of *ba'alei t'shuvah* are Ashkenazi Israelis whose *t'shuvah* can be understood only in light of the Six-Day War of 1967 and the Yom Kippur War of 1973. These two wars brought about a time of reflection among many Israelis. After the occupation of the West Bank in 1967, Israel became isolated from the rest of the world, and the survival of the state seemed to have come to depend on the Jewish people. Fear of the extinction of Judaism surfaced among some. It was at that time that questions arose in Israel about the meaning of being Jewish, about the purpose of the Jewish state, and about its continued existence. Even socialist Zionists connected the questions about the legitimacy of the state Israel (*Medinat Yisrael*) and its relation to the land (*Eretz Yisrael*) to the Jewish religion. Many of them converted because they were convinced that the most important reason for the establishment of a Jewish state in Palestine had been the Jewish religion—this was contrary to what the socialist Zionists had advocated earlier. The *t'shuvah* movement offered the "spiritual" solution to many people at this time and it answered many of their questions.

One of these people is the Israeli sculptor I. A. (1957). He "returned" when his brother was wounded in 1973. Like many others who were searching for God at the time, he wanted to make a fundamental change in Israeli society. "I discovered that in order to reach the ultimate goal of the Jewish state more was needed than the materialistic reality in which I too had lost myself. I was a freak with long hair, a joint, and an earring." During a walk near his home in a rural town northeast of Jerusalem, I. A. shows me the little hole in his ear.

> I was always searching for the truth, but since my brother was wounded, this need became more urgent. First I thought I had found the truth in Zen. On Friday evenings we'd get together like Bohemians in a café in Tel Aviv where I heard that two of the group were studying at Or Sameach. I was curious and went to see them. They convinced me that I should seek the truth at "home" and not in Zen. After that God came quickly into my life. He prepared the way for me, and I offered my girlfriend the choice: come with me or separate. She chose me and therefore God. We got married and had seven children, five of whom have remained Orthodox. Meanwhile we have divorced because she evolved toward a secular life of pleasure and fun. That kind of life is not compatible with my Orthodox, more spiritual life.

At first I studied for days on end and well into the night at Or Sameach. The atmosphere was competitive but stimulating. There was always the challenge of who would turn off the light at night. It was difficult, but after three months I took off my earring; I cut off my hair that had been to my waist before I started to study. During that period the relationship with my parents was awkward, but it's better now. We are used to our spiritual alienation, and I accept the fact that they haven't followed me. In the beginning they didn't know what to do with me. They spoke with the head of the yeshiva, rabbi Nota Schiller, who convinced them I was following an academic course of study. In less than a year I was able to understand and explain the Gemara, a book that isn't accessible to everyone in the yeshiva. After a year I had reached a level that was high enough so that I could *lern* with the boys of a regular yeshiva. I learned Yiddish and began to *lern* in Mir, a Lithuanian yeshiva where Avraham Ravitz of Degel haTorah was still teaching. Only Yiddish was spoken. There I saw people study holy texts with enthusiasm, day and night. I had never experienced such a feeling of fellowship. I knew immediately that this was a way of studying that appealed to me. It was not a solitary activity. Everyone enjoyed participating in the discussions. The vitality of the study hall was incredible. And to think that this vitality has a holy origin!

There were always new questions; we spoke about secular subjects as well and of course about the nonobservant who neglect their duties, the mitzvot. I became acquainted with pure Judaism which is unknown to most Israelis. During that time I came to the conclusion that we should separate the state from religion to prevent Judaism from becoming increasingly eroded by politics and brilliant Talmud scholars like rabbi Ovadia Yossef from being corrupted. We're now twenty years along, and the secularists are still absorbing our energy; they live off our Judaism. A separation could keep Judaism pure, and the secular Jews would miss Judaism and would quickly return to the faith.

The Israeli *ba'alei t'shuvah* often remind others that they have led a completely secular "sinful" life: their absolute freedom meant a "dissipated lifestyle" and a "constant violation of God's law." They're often proud of having taken this step and usually carry with them a photo from their "sinful" time to prove their metamorphosis. This is part of their confession of guilt. They want to cleanse their soul and often do this in a more extreme manner than Jews who were Orthodox to start with. Studying in the yeshiva is their responsibility as Jews. I. A. continues:

> The secularists deny their responsibility as Jews. This is the basis of the present conflict between the Orthodox and the secularists. We, the Orthodox, preserve the Jewish people. Being Jewish isn't exactly fun. We bear the heavy burden of the law. The *hilonim*, the Zionists, have betrayed us, but we continue to do our work as Jews. At home I try, without forcing my ideas on people, to explain the importance of the mitzvot to twenty people every month. After a number of meetings I ask them if they could observe a few from now on. If they can't or won't, then I regret to have to tell them that they'd better not come again next time. You have to start somewhere.

The well-known Sephardic yeshiva for the newly Orthodox, Or haChaim (light of life), is housed in a dilapidated building in Mea Shearim in Jerusalem. In front of the office of Rabbi Reuven Elbaz from Morocco (1945), there is a notice from a building contractor that shows a picture of the new yeshiva complex with dormitories and lecture halls, all financed from abroad and by the government. At present Elbaz gives his lectures, which are usually well attended, in old dilapidated rooms. Rabbi Elbaz, who is known for his charisma and his persuasiveness, usually doesn't beat about the bush during his lectures:

> The European, materialistic, animal-like, secular lifestyle is good for the goyim but not for Jews, and certainly not for Sephardic Jews. The Western criteria for success—a car, a large apartment, vacations in distant places—are false. The Jews must be called back to their own culture. The Jewish people can live without land and without money, but not without the Torah. The angels in heaven don't make a distinction between believing and nonbelieving Jews. In the belly of the Jewish mother they already learn about the meaning of being Jewish.

Rabbi Elbaz came to Israel via France in 1956 and founded his yeshiva in 1967 after the Six-Day War. It is the largest yeshiva for new Sephardic believers in Jerusalem and has approximately four hundred students. Rabbi Rafael Eliyahu came from Morocco around the same time as Elbaz and was involved in the establishment of Or haChaim and is Elbaz's right-hand man. In a small, cluttered office that is filled to bursting with tapes of Orthodox texts, Orthodox text-books, and propaganda material, he answers a constantly ringing telephone. "It's like this all day long," says Eliyahu as he notes down an appointment with 250 youths from Ramat Gan who, as he says, "want *t'shuvah.*" Meanwhile some new believers appear at his door, looking in with curiosity, and ask Eliyahu for money. "They're going to schools to talk about repentance with the children," explains Eliyahu.

Rabbi Ovadia Yossef is their spiritual leader. Since 1984 Eliyahu and Elbaz have voted for Shas, the party that promulgates pride and self-awareness of the Oriental Jews in Israel—as Elbaz does in his lessons. Elbaz concentrates on the "return" of the Oriental youths in the neglected districts in Israel. According to him these youths have started using drugs because of their "contact with modern Ashkenazi culture." He tries to convince them that the lifestyle of their grandfathers is the only one that is good for the Jews. Once they are in the yeshiva where they often get housing, they become convinced that they can save themselves and their souls through repentance. To illustrate this he gives a rough outline of the life that awaits those who don't change. Elbaz teaches throughout he country. He appeals to the feelings of inferiority of many Sephardic Jews, stimulates their interest in mysticism and spirituality, and strengthens their solidarity. Talmud and Torah study is compelling, and the students who are between fifteen and twenty-five years old see regular, intensive study as a means of developing. Elbaz points out the dangers of a nonspiritual life and shows photos of youths who actually went through the transformation—in three weeks he makes them into different people. Full-time study in the yeshiva is the best use of time for the *ba'al t'shuvah.*

To the exasperation of left-wing secular Israel, the Israeli government pays for the training of Orthodox Jews, therefore also for that of the new Orthodox. In total it spends at least 200 million shekels yearly on "recruitment activities." Money for Bible lessons and lectures comes from funds with names like Biblical Culture, Reception of Spiritual Immigrants, Supplementary Religious Education of the Ministry of Religious Affairs, and *Haredi* Culture of the Ministry of Education. These amounts have decreased since Meretz leader Yossi Sarid became minister of education, but they continue to account for a considerable part of the total budget.

In 1998 *Ha'aretz* investigated the financing of these recruitment activities. Shahar Ilan, the previously mentioned correspondent for religious affairs who was assigned this investigation, is accused of anti-Semitism by some *haredim*. In 1998 he wrote a series of articles about the *haredi* and Orthodox communities for which he received a journalism prize. The Ministry of Religious Affairs considers him "unreliable" because, according to a spokesperson of the ministry, "as a representative of the left-wing secular establishment he intends to place us in a bad light by depicting us as a parasitic minority, even though we demand only what is due to us."

Secular Jewish adolescents from home and abroad and Israeli soldiers are easy prey for ultra-Orthodox preachers. The first step to an Orthodox life is often a conversation with such a preacher or with a rabbi, a discussion with friends, or a visit to a yeshiva. The hospitality of Orthodox families who invite the "searchers" for a Sabbath meal often clinches things. A Jewish student from abroad walking around near the Wailing Wall on Friday evening has a good chance of being invited to such a meal by Jeffrey Seidel, a former hippie from Chicago. He became Orthodox and in 1981 immigrated to Israel, where he has been working for the Jewish Student Information Center since 1996. His office is in the old city of Jerusalem, but his work area is the Wailing Wall. He is especially busy on Friday evenings when large crowds of praying and dancing people congregate there.

"Preachers" like Seidel have as their goal to change Jewish unbelievers into Jewish believers who wear their Jewish identity with pride. Armed with flyers, he goes daily to the Wailing Wall, but he also recruits on the streets, at the universities, and in bus stations. "It is our spiritual duty to invite Jewish travelers and students. Their souls, and with it the Jewish people, must be saved. If I approach non-Jews, I get into trouble with the Ministry of Religious Affairs, which considers contact with goyim as doing missionary work. I can accept a Christian who is in the process of converting, but I always have to ask if someone is Jewish before I offer him a meal."

The above-mentioned yeshivas are active in this area too. In addition, they recruit abroad, where most yeshivas for the newly religious have branches. They try to attract the attention of nonreligious Jews through the Internet and with flyers written in easily accessible English. The newest development in this area is the possibility of being photographed at the Wailing Wall via the Internet. Since the end of 1999, a new photo of the Wailing Wall appears every minute in a special window on the Web site, www.thewall.org. With a special camera—which, by the way, is pointed only at the area of the Wall where the men pray—those at home can photograph their friends at a certain point in time and then print it immediately afterward.

The initiative for this activity came from *Aish haTorah* (Fire of the Torah), a yeshiva for new believers that was founded in 1974 by an American rabbi, Noah Weinberg. In the course of the years this rabbi has established a worldwide organization, with branches in 120 cities. The main building is across from the Wailing Wall. The purpose of the organization is to prevent the assimilation of Jews into other cultures and to link Jewish believers all over the world to their Jewish identity. In their lectures, rabbis from the organization usually approach young Jews with questions like "In what way is Judaism relevant in my life?"; "Who is God?"; and "Why should I have to marry a Jew?"

In the hall of the main building in the old city of Jerusalem lie glossy magazines with articles by rabbis, and flyers with stories of "returnees." There is also a small brochure titled "Four misconceptions Jews have about Judaism." Inside the folder is the assertion that the yeshiva has been confronted for twenty years with the question "Why be Jewish?" The advice in the folder is as follows: "If you want to deepen your appreciation of the joy and meaning in being Jewish, here's how you can get some information about our seminars and learning opportunities." One of the previously mentioned misconceptions, printed in four different colors, says, "Being religious is an escape." "Absolutely untrue," says Seidel, who is standing near the Wailing Wall. "Judaism teaches us that we are responsible for the whole world. In the Talmud it says that each one of us must feel that the world has been created for him and that we must take care of it." The second misconception is "Religion takes the fun out of life." Seidel shakes his head and says that God, like our parents, wants us to have as much pleasure as possible in life.

On Friday afternoon activists of Shas and Chabad (a contraction of the Hebrew *chochma* [wisdom], *bina* [insight], and *da'at* [knowledge]) stand near the entrances of shopping centers—even in the seaside resort Eilat!—to bring secular Jews back to religious Judaism. These activists are usually Sephardic Jews who got in touch with

Judaism in the same way. They set up a small table on which they place yarmulkes, tefillin, and prayer books. In addition, they offer tapes with religious music and books for sale. From time to time they help a secular passer-by to put on the tefillin and to say a prayer, or they try to convince someone through a serious conversation. Such a brief experience can be the start of a change of identity at a later time in life. The Messianic Chabad movement is especially active in this way. For many years Menachem Mendel Schneerson, the Lubav-itcher rabbi who died in New York in 1994, regularly sent a number of his followers to Israel. These were always young, just-married men who were to bring alive Orthodox Judaism and to start a large Jewish family. Rabbi Yossef Hecht from Eilat is proud as a peacock. Together with fifty other just-married rabbis without children, he was sent out by the rebbe himself to turn nonreligious Jews into Orthodox Jews and to start a large family in Israel.

> When we came to Eilat in 1980, there was nothing but sun and sand. There were four synagogues, the city council was *hiloni*, and there was no *haredi* like me, and the Sabbath was violated on a large scale. There were no mikvot and the kashrut level was low. Now we have twenty-four synagogues, two mikvot, and women wearing wigs push baby carriages *beEzrat haShem* on Friday evening, hundreds of homes have been made kosher, and our food is ultra-kosher. Soon we will have a store selling wigs and a clothing store for Orthodox men. All the elements for an Orthodox life are present for the inhab-itants of Eilat. In the city council there are two Shas representatives and two Orthodox, including one *ba'al t'shuvah*.

The rebbe sent Hecht and his wife first to Safed where 95 percent of the population now is newly religious and supports Chabad. After he had been in Safed (two of his eleven children were born there) for two years, he received a letter from the rebbe. "He wanted me to apply for a job as a rabbi," says Hecht from behind his desk which is covered by documents, scribbled notes, and books. From the wall, the life-sized, bearded rabbi looks into the room. Hecht looks at him with affection and picks up a photo album of his departure for the Holy Land. The photos show the farewell of the rebbe. "He launched a revolution by directing us to start talking to non-Orthodox Jews. In that way I became the Ashkenazi chief rabbi of Eilat."

For Orthodox Jewish Israelis, Eilat is the twentieth-century

Sodom and Gomorrah. Hecht says, "Of course we were aware of the stigma of Eilat, but we bring its inhabitants the Judaism that is theirs. They have forgotten their roots but they are Jewish nonetheless, and they are still one with us. We miss the atmosphere of Bnei Brak, Mea Shearim, and Safed, but it's our task to bring the Torah and the mitzvot to non-Orthodox Jews." It is over 104 degrees Fahrenheit outside, but Hecht is dressed suitably for his trip to the synagogue later in the day, a fifteen-minute uphill walk. "We organize lectures with speakers from Bnei Brak and Kfar Chabad, we invite non-Orthodox Jews to celebrate the holidays with us, we blow the shofar in hospitals and in the city, and we ask the minister for money for education and synagogues."

"We're not Messianic—the rebbe wouldn't approve of that—but every Jew who is not involved in Judaism feels a lack," says Hecht with conviction. "Jewish standards and values have suffered a decline. All of our grandparents were rabbis or at least lived according to Jewish laws. The return is a part of our tradition which many of us have left behind. Everyone has rules in his life, every job brings with it certain dress codes, and every person needs a structure. Everyone needs something to hold on to, and Judaism is such a thing for us."

Hemmed in by the Gemara, the *Shulchan Arukh*, and books by Maimonides, two of his sons *"lern."* Another son is playing a computer game in the adjoining room that houses a television set and numerous videos of the rabbi's appearances. The lady of the house brings a glass of water. She helps her husband with his work. She not only prepares all the meals but in schools she tells women about family hygiene and about the use of the *mikvah*. She talks to non-Orthodox parents, and she was responsible for the establishment of a religious day-care center in Eilat. The first *mikvah* in town was built in the eighties with money from the Ministry of Religious Affairs; she is very proud of it because of the rebbe's role. Beaming, Rabbi Hecht continues: "Rain never falls in Eilat, and nine hundred liters of water are supposed to run in a *mikvah*—without human intervention. I prayed for rain. Then it rained for nine hours. Ritual cleansing can be done in the sea, but women prefer not to because it has to be done at night under the supervision of a woman who makes sure that the hair goes completely under water and that the woman's body is uncovered." (Construction of the third *mikvah* has meanwhile been started.)

As "Master of the Answer" Hecht has an explanation for the great number of nonbelieving Jews on earth:

> God has sent millions of Jews into the secular world in order to enrich the Orthodox community with knowledge. This means that the use of the returned is as someone with a secular past who can add modernity to Orthodox life. We don't worry about the Jewish soul because in every secular Jew there is a religious soul which will eventually take him to God. Everyone will study the Torah when the rebbe declares himself as the Messiah. That is his task, just like the rebuilding of the Temple, the third one in Jewish history. As long as that hasn't happened, he still lives. His departure doesn't have the usual meaning of departing from the earth, or dying.

According to Hecht, the greatest proof of the success of his efforts is the establishment of the Organization against Harediza-tion. Rachel Gilad, an Argentine Jewish doctor who moved to Eilat ten years ago, has been the chair of this organization for a year. She regularly organizes demonstrations in Eilat in front of schools and synagogues, she prints flyers against the expansion of Orthodox Judaism in Eilat and in Israel, and she gives lectures. She attributes the increasing *haredization* to the composition of the population of Eilat. Sitting on one of the sun-drenched terraces of Eilat, Gilad says,

> Poor people with a Sephardic background are receptive to the rhet-oric of the Orthodox city council member Samuel Pilus. The char-acter of the city is changing. Ten years ago there wasn't any pre-torn toilet paper for sale in supermarkets [the Jewish law forbids work on the Sabbath and therefore forbids tearing off toilet paper] and you could still order an espresso in Eilat on Saturday. Now pre-torn toilet paper is sold and you can no longer order espresso on Saturday. At the gates of the high schools there are "preachers" who are trying to influence the children. Whole families in Eilat, a city that lives on tourism, are going over to Orthodox Judaism. That's why we are demonstrating against this "khomeinization."

Some army bases also have synagogues, yarmulkes and prayer books lie ready, and rabbis come by to give out flyers and other propaganda material. An Orthodox officer can ask a soldier, who finds it hard to refuse, to form a minyan one time; he can do this a second time, and after a few serious conversations the soldier may become Orthodox. The Israeli army command doesn't want to reveal anything about these practices. It's impossible for a non-Jew to visit an army base, and for a Jew it's difficult to get in as well. Nevertheless the Israeli journalist Yossi Bar-Mocha of *Ha'aretz*, who wears a crocheted yarmulke, published an article about this phenomenon in 1998. He did a report on the Shimshon army base in the Galilee. He knew that there was a synagogue there because he did his retraining exercises there in the eighties. That synagogue even won an architecture prize. During the eighties the synagogue was closed because there weren't enough Orthodox Jews, but today there is no problem getting a minyan.

The people with whom Bar-Mocha spoke for the article are angry with him and have announced that they are not allowed to say anything about this article and about life on the base. Bar-Mocha explains:

> When I asked the army command for approval of a visit to the base, I said that I was interested in the synagogue and in the Orthodox life on the base. It's a great advantage that I wear a yarmulke and that I'm Sephardic because it's Shas which is primarily active there. I traveled there with a young lady of the army who was present during all the conversations. No one knew that I wanted to write an article about the *ba'alei t'shuvah* movement on the base. I didn't even need to ask questions: the office of the sergeant made you feel as if you were in the office of a rabbi or a Shas activist. Life-size pictures of Kedouri the Kabalist, the Lubavitcher rebbe, and of Ovadia Yossef hang on the walls. When I started to ask questions, no one refused to answer. The commandant of the base even said: "The Orthodox life here is terrific."

"We lost our son through the army base," say Sophia and Dan Mahler. Sophia works as an educator, and Dan is a surgeon.

> He came home with flyers, with halakhic analyses by various rabbis, and with commentaries on the "Bible texts of the week." These things were filled with political messages and the need for "return" of the Jewish people and the coming of the Messiah. Although he had never shown any interest in religious rituals, he suddenly started to lay tefillin. He said that we didn't devote ourselves to things for which Jews are born, and according to him it was supposed to be our task to live according to God's law, and

because we didn't do that we were not Jewish enough. Our kitchen wasn't kosher; he no longer wanted to eat at home. We built two sinks, cleaned our pans and our cutlery, and we bought an extra set of dishes. Yet he hardly ever came home: we weren't dressed modestly enough. We adapted and no longer wore short-sleeved T-shirts. And when I knew that he was coming, I'd put on a long skirt. Still he didn't come. Now the reason was that we traveled on the Sabbath.

This happened twenty years ago, but these parents are still perplexed.

It's unbelievable that one of our children whom we brought up with universal values and whom we taught knowledge of science and technology and fine arts is now concerned only with the Torah. The humanist prophets Jeremiah and Isaiah are ignored! It's painful that our son let himself be dragged into the irrational limited world of mysticism. He has returned to the first millennium while we're entering the third. Since he's had children, he no longer comes at all. Our world is a threat to his family.

Dan points to the bookcase:

Our library is irreligious, our art is irreligious, our food is not kosher enough, and our clothing remains strange. Moreover, we delay the coming of the Messiah with our sinful way of life. He is especially afraid that we'll give his children the wrong answers to their questions and that we'll express ourselves in a negative way about Judaism. But I'm not antireligious, I'm only against missionary work among the Jews. We invited them for Purim, and we promised to go to Bnei Brak with their shopping list and that we would dress as he wished. I told him that I won't talk about God with his children and that I won't mention Darwin. But he isn't coming.

The Mahlers feel that the born-again network has expanded into a self-assured, efficient "missionary machine" that is subsidized by the government. Dan continues:

The ultra-Orthodox "preachers" all express themselves in the same way and are good at using their charm and their rhetorical skills. They appeal to the insecurities of adolescents who are easy to influence, and they say repeatedly that the secular existence has no meaning. Moreover, the "preachers" are masters in avoiding critical questions, and they try to detach the newly religious as quickly as possible from his old surroundings.

"The *mitzvot* lend themselves well to brainwashing," says Sophia.

> They don't leave you alone for a moment. There's a prayer for everything you do—going to the toilet, dressing, or eating. Through this brainwashing the "candidates" are quick as lightning "re-educated" into Orthodox Jews. People who let their faith depend on the observance of the 613 commands and prohibitions close themselves off all day and all night long in a world that is dictated by axioms: God's truths. Everything that's outside the divine paradigm is a lie, and everyone who associates with non-Orthodox people sins. And the worst thing is that our secular leaders betray the Zionist, humanist, and democratic values of Israeli society. The government of Netanyahu placed the Ministry of Education in the hands of Shas. Fortunately it's now in the hands of Meretz leader Sarid, who gives the Orthodox less money. It's time in Israel for a constitution that removes religion from politics.

The anger of the Mahlers has not yet cooled off; in 1998 they published a book called *The Soul's Hunters*. "We wrote the book because 'recruiting' is a big social problem." Since 1984 the authors have been active in Aleh, the Organization against ultra-Orthodox Domination. Through Aleh the Mahlers are often approached by fellow sufferers who ask for advice. Sometimes they refer them to a psychologist, to a secular Bible expert, or to a lawyer, and once in a great while they invite the parents. The families always seem to be wrestling with feelings of guilt, and they try to break through the logic of the newly religious family member. The latter action is useless, say the Mahlers, because it is impossible to refute religious logic with arguments—faith doesn't accept reason. In the last two years the Mahlers received an average of three telephone calls per day, and they began to find this too difficult. Besides, they kept repeating themselves. That's the reason they decided to write everything down in a book which they hope "might be able to serve as handbook for families who are in danger of losing one or two children to religion."

"This book hurts," says Dov Elboim, and you can see in his eyes that he means what he says, for Elboim is a *chozer bish'elah*. He lights up a cigarette in a café of Tel Aviv University where he is working on a dissertation on Maimonides.

> I understand the pain of the Mahler family and I can even identify with the break in the family. My decision to lead a secular life has cost me my relationship with my parents. This loss is barely made up by the difficult contacts with the secularists. They don't understand that the war against winning souls by devious methods, deceptions, and other dirty tricks can only be carried out by obtaining reliable information about the *haredi* community—that means without the aggression and the rancorous feelings shown by the Mahlers. With this information the youths who are seduced by the messages of the missionaries and are considering the "return" can learn where they will end up and can then still reconsider this step.
>
> This book hurts because it offends numerous families; it hurts because of the ignorance with which the subject is treated; and it hurts because it is based on prejudices. The book is disappointing because it doesn't fill the need for a book that provides the means to approach the newly faithful. Yet they call this book a "manual." There is a need for ways to oppose the propaganda machine of the Orthodox Jews. But the secularists have to try and understand that the *haredim*, just like I, were born in surroundings where it is usual not to serve in the army but to go to a yeshiva and to speak Yiddish. All this is changing, but you can't blame them for it.

Elboim has a hard time forgiving the authors for depicting the milieu where he grew up as being against Western culture. And he thinks it's even worse that the *haredi* family is shown as one that takes violence and hate for granted. "Some illustrations in the book belong in anti-Semitic publications," says Elboim. Despite the comments he is making now, he finds it difficult to talk about this subject. He feels that the most hateful cartoon (on p. 279) shows an Orthodox man in a window who is inviting a child for the Sabbath. On the wall of the house are the words: "destruction, hooliganism, embezzlement, violence, fraud, deception, sabotage, arson, throwing rocks, disgusting actions."

According to Elboim these secular prejudices are formed by an accumulation of quotations from newspapers, especially from left-wing newspapers. "Shahar Ilan [the correspondent for religious affairs of *Ha'aretz*], for example, is an anti-Semite. He writes series of articles against the *haredim* without knowing this community from the inside. He says for example that ultra-Orthodox families want to have more children because they will then receive more money from the government. That's a racist remark." Elboim seems hurt rather than angry when he speaks of this. Dan Mahler, who drew the cartoon, is angry: "The ultra-Orthodox family isn't all sweetness and warmth as they always try to portray it. They study, they help one another, and they pray, but on Saturdays they throw bags with shit and stones at people who drive into Bar-Ilan Street, they set fire to rooms of those who leave, and in Jerusalem they beat up a man who looked at television on Saturday. Everything occurs there which occurs in other communities, but it's done in the name of God."

It's precisely this ultrasecularism, the explicitly anti-*haredi* attitude that stirs up the *Kulturkampf* (culture war) in Israel, according to Elboim. He feels that the book shows all sorts of arrogance and ignorance with respect to the Jewish religion and the *haredi* community that are at the bottom of the *Kulturkampf*. Elboim comments:

> Some young Israelis who were brought up in an absolutely secular system and who are influenced by an arrogant, prejudiced, and fanatically anti-*haredi* attitude at home and in their surroundings, are surprised when they become acquainted with holy texts—even if it's through the cunning agents of the "missionary industry." Suddenly they see the beauty, the wisdom, the depth, and the literary value of these writings. Sometimes one text by rabbi Nachman or by Breslav is sufficient to accept everything, everything that passes for real Judaism according to the *haredim*. I know what I'm talking about because I've seen it happen.

"That's what happened to me," says Moshe Chaim Levy. He says a prayer and with a piece of pita bread he takes some hummus from a bowl. With a number of new believers he drinks wine and eats homemade food in a small restaurant—kosher, of course—in the mystic city of Safed. For years Levy disobeyed God. It's an episode in his life that he regrets, but he's unwilling to say more about it than that he drove a car without a license, dealt in drugs, and that he hung around in "shady places of entertainment" as he now calls them. Levy says: "HaShem called me to Him before things really went wrong. For three years I've been living in an orderly world that has a three-thousand-year-old, black-and-white tradition. No one in the gray-tinted Western world dares to distinguish good from evil. I am reborn; I'm only three years old but I have more answers to my questions than I had in all thirty-three years of my secular life." In 1965 Levy was born as Moshe Grass in the southern California city of Carlsbad, where he graduated from the Academy of Arts. He blesses the meal with the words "Blessed art Thou, our God. . . ." and continues to eat.

Both of his table companions feel reborn as well: thirty-one-year-old Rachel Levine from South Africa, who is called Rifka in Israel and works in a candle factory, and an American youth who wants to remain anonymous but admits frankly that he used to lead a sinful life. God showed them the right path, too, and he has preserved them from a licentious and wicked life. "I was constantly breaking God's law," says Rifka. "For example, I ate ice cream after meals with meat. In Johannesburg there was some *Yiddishkeit* in our home: we celebrated Pesach and Hanukkah, and I lit candles every Friday night, but after that I went out and ate shrimp. God placed me on the road to Safed." She kisses her siddur, opens it, and murmurs some prayers while the others continue to talk.

The restaurant has a partly secular, partly Orthodox atmosphere; its owner is newly religious and is from the United States. The language is English mixed with Hebrew religious terms. The conversation is interspersed with Bible verses, sayings from old rabbinical sources, and a large number of clichés. All the guests have gone through the major turnaround from a secular to a religious life. Zalmon Bear Halevy Tornek sits at a table in front of the window with his wife. "He was a cowboy," says Levy. Then Zalmon pulls from his inside pocket a photo of a bearded man with long hair and a cowboy hat sitting on a horse. "That's me," says Zalmon, beaming. "As a cowboy I had a large ranch in Colorado, and now I work here as a *sofer*." As it says on his business card, he buys and sells Torahs, repairs tefillin, mezuzot, tallitot, and *kippot*. "All of us are ambassadors of HaShem Who has called us to Him," he says seriously. "After the *Kadosh haBaruch* called me for this task, I simply put on another hat," he smiles and taps his black high hat. His wife is also newly Orthodox and is from the United States. She wears a charming wig and works at the Ascent, a hotel in Safed where Jews who want to "return" can stay for free and can follow lessons in Judaism; this is set up by the director, Rabbi Samuel Leiter, a "returned" American ex-hippie.

In front of the faucet in the corner the guests are waiting their turn to wash their hands and say a prayer. Some don't know yet exactly how the water has to run over their hands and they get help from those more advanced in Jewish doctrine. "The life of a *ba'al t'shuvah* isn't easy," says Levy as he sits back down at the table.

> We're afraid to make mistakes. Last week I was invited by an Orthodox family to learn how to ready the house for the Sabbath. For five minutes I stood with bags of kitchen waste in my left and my right hands because I didn't know which bag contained milk waste and which contained meat waste. Sometimes I turn on the light at times when it is forbidden, I tear toilet paper on the Sabbath, or I just stick something in my mouth. All that isn't allowed.
>
> All of us are in the same boat, and we know what it's like to look at women. A "real" yeshiva boy isn't used to that. That's one of the most difficult things.

Levy, his head covered with a brightly colored yarmulke, continues: "We *frum* ones aren't supposed to appreciate female beauty." He pulls out his journal and opens it to a page where he has pasted in a picture of the German model Claudia Schiffer. His table companions watch. Rifka says, "Women distract your thoughts from God, and married men can be tempted. . . ." Levy interrupts her: "But why do married women make themselves beautiful with expensive wigs, and why can't they be beautiful with their own real hair?" Rifka replies, "It is written that a married woman without a head cover is like a naked woman. And if we ask the whys and wherefores we no longer need God and religion."

A middle-aged Hasidic Jew appears in the doorway with two identically dressed boys. They are greeted enthusiastically. "Everything is going well, *baruch haShem*," says the man. He is an Englishman who turns out to be married to a newly Orthodox Dutch Jew and who lived in the Netherlands for nine years. In 1998 they opened a store across from Zalmon's business, where they sell homemade cheese and buttermilk. In contrast to the others, A. B.

comes from an Orthodox environment but was secular for nine years—then twenty years ago he became Orthodox again.

When he was sixteen and living in London, he became interested in secular subjects like sociology, history, and geography. His parents sent him to a public school because they wanted him to get a good job. Then, as he says, he realized how primitive religion is. He studied sociology, immersed himself in Zen Buddhism, smoked hash, and used LSD a few times. But he came to the conclusion that the modern Western world was "sick" and "empty." He calls the ten secular years of his life "destructive" and "superficial." He missed the religious duties that he had originally been relieved to shake off. He lived for his own pleasure. But a Jew is not on earth to have fun in life.

"Now, *baruch haShem*, I've been Orthodox for more than twenty years," says A. B. the next day in the cheese store, where he helps his wife from time to time.

> After some years I wondered what was wrong with primitiveness. Real primitiveness is linked to the divine. And what is progress after all? Didn't the Germans use technology to murder? Is there much difference in outlook between the years 1919 and 1999? Has humanity progressed? Are we less cruel? Is there peace? Progress isn't bad, but what do we do with it? The secular world is separate from God. The secularists and the goys enjoy the present without a spiritual goal. Jews live to serve the Creator. By nature the Jewish people has a greater spiritual capacity. God clearly trusts the Jewish people to obey all 613 mitzvot. God asked other peoples to accept the mitzvot, but only the Jews answered: "all that the Eternal one has spoken, we will do, and after that we shall hear" [Exod. 24:7], in that order. The non-Jews are not inferior; they can reach the same level by observing the seven Noahide laws. Actually it's just like in a family—the parents expect more from the talented child. That's how it is with the Jews as well: God has chosen us.

The return is not an unqualified success for every searching Jewish youth. For example, the previously mentioned Moshe Levy from Safed, who studied in Or Sameach and in some yeshivas in Jerusalem and in Safed, decided to stop.

> I must admit that I let myself be influenced. I literally felt I was a "master of the answer." When I started *"lernen"* in Or Sameach

after a meeting with Jeffrey Seidel, I knew very little—my *Yid-dishkeit* didn't extend beyond eating bagels. Therefore I was an easy prey for the rabbis. They tell you that you have to surrender your personal freedom and that you have to live for God and for the Jewish community. They offered us—weak and searching youths—an antiscientific, antidemocratic way of thinking and presented it in an un-academic way. They compare the university to the yeshiva: the former teaches doubt and the latter teaches truth. And the rabbis don't like individuals who ask the why and wherefore. That's how it was with many subjects. I had this arrogant attitude also, and because of it I lost friends. One of them married a non-Jew, and I wrote him what the rabbis told me: "Hitler's wish will be granted if many Jews make such a marriage."

The Torah is fantastic, but it contains a lot of dogmatic junk, and in the yeshivas they have "good stuff on gentiles." When I noticed that anti-Gentile feelings were drummed into us in the yeshiva, I started asking questions. For example, I'm still wondering in what aspect Israel has to be, as the Orthodox say, "a light for all the nations." Remarks that are made here about the spiritual and moral inferiority of goyim would be called racist elsewhere. They want to prevent contacts between unmarried pupils and goyim of the other sex as much as possible. Once I asked during a class if a gentile has a soul. The rabbi mentioned the massacres near the Rhine in the Middle Ages, the inquisition in Spain, and the Holocaust, and then said he doubted that people who did such things could have a soul.

I found these statements so shocking that I made a kind of study of them because I wanted to know for sure. For example, I asked one hundred Orthodox Jews if it is a mitzvah to save the life of a unbeliever. Six of them answered "yes" but rushed to add that saving on the Sabbath is a problem. The life of a goy is apparently less important than the Sabbath. I became frustrated by their arrogance. I made the rounds of yeshivas to find out more about the attitude toward unbelievers. They pride themselves on the fact that after three weeks of *lernen* day and night, no student would get it into his head to marry a non-Jew. And if that were to happen, a "whole generation of Jews would be lost."

I am a *chozer b't'shuvah* and *bish'elah*—not that I'm turning my back on God, but I want to keep my own character and be able to give my own answers and above all be able to ask my own questions. I don't need a yeshiva to be observant. Besides, the rabbis are training a generation of voters who have antidemocratic thoughts. The lessons are not apolitical: many yeshivas are linked to an

Orthodox political party. In addition, the yeshiva heads themselves—and their students in imitation—follow the advice of the
spiritual leader without asking questions. As soon as the rabbis
noticed that I asked critical questions I was shut up, or they were
tolerated at the end of the lesson, or I was told to reformulate them.
As if questions and answers are supposed to take place according
to a certain pattern. When the rabbi said that you asked a clever
question you had to be on your guard because with this he meant
nothing more than to say that this was an age-old question for
which he had an age-old answer.

The attempt of the government to bring together opposites that are
increasingly growing apart, the religious and the secular, shows that
religion is a government affair and will most likely remain so. It
wants above all to preserve the unity within the state, but the
struggle for dominance between these two poles has led to extreme
polarization during the last years. The government of Prime Minister Netanyahu, who sympathized with the Orthodox right-wing of
the Israeli people, spent a lot of money on religious education,
yeshivas, and other religious institutions. The government of Barak,
who appointed an ultra-secular minister of education, gave money
to Hillel, which helps the newly secular for the first time in Israel's
history. Prime Minister Sharon's nominations of Limor Livnat and
Avraham Ravitz as minister of education and deputy minister of
education respectively show that he is not hostile toward the religious part of the population. The independent position of
Meshulam Nahari, who is responsible for the educational system of
Shas, also points in that direction. It can rightfully be said that the
extremes are growing increasingly apart and that no group will ever
feel at home with a government— of whatever character—that continues to compromise. Because this situation continues, the separation of religion and state that is desired by many secular Israelis will
for the time being remain an idle hope.

SIX

THE WEST BANK

a false messiah?

"Prepare to cross the Jordan, together with all this people, into the
land that I am giving to the Israelites."

Joshua 1:2

"A season is set for everything, a time for every experience under
heaven: . . . a time for planting and a time for uprooting the
planted."

Ecclesiastes 3:1, 2

"'Wye' is a dangerous agreement," says the settler
Chanan Porat as he gazes into the distance of
Judea from his birth place Kfar Etzion. As a Knesset member of the
National Religious Party, Porat caused the fall of Prime Minister
Benjamin Netanyahu's government in February 1999 because of his
dissatisfaction with the Wye accord that was signed on October 23,
1998. This step caused a historic decline in Porat's popularity in the
National Religious Party and also marked his political downfall.

After spending half a year opposing Barak from within Tekuma (literally, "rebellion," "renewal"), a party established in March 1999, Porat decided in November of that year to leave politics.

> Being in the opposition under Prime Minister Barak is wasted time, and I could no longer participate in Netanyahu's government. After all, it says "You shall love the Lord your God with all your heart and with all your soul and with all your might" [Deut. 6:5]. How could Netanyahu, who once was our leader, sign an agreement that draws the line with the Palestinian territory at barely five kilometers from my home here in Judea? Netanyahu has "made a covenant with Death, concluded a pact with the kingdom of Death" [Isaiah 28:15] and in this way he helped Barak come to power.
>
> After the transfer of 13 percent of the West Bank, Yasir Arafat will have as much as 18 percent of our land in his hands! Why do they need a state? The Palestinians can live here in *Medinat Yisrael* if they demonstrate their loyalty to the Jewish state with a test.

Porat feels that this also applies to the Arabs who live within the "Green Line"—the temporary eastern border of Israel that was drawn in 1967 after the Six-Day War. "Why do Arabs have an automatic right to vote even though they're against the state? In Israel they can get autonomy, but no army and no Ministry of Foreign Affairs. I'm against 'Wye' because it leads to an independent Palestinian state and, in addition, it conflicts with the frame of mind of the Jewish people which wants to let the Zionist flame burn and has a definite need for 'action.'"

The silence on the hill is broken by the call to prayer in the Arab villages Ohal Choel, Bet Omar, and Bet Fadjar. According to Wye, these villages form the border with Kfar Etzion. Porat walks slowly; he limps slightly because he was wounded in the Sinai during the Yom Kippur War. He seems plunged in his own world in which every Jew still resists tooth and nail giving away Jewish land. A world in which all Jews have reached the spiritual level that gives them the understanding that *Eretz Yisrael* is of vital importance for the continued existence of the Jewish people. It is unclear if Porat realizes that it's that very frame of mind of the Jewish people as well as that of the National Religious Party that has changed and that he's the one who hasn't adapted to the new reality. In actual fact,

Porat's war is over. The National Religious Party has become more moderate, and negotiating with the Palestinian Liberation Front hasn't been taboo for a long time. But Porat—a father of ten children, not all of whom have remained Orthodox—continues fighting and has chosen to continue the battle outside parliament by concentrating on training a new generation of religious Zionists. A long historic development, as he calls it, will make the Jewish people realize that possession of the biblical land is essential for Jewish identity.

Porat wanted to keep the flame of pure religious Zionism burning at any price, and that's why, as chairman of the Knesset Constitution, Law, and Justice Commission, he proposed a call for early elections three days after the Wye accord was signed. Porat's proposal was approved on December 21, 1998. He had hoped that his party would be stronger after the elections and didn't imagine at all that he would be pushed out. After the last domestic elections, Porat ended up in eleventh place. The National Religious Party turned out to consist of an extreme minority and a moderate majority. On March 4 Porat left the party, because the "National Religious Party no longer battles with heart and soul for *Eretz Yisrael*," and joined the previously mentioned Tekuma party. On May 17, 1998—the day of the elections—the National Religious Party obtained five seats. Tekuma, together with three other right-wing, splinter parties—Herut (Freedom), Moledet (Motherland), and Ichud Leumi (National Unity)—formed the new right-wing block that won four seats.

After being in the opposition for a number of months, Porat retired from politics in order to take the message of religious Zionist activism to the younger generation by means of lectures throughout the country and lessons in yeshivas. In addition he is editor of the newspaper *Me'at min ha'Or* (A Fraction of the Light). Porat says,

> It is of great importance to try and make the Torah accessible to the younger generation and to foster more love for the Torah. Yesterday, for example, I gave a lecture in the north of the country to secular eighteen-year-olds. I told them that the Torah isn't only for believers and that you don't have to be Orthodox to love the Torah. I advised them to involve the Torah in our presence in *Eretz Yisrael*. When we started discussing the peace talks, one of the boys asked what I think about *Shalom Achshav* (Peace Now). I told them that I love "peace" but that I hate the idea that it has to be established

"now." It would be naive to think that this is possible. It's the same mistake made by the Jews who want the Messiah now. I stressed the importance of the historical process and said that it will certainly take one or two more generations before we can make peace. Meanwhile we will continue to develop the land. And I told them that we're working on relations among the Jews themselves and on relations between Jews and Arabs. But I said emphatically that this is the land of the Jews, just as God said to Esau that his "own dwelling was far away." The Arabs may stay here and be happy, but they will have to accept the fact that they are subjects of the state of Israel to which they have to be loyal.

Supporters and opponents of Porat call his fall even more tragic than that of Netanyahu. For thirty years Porat was an influential, pious Zionist. During the War of Independence in 1948 he was three years old when he was evacuated from Kfar Etzion right before it was captured by the Jordanian Legion. During the Six-Day War in 1967, he was one of the parachutists who "liberated" the Old City of Jerusalem and the Temple Mount. At the Wailing Wall he heard the legendary phrase *Yerushalayim beYadenu* (Jerusalem is in our hands). Three months after the end of that war, after the recapture of the area by the Israeli army, he returned to the village where he was born—it had in the meantime been destroyed and deserted. From a tent he founded the settlement where seven years later, in 1974, the plan for the establishment of Gush Emunim (Block of the Faithful) originated.

The occupation of the West Bank caused the greatest psychological change of climate that has taken place in the history of Israel. The occupation—or, in the opinion of the religious Zionists, the liberation—of the West Bank of the Jordan and the Gaza Strip made Israel complete in a religious sense and heralded the beginning of the Messianic era. Now the state covered the whole land of Israel: East Jerusalem, the graves of the Patriarchs in Hebron, the grave of Rachel, and the Temple Mount. For many Israelis this victory was the proof of the indestructibility of Israel, and many religious Zionists interpreted the territorial expansion as proof that God "did remain on our side." After all, many religious Zionists had with pain in their hearts distanced themselves from the religious conviction that only the Messiah could establish the "Jewish Kingdom." This compromise always bothered them from a religious viewpoint; the ultra-Orthodox Aguda members didn't make this compromise because the state of Israel had no spiritual meaning for them. However, according to many of them, like Porat, it was the voice of God that rang out in the 1967 victory—giving his approval of the establishment of the state.

An era of pride began, and the radicalization of the National Religious Party that still ruled the country in a coalition with the Labor Party caused unrest about the occupied territories within the coalition. (In 1977 this unrest would lead to a definitive end of the traditional alliance between these two parties, because the National Religious Party tended increasingly toward a coalition with Likud, which wanted to retain the occupied territories as well.) To the great displeasure of the supporters of the concept Greater Israel, which took shape in 1977 under the leadership of Porat and meant that the land of Israel had to remain whole, the army commander Moshe Dayan (1915–1981, Kibbutz Deganya, Palestine) put the Temple Mount under the control of Jordan because of the Islamic shrines that are located there. The settlers were dismayed by this decision and, confident that the just-recaptured land must remain in Jewish hands, they started the colonization of the West Bank and the stimulation of Jewish studies in Zionist yeshivas throughout the country. The victory encouraged Talmud students; after all it was through their devotion and their dialogue with God that the West Bank had been liberated.

The more intensely a noisy Zionist minority experienced the state as the beginning of redemption, the greater became the contrast between their opinions about this and the unchanged reality. Despite the religious revival of religious Zionists, the state remained as secular as before 1967; this caused some of them to lose patience. They wanted to break the Messianic tension themselves, and in order to do this they felt justified in breaking the law. Henceforth, these Messianists listened only to the voice of God. Convinced that God needed help in completing the redemption, they united in a clandestine movement. This movement undertook attempts to blow up the mosque on the Temple Mount where, in their opinion, the Third Temple should be built. In the opinion of some Messianic settlers, attempts to clear away this mosque would bring closer the coming of the Messiah. Because returning any area of the West Bank would delay the glorious day of his coming, these settlers became fierce opponents of any politician who showed willingness to relinquish parts of the Holy Land. In the eyes of these anti-Arab Jews, a government that inclined to a compromise with the Arabs violated a divine command, and every Jewish leader who signed an agreement to give the West Bank or a part of it to the Palestinian Arabs was guilty of high treason. (Such actions by Yitzhak Rabin, who signed the Oslo accords in 1994, resulted in his death in November 1995. The murderer, Yigal Amir, called Rabin a traitor.)

Yeshayahu Leibowitz, mentioned in the first chapter, publicly resisted declaring the land and the state holy. He warned the state that the "military occupation would change the Israelis into "Judeo-Nazis." He deemed mixing halakhah with nationalism "pure idolatry" and compared the religiosity of the extremist religious Zionists to that of the "worshippers of the golden calf."

However, the radicalization of the right-wing nationalist movements continued after the Egyptian-Syrian attack in October 1973 that took Israel completely by surprise. Until this very day this war, the Yom Kippur War, evokes memories of the country's darkest hour and the overconfidence of the army and the government. During this war many Zionist citizens and soldiers chose God's side so that Zionism and Orthodoxy, which seemed to have parted for good in the nineteenth century, found each other once again. One year after the war, in 1974, the first generation of students trained in religious-nationalist yeshivas founded Gush Emunim, a movement that gave Israeli politics (but especially the National Religious Party) a push to the right.

This movement had as its purpose to serve "an authority higher than the state" by using the Zionist tactics and ideals of the original pioneers. Under Porat's inspiring leadership, this extremist rightist apolitical wing of the National Religious Party began to build settlements in Judea and Samaria. The Orthodox still had to catch up compared to the secular Zionists. Building settlements and living in them was actually part of the time of the pioneers, and in fact the Orthodox had played no role in it. For the secular politicians of the Labor Party it seemed as if their past was coming back to life. Although their political credo was "territories in exchange for peace," the government didn't contradict the religious motivation of Gush Emunim. At that time the majority of the Israeli population would have considered a negative attitude as anti-Zionist. In 2000 there were about 144 settlements, and a total of 170,000 Jews (3 percent of the total population) lived on the West Bank, which had approximately 20,000 homes. Twenty families lived in Kfar Etzion, which is part of Gush Etzion, a conglomerate of settlements south of Jerusalem. Just as in other settlements, the number of inhabitants is not counted by individuals but by families, which, according to accepted Jewish custom, are the core of the settlements, where community spirit and solidarity are important concepts. According to them, the settlements are traditional enclaves in a world that is degenerating. Within the gates of the settlements no one says "I," everything is "we," although it must be said that this attitude is changing.

The National Religious Party and the "liberation" of the West Bank—or the "occupation" as his opponents called it—were Porat's ruling passion. After the Six-Day War a climate was created in which religious Zionist ideology, and therefore its followers, could thrive. Porat took full advantage of this climate, and he has become a legend for a whole generation of religious Zionists with crocheted yarmulkes. The illegal construction of settlements that started after 1967 resulted in the group of settlements of Gush Etzion and Kyriat Arba. The government of the Labor Party, which was opposed to building settlements, had to legalize these settlements under pressure of representatives of the National Religious Party in the Knesset. After the Yom Kippur War in 1973 and certainly after the political upheaval in 1977 (when Menachem Begin with Likud came to power), the extremists could go their own way on the West Bank. It wasn't until Begin that religious Zionism came definitively out of its isolation and thus proved its success: the modern religious Jew held positions in all professional groups, he lived everywhere in the country, and he was integrated in secular Israeli society where until the early seventies the secular form of Zionism had dominated. For many people Porat embodied the breakthrough of religious Zionism that put an end to the domination of secular Zionism. Until 1981, when Begin and Defense Minister Ariel Sharon cleared the Yamit settlement in the Sinai, no government had relinquished any settlements. The tensions in the years that followed resulted in the Palestinian revolt, the *intifada* in 1987. The peace negotiations with Palestinian leader Yasir Arafat were pursued at the end of the eighties, and finally in 1993 the peace accord was signed in Oslo by Arafat, Shimon Peres (who was minister of foreign affairs at the time), and by Prime Minister Yitzhak Rabin. During these years it was Rabin in particular, with his hurried plans to reach a peace accord, who caused bad blood among many pious Zionists, some of whom had increasingly radical points of view. All Israelis still have clear memories of the events that took place after the Oslo peace accords were signed.

On Friday morning, February 25, 1994, the Orthodox Jewish doctor Baruch Goldstein from Kyriat Arba emptied his gun on 500 Muslims who were kneeling in prayer in the Isaac Hall in the Grotto of the Patriarchs in Hebron. Twenty-one were killed instantly and many were wounded. Those who were uninjured aimed the fire hose on Goldstein, knocked him to the floor, and beat him until he died. Prime Minister Rabin declared that Goldstein was "crazy" and said that this man "couldn't possibly be a normal Jew." He suggested removing the Jews from Hebron, but because he had no majority for this and because he feared a "small civil war," he didn't risk it. Yesha, the council that represents the right-wingers of Judea, Samaria, and Gaza, declared that Goldstein represented only himself, but did add that the "Rabin government had provoked Arab terrorism which Goldstein had answered with this deed." The banned anti-Arab movement Kach expressed itself in halakhic terms about the bloodbath and called it the "sanctification of God's name," *kiddush haShem*. According to them, Goldstein had wanted to warn Rabin because he was going too far in peace negotiations with the Palestinians. In October 1998, in the Israeli newspaper *Ma'ariv*, the extremist right-wing activist Baruch Marzel remembered Goldstein as follows: "He carried out the extreme act out of total devotion, *m'sirut ha'nefesh*, a level that I'll never reach. He was an example for all of us, but I have another level of devotion. Everything that I could say about Goldstein is illegal—therefore I won't say anything." (This was his reaction to the Wye accord that he thought could produce a second Goldstein.)

In the days following Goldstein's assault, violent confrontations took place on the West Bank between Israeli soldiers and Palestinians. During these confrontations nine Palestinians were killed and almost two hundred were wounded. The continuation of negotiations about Palestinian autonomy, the terrorist assaults of the Palestinians, and the withdrawal of the Israeli army and Shin Beth (the Israeli secret service) from part of biblical Israel drove the extremist residents of settlements that bordered Palestinian autonomous territory to despair. Moderate residents held their breath, but many settlers expressed their feelings in demonstrations against peace and against the gulf of Palestinian terrorism that had started in 1993. They called the government "not legitimate" and its leaders "murderers who collaborate with terrorists." Peres and Rabin "bore responsibility for the death of many innocent Israeli Jews." At any rate, that's what was being said in these circles.

During that time the antipeace demonstrations alternated with peace demonstrations, one of which—on November 4, 1995, in Tel Aviv—resulted in the murder of Rabin. The law student Yigal Amir (1965) assassinated Rabin because he considered Rabin a *rodef* (literally, "pursuer"). Extremist rabbis debated, with respect to Shimon Peres and Yitzhak Rabin, about the *din rodef* (a halakhic conviction of the pursuer) and the *din moser* (*moser* means messenger; *din moser* is a halakhic conviction of the messenger). The messenger is suspected of giving unbelievers information about Jews or of illegally giving them Jewish possessions. A *rodef* is someone who is on the verge of murder or who makes a murder possible. The only halakhic verdict that permits a Jew to kill another Jew without administration of justice is the *din rodef*. Amir asserted that according to Jewish law *rodfim* and *mosrim* (Hebrew plurals) could be sentenced to death and killed in extreme circumstances.

After a short interim period during which Peres took Rabin's place, Likud leader Benjamin Netanyahu was chosen as prime minister in 1996. Circumstances were favorable to him: the population needed a strong man who would offer security and allow the peace process to continue at a slower pace. Moreover the separate elections (one round for the parliament and one for the prime minister), which were held for the first time that year, worked in his favor (see chapter 2). During the election campaign he had capitalized on the fears of the inhabitants of the West Bank, and he promised them that he would "make a safe peace." Their disappointment was even greater when Netanyahu began to prepare a partial withdrawal from Hebron shortly after coming to office. However, Netanyahu thought that with this political step he would be giving "Oslo" a solid basis by placing the settlers and the moderates who had voted for him in 1996 with the doves under the wings of "Oslo." The withdrawal was carried out in January 1997.

The prime minister received the benefit of the doubt; after all, he had come to power with great support of Yesha and was still called "one of us" on the West Bank. After all, this order was a legacy of the Rabin government. The rest of 1997 continued without terrorist assaults, and Netanyahu maintained his contacts with the settlers whom he thought he could keep as friends. He promised the settlers who were afraid that some settlements would become "Jewish enclaves" in Palestinian territory that he would offer them extra protection right before the withdrawal. This concerned six settlements and the construction of twelve roads around the territories of the Palestinian Authority for safe access to the settlements.

The friendship between Netanyahu and the Zionist residents of the West Bank held up until October 23, 1998, the day when Netanyahu signed the Wye accord. The leader of the nationalist block had taken a step that many in Israel would have expected of a left-wing leader. Their leader "bartered" away land, and in their eyes he showed that he had forgotten what it means to be a Jew. Benny Kashriel, then chairman of Yesha and mayor of the Ma'ale Adumim settlement in the Judean wilderness, called this accord, signed "under pressure of the U.S.," a "disaster for the state of Israel." He called on Netanyahu to "stop the negotiations and to fight against terror and against the humiliation that an independent Palestinian state means for us." Netanyahu was accused of a humiliating surrender to Arafat. A representative of Yesha announced: "One thing is sure, if he signs he's a king without a country"—initially this was the official standpoint of Yesha.

After a short time Yesha and the moderate members of the National Religious Party seemed to reconcile themselves to the thought that withdrawal would be inevitable. The most important thing was to limit to a minimum the damage that the inhabitants of the West Bank would suffer. Even the hardliners kept quiet—in contrast with the situation on the eve of the withdrawal in the summer of 1995. It's possible that collective guilt after Goldstein and Amir had moderated the protest.

The change in Netanyahu's behavior was difficult to understand, particularly because he had at that time granted permission to build a great number of houses in Judea and Samaria. Determining the right attitude toward Netanyahu was therefore the greatest dilemma of the religious Zionists: on the one hand, his fall would help Barak into power, but on the other hand, the continuation of his government would mean the complete implementation of "Wye." David Levy, the minister of foreign affairs, was the first in a succession of five Likud members who resigned because of dissatisfaction with Netanyahu's decisions. The surprise of both left and right was great when Netanyahu, in the midst of the peace negotiations, designated the hawk Ariel Sharon as Levy's successor. For the opposition, this appointment was a sign that Netanyahu didn't want peace, but Sharon was a gift for the National Religious Party because he was known as a supporter of the Greater Israel concept. On November 16, 1998, only five days after taking office, Sharon encouraged the settlers to "take the hills that would otherwise fall under Palestinian control." While the extremist settlers continued building, Arafat's parliament approved the Wye accords, road blockades occurred on the West Bank, and a bomb that wounded twenty people exploded in the Mahaneh Yehuda market in Jerusalem. The perpetrators, two Islamic jihad terrorists, were killed. During a postponed vote, "Wye" was approved by a large majority of the Israeli government. Of course the National Religious Party voted against it and stipulated a number of conditions: the Palestinian Authority had to repeal the clause in its charter that called for the destruction of the state of Israel, the third withdrawal could not involve more than 1 percent of the territory, the Palestinian Authority had to arrest thirty terrorists who had been freed, and Israel had the right to annex Judea and Samaria if the Palestinian Authority would unilaterally proclaim the Palestinian state on May 4, 1999.

Tens of thousands of Israelis demonstrated against "Wye" on Rabin Square in Tel Aviv. Sharon and Netanyahu were the villains. A banner with photos of the two politicians read as follows: "You are responsible for this shameful agreement." And referring to Netanyahu: " We voted for you, we brought you to power; we won't forget or forgive." The right-wing English-language newspaper the *Jerusalem Post* had full-page ads by extremist factions.

Arafat threw oil on the fire with his speech of November 15, 1998, to commemorate the tenth anniversary of the declaration of Palestinian independence. Thousands of cheering Palestinians had assembled in Nablus for the occasion. Arafat announced, "Step by step we will return to the Holy Land until we proclaim our state on May 4, 1999." Two days before the Knesset would approve "Wye" and four days before the government would approve the first with-drawal, Arafat spoke the following words with trembling lips: "In a few days we will control half of the West Bank of the Jordan and Gaza, and all the Palestinian land will come into our hands. Stone by stone we will build our state until it reaches Jerusalem where the Palestinian flag will fly. . . . They let us see Jerusalem from afar, but we will see it from close up."

On November 20 the Israeli army, slightly delayed by the distur-bances, withdrew from the area around Jenin in Northern Samaria. Because of this withdrawal two settlements, Kadim and Ganin, sit-uated five kilometers from Jenin, became isolated. The inhabitants—a total of twenty moderate families who lived in both settlements—felt betrayed and demanded compensation from the government in order to be able to move; the government has not agreed to this demand. Two hundred and fifty Palestinians were freed, and the first Palestinian airport was opened in Dahaniye in Gaza without any disturbances.

On the hills of Judea and Samaria, mindful of Sharon's encour-agement, the settlers placed mobile homes where there were no set-tlements yet. Sharon hastened to say that his encouragement to "occupy hilltops applied only to areas within the borders for expan-sion of the settlements." Nevertheless thirty Jews from Shavei in Samaria occupied Sebastia, where the capital of the old kingdom of Samaria had been situated and which had been one of the most important places for activities of Gush Emunim in 1975. On being asked, Prime Minister Netanyahu and Minister of Defense Yitzhak Mordechai gave them permission to open a yeshiva and a museum. (This is incidentally the way in which many of the present-day set-tlements came into existence.) That same day secular Israelis set up tents on a hill near Itamar, very close to Nablus, with the purpose of establishing a secular settlement. On another hill, right near the set-tlement of Elon Moré, another group of Israelis erected a tent camp and ignored the commands of the army to leave.

At the same time the Palestinians continued building, planting trees, and constructing roads. The Palestinian authority had mean-while voted on a letter from Arafat to President Clinton in which Arafat retracted the clause about the destruction of Israel in its charter. According to the conditions of "Wye," a second vote had to be taken about this letter, but Arafat refused this for the time being.

During the following days clashes occurred on the West Bank between Israeli soldiers and Palestinians. In Qalqilya, a Palestinian city not far from Tel Aviv, three Palestinians were killed. Many Palestinians were wounded, rocks were thrown on the road from Jerusalem to Judea, and three Molotov cocktails were thrown at a building of Hebrew University in Jerusalem.

Prime Minister Netanyahu told President Clinton that the second withdrawal would not be carried out on December 18 as agreed "because the Palestinians are not observing the 'Wye' agreements." Shortly afterward, on December 21, 1998, the Palestinian Authority reconfirmed the letter to Clinton—subsequently thousands of Palestinians in refugee camps in Syria and Lebanon demonstrated against this. A week later the Knesset approved Porat's plan to hold early elections. Less than a month later the right-wing spectrum of Israeli politics was completely changed. One member after the other left Likud, as though Netanyahu's party had long been shattered. A number of small right-wing parties came into being; these parties were made up of former Likud and former National Religious Party members who united in the above-mentioned Ichud Leumi (a national unity block with right-wing splinter parties: Tekuma, Moledet, and Herut). Their principal unifying bond was their aversion to Netanyahu and his obscure, changeable politics.

After the 1999 elections, twelve religious Zionists, distributed among different religious parties, were members of the Knesset; among them were five members of the National Religious Party. Even though this party emerged weakened from the elections, the religious Zionists can nevertheless look back with satisfaction over the last twenty years. After all, their goals have been reached: they are completely integrated into secular society, they have their own school system, and they have created settlements all over the West Bank. They will be able to hold onto these achievements without too much difficulty, but the question is whether new life can be breathed into the traditional religious Zionist fervor as it was once carried out by a number of Zionists, Porat among them. Now that the government of Barak is heading for an accord with Arafat, the role of the religious Zionists seems to be finished. After all it's no longer possible to gain the same honor with the struggle for the biblical land as was possible in the 1970s and 1980s. Moreover, spreading the love for *Eretz Yisrael* takes up a lot of time, which the religious Zionist youth is no longer willing to give. Dragging mobile homes, installing electricity and water pipes, consulting with Yesha and with mayors of Samaria and Judea, and organizing demonstrations—all these activities are practically a full-time job. And you also need guts, because a great many of the activities are illegal. Many children who were brought up in the religious Zionist milieu don't stay on the West Bank; they have other ideals and abandon the faith (as was described in chapter 5).

The old guard of the religious Zionist movement to which Porat belongs would rather not know, but even Yesha wants to distance itself from the extremist nationalist ideas. Benny Kashriel, the previously mentioned chairman of Yesha and secular mayor of Ma'ale Adumim, a settlement that borders Jerusalem, has said that the "post-ideological era has begun" and that "Yesha wants to dissociate itself from radical points of view and militant personalities who in the past linked their names to Judea and Samaria." With this statement he alludes to the increasing political variety of the residents of the West Bank, among whom are Russians, Ethiopians, Sephardic Jews, Ashkenazi Jews, Orthodox, secularists, Zionists, and left- and right-wingers.

Nevertheless the activist Zionists fight for a Greater Israel with as much energy as in the time when these ideas were heard on a large scale. The extremist religious Zionists who have united in the National Block will continue to put down mobile homes and block roads in the name of God. Proudly they hold to the word of God: "When you cross the Jordan into the land of Canaan, you shall dispossess all the inhabitants of the land . . . and you shall take possession of the land and settle in it, for I have assigned the land to you to possess" [Num. 33:51, 52, 53]. The extremists on the West Bank were absolutely against a Palestinian state and put their hopes in the secular Jews—who have gone astray according to them—but who, when they repent, will bring better times for the Jewish people. They reason that if the Jews don't make an effort to retain the biblical places, they might as well have stayed in Europe.

Prof. Ehud Sprinzak of the Hebrew University says, "The National Religious Party has known enough low points to be able to surmount such a crisis. The mutual relationships will increase, and therefore there is little reason for despair for the settlers." Sprinzak is an expert on the extremist right, and recently published the book *Brother against Brother: Violence and extremism in Israeli politics, from 'Altalena' to the Rabin assassination*. He is also the author of *The Ascendance of the Extreme Right*. "Moreover, prime minister Barak is sympathetic to the settlements, and it is known that Shilo Gal, his advisor in this area, has a soft spot for the settlers. Barak will give the Palestinians very little. At the moment the settlers are waiting to see what Barak will do." Then Sprinzak emphasizes,

> And we shouldn't forget that the settlers have become Israel's bourgeoisie: they have a good life; peace and quiet [of course this is true only if the peace negotiations with the Palestinians turn out well]; they live comfortably and pay low rents and low mortgages. The bourgeoisie doesn't fight. They now spend their time making plans. Every day they work on retaining settlements and spreading ideology, and they prepare demonstrations that will take place if it looks like their security is endangered.

According to Sprinzak it's true that several years ago the National Religious Party promoted the settlers' interests without asking any questions. In some aspects the National Religious Party members were extremists, but after Rabin's murder the National Religious Party has become a party for moderate Zionists who are willing to compromise and who understand that it is difficult to retain all of *Eretz Yisrael*. Sprinzak feels that it's because of this that the extremists who don't share this opinion have gotten into difficulties. However, Sprinzak doesn't want to call it a crisis because this group will always remain close-knit: "Porat has partially dug his own grave, but he can still count on the support of the extremists like the Gush Emunim supporters, who are loyal and still form an exceptionally strong group."

Sprinzak explains that the group in Israel that was always called extreme right is now broken down into four groups: terrorists, extremists, pragmatists, and moderates. According to Sprinzak, Israel doesn't have any real terrorists, but Rabbi Meir Kahane, who was assassinated in 1991, approved of terror against Arabs and greatly admired someone like Goldstein. Sprinzak thinks that if Kahane's followers had enough reasons and were sufficiently numerous, they could become terrorists. The extremists, a close-knit groups of activists among whom Sprinzak counts the secular jurist Elyakim

Ha'etzni and Rabbi Chaim Druckman, could in certain circumstances cross the line of terrorism. They don't shrink from breaking the law— some of them have at times been arrested for that. They build on hill-tops and then ignore commands of the army to clear what they have built. With his eighteen years of political service to the state, Porat actually stands between these extremists and the largest group, the pragmatists. The latter negotiate with the government and are dependent on the support of the population. Sprinzak says,

> Now that Porat has left politics, the extremist Porat from the past comes through, and he will certainly not reconcile himself to acquiesce in the establishment of a Palestinian state as most pragmatists—certainly those in the government—will. Their opinions as regards the Jewish presence on the West Bank are not too different from those of the extremists, but they are inclined to accept the decisions of Barak with whom they consult. An example is Benny Kashriel, who confers with Barak about the withdrawal from the West Bank.
>
> The moderate extremists, who have as their highest goal to reach a consensus, belong to this last group. They don't exclusively inhabit the West Bank but are spread over large parts of the country and don't wear yarmulkes.

According to Sprinzak, the majority of the people who live on the West Bank are not religious, and that's why he doesn't want to call it an ideological crisis: "Most of the inhabitants of settlements like Ariel, Kyriat Arba [literally, "city of four"; refers to four Old Testament couples who are buried in Hebron according to tradition], Ma'aleh Adumim [literally: "red or bloody slope"; Joshua 15:7, 18:17], don't wear a yarmulke. They base their presence on the West Bank not on religious arguments, and they don't have the feeling that religious Zionism has failed. This is different for the settlers from such places as Hebron or Kfar Etzion who do wear yarmulkes, and that's about one-third."

In principle every Jew who lives outside the 1948 borders, the so-called Green Line, is a settler. But not everyone in the territory conquered by Israel in 1967—called "biblical Judea and Samaria" by religious Zionists, or "occupied territories" by left-wing Israelis, or "on the West Bank," the most neutral term—call themselves settlers. This word calls up images of Gush Emunim members like Porat, for whom many inhabitants of the West Bank have no sympathy at all. Porat calls himself a settler (*mitnachel* in Hebrew, from the biblical word *nachala*, which means heritage), and abroad and often in Israel itself as well he is still erroneously considered the typical settler. Yet many "settlers" are moderately right-wing or even secular and are therefore not living on the West Bank for religious reasons. After all, there are other reasons for living on the West Bank, like the scenery and the low prices for housing. It's true that most of the residents of the West Bank were raised with religious Zionist ideas or started to support them later, but this definitely doesn't mean that only extremists live there.

There are ideological differences among settlements that are expressed in the degree of religiosity and nationalism of the inhabitants. For example, the inhabitants of Elkana (near Tel Aviv) are predominantly moderately right-wing (10 percent of the inhabitants are secular); in Efrat (near Jerusalem) live mainly English-speaking Jews who have mostly moderately right-wing opinions; the population of Ma'aleh Adumim (near Jerusalem) is 75 percent secular; and that of Ariel (near Tel Aviv) is mostly mixed, varying from the extreme right to the extreme left. The residents of these settlements usually call themselves *mityashvim* (singular: *mityashev*, from *lehityashev*, "to settle") and not *mitnachelim* (plural of *mitnachel*). They were, and are, less involved with the activist occupation of Samaria and Judea, and in the rest of Israel they don't evoke associations with Gush Emunim, that is to say with building settlements, occupying hilltops, and demonstrations against the peace negotiations.

However, someone who chooses to live in Kyriat Arba or in Hebron can—from the very choice of city of residence—count on little sympathy from most inhabitants of Tel Aviv and from those living in so-called moderate settlements. Such a person is often, but not always, strongly nationalistic and therefore against the Palestinian state, and such a person can be strictly Orthodox but generally is moderately Orthodox. The image that inhabitants of Kyriat Arba of Hebron have of themselves is that of active nationalist Jews who will fight to keep Judea and Samaria in Jewish hands. This is why they call themselves *mitnachelim* and receive ideological support from inhabitants of places like Ofra, Tapuach, and Alon Moré, extremist settlements in Judea that were established near Palestinian villages. The situation in Hebron is the most explosive, partially because the Jews in this place live in close proximity to the Palestinians. The atmosphere there is permanently tense because of the presence of Arab and Jewish soldiers. The settlers here are confronted almost daily by the question of which people can call itself the rightful owner of the graves of the patriarchs and matriarchs that are located in this city.

"The graves of our patriarchs and matriarchs are very important, and someone like Rabin, who wanted to leave Hebron and who froze the settlement politics, has a counterproductive effect on the Jews in this area," says Noam Arnon from Hebron, where he is the chairman of the Jewish community of fifty-two families, approximately 400 people.

> In other places I would no longer be able to pray. Being Jewish in Hebron is different from being Jewish in Tel Aviv where there are goyim who speak Hebrew. Despite everything, I feel more at home here among the Arabs who live like our forefathers: they have a modest lifestyle and are religious. We could have become good friends, but everything has gone wrong since the *Intifada*. Goldstein murdered the Palestinians to avenge their murder in January 1994 of Pinchas Lapid, Goldstein's friend from Kyriat Arba, and his son Shalom Lapid, a yeshiva student. Rabin threw oil on the fire with "Oslo," Netanyahu vacated Hebron and signed Wye—a disaster.

Arnon sighs while he takes loose pages from a Hebrew prayer book covered with swastikas and Arabic phrases out of a folder: "How can we ever trust Palestinians who write this? It says here, 'We'll make slaves of you.'"

"That sort of statement is frightening, but why do these Jews stay there?" asks J. B. A. from the Efrat settlement. He covers his head with a crocheted yarmulke and calls himself a "proud settler," but he wants nothing to do with extremism. He worries about the distinction between theory and practice that many rabbis in yeshivas don't make very clearly. He emphasizes that he wants nothing to do with Gush Emunim or with whatever is left of it. He is worried about the influence of the radical rabbis:

> My son heard from his rabbi that the men of the Jewish underground and of Gush Emunim who prepared assaults on the

mayors of Arab villages in the eighties were heroes. This is dangerous! And besides, one of the important rabbis, Nahum Rabinowitz from the Ma'ale Adumim settlement, said to Yigal Amir that Rabin is a *rodef*. And worse: after the murder Rabinowitz affirmed this again during a radio broadcast, but he added that he "had never said that the law should be applied." In 1997 when Netanyahu ordered the army to leave Hebron, Rabinowitz also said that "soldiers should not carry out this Nazi order." This kind of view is dangerous for our democracy.

Hillel Weiss, professor of Israeli and Jewish literature at Bar Ilan University in Ramat Gan, says, "The Jews have every right to live in Judea and Samaria and to refuse the order to withdraw." Weiss is one of Israel's most strongly opinionated intellectuals and lives in the Elkana settlement on the West Bank. Weiss, who in the nineties wrote for daily papers like *Dawar* and *Chadashot* (now defunct), is accused of having called Rabin an SS member during demonstrations in 1992:

> They say that I'm guilty of Rabin's murder. What I said about him was taken from a satirical piece, and moreover remarks about Rabin are legitimate. Rabin didn't understand the Jewish claim to the West Bank at all. He contributed to the decline of Zionist values and also to the terrible thing that happened to him. According to him, peace was possible only in exchange for land, but we have to remember that we have to act as Jews—otherwise we lose our right to live in Judea and Samaria. Rabin was a Hebrew-speaking goy and didn't understand the spiritual meaning of the peace process, or of the Biblical land. He was a general—not an intellectual.

Not everyone on the West Bank has a strong opinion about Rabin. S. R. was still living in the Netherlands during the demonstrations against Rabin and the peace negotiations. Since 1998 she has lived on the West Bank in the ultra-Orthodox settlement of Beitar. She won't say with pride—most ultra-Orthodox won't—that she lives in Judea or Samaria. After all, these territories can be called that only after the coming of the Messiah, and for them Beitar, Kyriat Sefer, and Emmanuel are extensions of Mea Shearim and Bnei Brak where there is no more space. Many *haredim* live in these places, not for religious reasons but because housing is cheap there and because it is less hot and dusty than in Mea Shearim and Bnei Brak, and because it is quiet. Besides, the government subsidizes living in one of these three *haredi* "settlements." New immigrants like the *haredi* R. family, which has four children, receive money. "I'm not too happy that we live in the 'territories,'" says S. R. who returned to ultra-Orthodoxy years ago in the Netherlands. "But those fifty thousand dollars, half of which we may keep and the other half we have to pay back in eighteen years with an interest rate of 4 percent, is attractive. We didn't want to live in Bnei Brak because it's dirty, dusty, and hot. The houses there are small and you don't receive a subsidy like you do here."

S. R. continues: "We don't sympathize with the religious Zionists' ideological struggle for the land." She walks to her balcony and points to a hill right in front of her house where a bulldozer is leveling the ground. "We want to live in security, and we've received bullet-proof glass for our car. But I'm *haredi*, perhaps I'm a *haredi* Zionist, and I think that we Jews are entitled to pray in the cave of Machpela in Hebron and on the Temple Mount. The world thinks that we are trampling the poor souls of the Palestinians, but we don't have freedom of religion in our own land. I won't blow up the mosque, but Israel has every right to do that."

In 1998 when the National Religious Party was greatly reduced in its representation in the Knesset and on the West Bank, the obvious question was whether the party would return to its alliance with the Labor Party that had lasted from 1948 to 1977. Ninety-two-year-old Zerah Wahrhaftig from Jerusalem, an old-time member of the National Religious Party, who was minister of religious affairs from 1948 to 1977 and Knesset member until 1977 and died in 2002, didn't think so.

> Too many extremist elements have come into the party in the course of the years. Although the settlement policy of the National Religious Party and its attitude toward the Palestinians has moderated in recent years in comparison to the nineteen-seventies and eighties, the taint of Gush Emunim still sticks to it. At the time we pleaded for Jewish settlement on a limited scale in parts of Samaria and Judea, but not in the whole area and on every hilltop. I was the only minister who was present at the establishment in 1967 of the first settlement, Kfar Etzion. This village had been destroyed by the Jordanians, and I felt that we should go and live there again.

And certainly I felt that we were allowed to build settlements as long as the Palestinians refused to accept the Partition plan of the United Nations. But it wasn't the intention to build a settlement for ten families on every empty hilltop.

One of the two signers of the Declaration of Independence who were still alive at the time, Wahrhaftig said, "The Palestinians have a right to autonomy, but having their own state is problematic."

Wahrhaftig was a religious Zionist in heart and soul who covers his gray hair with a large black yarmulke, not a crocheted one like the younger religious Zionists. Since 1974 the position of the National Religious Party has become weaker. This is no accident, since that was the year when the extremist organization Gush Emunim was founded. Wahrhaftig thinks that the cause was the emergence of extremist nationalists in the party; they wanted, as he puts it,

> to colonize all of the West Bank. In this respect the National Religious Party became more fanatic from a nationalistic viewpoint and less strict from a religious viewpoint. The National Religious Party hardliners, like Chanan Porat, felt that the life of every Jew had to be in the service of the Jewish trinity: *Am Yisrael* [the people of Israel] and *Torat Yisrael* [the Torah of Israel] in *Eretz Yisrael* [the land of Israel]. They began to concentrate more on the last component at the expense of the religious one. According to them the holy state as a part of redemption had to stimulate its subjects in a more active way to lead Orthodox lives. I disagree with that—I'm for a wait-and-see attitude. Nowadays I'm no longer involved in politics, I support the National Religious Party only culturally, like Bar Ilan University for example. In 1967 the hardliners, Rabbi Kook's disciples, were the first ones when God gave the sign—as they explain it—to bring the *Eretz Yisrael* concept to the awareness of the Israeli public. According to them, after the reconquest of the Jewish land, the time was ripe to give Him a hand on the way to redemption, and Gush Emunim was a means.

"Gush Emunim was founded here," says Rabbi Chaim Druckman (1932 Poland) proudly from behind his desk in his home in the religious Zionist village Merkaz Shapira, near Ashkelon. "We were afraid of the signing of peace accords under pressure of Henry Kissinger, the American Secretary of State at the time. After all, Begin signed the Camp David accords, Rabin and Peres the Oslo accords, and Netanyahu the peace accords in Wye—all under pressure of the Americans. [According to this reasoning, Prime Minister Barak was ready for territorial concessions at Camp David in 2000 under pressure of President Clinton.] This is not a true peace. The true peace is the one of the Prophet Isaiah: the coming kingdom of peace." Druckman constantly strokes his long white beard as he picks up a leather-bound book from his cluttered desk and reads Isaiah 2:4: "'Thus He will judge among the nations and arbitrate for the many peoples, and they shall beat their swords into plowshares and their spears into pruning hooks: nation shall not take up sword against nation; they shall never again know war.' It is our task to bring redemption closer slowly but surely, because redemption of the Jewish people will bring peace to all of humanity."

Druckman is one of the few settlers in the Knesset. In 1984 he was already a member of the Knesset, but at that time he represented Matzad, a radical splinter of the National Religious Party. At present Druckman, who is known as a hardliner, represents the interests of the more moderate National Religious Party. As an extremist he is an odd man out, but after Porat's departure he was asked to join the National Religious Party in order not to lose the more extremist constituency of Hendel and Porat that is comparable to Druckman's. Druckman, a father of ten children, is also head of the Or Etzion (Light of Zion) yeshiva and teaches at the Meir Institute for newly religious Jews in Jerusalem.

Rabbi Druckman seems not to have lost any of his *Eretz Yisrael* enthusiasm. He is a convinced "Kookist":

> Kook was the only one in his era who understood that the state represents the complete messianic revelation. He saw the light of the Messiah in the state of Israel and taught us that this state is a holy state where the Jews must live. The Israeli army is still the army of God, just as Kook said. The tanks, the cannons, and the airplanes are tools that serve the ultimate goal of Jewish settlement in the Holy Land. Naturally we build on empty pieces of land; I emphasize empty because many Europeans compare the return to our land to Nazi activities.
>
> What Rabin did was wrong, and I think that soldiers should refuse all orders that conflict with Jewish law, like the withdrawal from Samaria and Judea. An Orthodox Jew cannot act against his beliefs. In such a case a clever officer gives the Orthodox soldiers

other orders. I've already told Barak that he should make it clear to the Palestinians that they won't get a state. Clinton feels that the Palestinians can return, but they already have twenty states. I want them to stay where they are. If they are loyal to the state of Israel they can become citizens, but most of the Palestinians want to destroy the Jewish state.

"Rabin was wrong, but he was not a *rodef*," says Druckman with conviction.

Too many Jews agreed with him to be able to call him that. Sometimes my students ask political questions, but I teach the ideology of the Jewish people, not its practice. Perhaps Rabin was a *rodef* in theory, but that has nothing to do with the political reality, and it certainly doesn't mean that he should have been killed. The principle of the *din rodef* can only become operative after other means to change the direction of the government have been used. Were telegrams and faxes sent to Rabin? Did fires burn on the hills of Samaria and Judea? Were there strikes? Was there public mourning? No. Therefore it was forbidden to call the government a *rodef*. Only if the people had unsuccessfully done everything that a normal people would do to change the direction of the government, then a *din rodef* could perhaps have been pronounced over it. In all other cases the government remains the legal representative of the people.

Undoubtedly this government is a low point for the National Religious Party. But everyone will see that we won't survive without Torah. Our ultimate goal is the sacrificial service in the Third Temple that will descend from heaven as soon as we truly master our task as Jews. We don't have to breed a "red cow" [ashes from the red cow are needed to cleanse Jews], but it is a duty to live in *Eretz Yisrael*, to return to *teshuvah*, and to lead a holy life. The National Religious Party is the ideal for the Jewish people. According to Rabbi Kook, from the inside out, that is by participating in the secular government, to save what can be saved in cooperation with the secularists. In 1983 I founded Matzad because *Eretz Yisrael* was being neglected at the time, but branching off does not help unity—just look at Tehiya, the party in which religious and secular Zionists united against the signing of the Camp David agreements. That party didn't make it.

The secular jurist Elyakim Ha'etzni (1926) from Kyriat Arba was one of the founders of Tehiya. Once he compared Shimon Peres, who was prime minister at the time, to General Pétain, who was convicted as traitor by the government of Charles De Gaulle. Until 1999 Ha'etzni led an action group, the Committee for the Abolition of Palestinian Autonomy, about which he now says that "it makes no sense to fight Palestinian autonomy because it's already too late. We are on the threshold of a great catastrophe, the Palestinian state." To show that he isn't giving up the battle, he has created the movement Shenit Gamla lo tipol (literally, "a Gamla shall not fall a second time"; Gamla is sometimes called the Masada of the north, because in the year 67 C.E. in a battle with the Romans, 4,000 Jews were killed there and 5,000 Jews committed suicide).

Ha'etzni is still against a Palestinian autonomy that will lead to their own state, which Menachem Begin first mentioned:

> Begin betrayed us and Netanyahu did too. He launched a big revolution in the national camp which he then left behind in confusion. We chose him because we thought that after two-and-one-half years of terror before and after the murder of Rabin he would bring deliverance. But he started with the withdrawal from Hebron, our Pearl Harbor because this decision came as a bolt from the blue. He ended with "Wye," an agreement that we'd seen coming and that is called a "positive development" here in Israel. The peace process is supposedly "irreversible," but we count ourselves out of this peace. It's called a "merit" that he was the first hawk who had his supporters accept the division of *Eretz Yisrael* and blew new life into the peace process. Just like the French remember Alsace-Lorraine or the Jews from Kfar Etzion the village they lost in 1984, we have to continue to remember every piece of ground that Barak will return and that Netanyahu has given back. Has the right also forgotten what it is to be Jewish? We don't want to govern with collaborators. We brought Netanyahu down with our own swords and we got kicked in the teeth. We gave Barak a chance, but the removal of one mobile home is a casus belli for us.

[Barak resigned in December 2000 after it became clear that he didn't have a majority for his readiness for far-reaching territorial concessions].

Ha'etzni is a confirmed supporter of the Greater Israel concept, and the establishment of an independent Palestinian state has been his greatest fear for many years. In 1974 he was in Druckman's house when Gush Emunim was founded, and for him the struggle continues. "Left-wing Israel thinks that our dream is over and done, but we're alive and kicking" says Ha'etzni as he drives his car through the streets of Kyriat Arba. On the rear bumper is a sticker that says, *"Hebron beYadenu"* (Hebron in our hands).

> Messianism is in our blood. Every Jew, even a left-wing secularist, loves *Eretz Yisrael*. After Netanyahu's fall, forty-two illegal settlements were built on hilltops. The three years of Netanyahu were good for Kyriat Arba, but in the end he dropped us. We're now back to square one, in 1967. We're now joining up with Shas, the *haredim*, and Lieberman and Sharansky's Russians. They're not against settlements either. Shas-voters live here; that's a hopeful new phenomenon in Judea and Samaria. Shas and United Torah Judaism are not against settlements.

Ha'etzni hopes that the "Zionization" of the ultra-Orthodox will lead to the formation of a new national bloc that will consist of *haredi* Zionists, called *hardalim* in Hebrew (contraction of *haredi* and *dati-leumi*, which means ultra-Orthodox religious Zionist), Shas supporters, right-wing Russians, and the extremist wing of the National Religious Party. According to him, the worry about security and the anxiety of living among Palestinian villages unites all Jews living on the West Bank. The future will show whether this is true, but at any rate the houses and other buildings that are mushrooming on the hills of Samaria and Judea symbolize for all the residents—perhaps unintentionally—the vitality of the Jewish people and its presence in the biblical land. With these remarks Ha'etzni refers to the increasing involvement of the *haredim* with the state. Some Israelis feel that the Arabs are the only anti-Zionists left in Israel. This observation is a consequence of two developments: first, the "Zionization" of the Orthodox mentioned by Ha'etzni, and second, the *"harediza-tion"* of the religious Zionists. The gap between the two extremes, the anti-Zionists and the Zionists, is becoming smaller because of these developments.

Ha'etzni is particularly elated about the 200 single-family homes under construction, the expansion of yeshivas, the construction of a recreation park, and the new roads. He points out exactly where Jewish landownership ends and where that of the Palestinians begins: "That hill belongs to us, but that vineyard and the land around it is Palestinian, and one of Arafat's ministers lives over there.

We are allowed to construct a road through the vineyard leading to the homes that will soon be constructed on that hill. The Arabs live there, and we live here. They help us build our houses and construct our roads." Turning onto a brand-new asphalted road that some Palestinians are finishing, Ha'etzni says, "For this road I was in prison for four months. Do you know how many Palestinians have work in the settlements? Countless numbers. We can't do without each other. Why should we separate? We have to live together. But an Arab minister? That won't be possible until the Messiah comes, when there is peace." He smiles. "This house was locked and bolted in 1992 after the left-wing government of Rabin came to power; they froze everything except the birth rate," says Ha'etzni, who knows all the tricks of the trade of settling. "We broke open the doors, put in water pipes, and connected electricity. Now a Russian family that used to live in a trailer home lives there. We moved the trailer home to a vacant Jewish lot; that's illegal, but we of Yesha believe in the usefulness of civil disobedience. For the rest we are obedient citizens."

Ha'etzni is not Orthodox, but he regularly quotes the *Tanakh*, which he calls "the genetic code of the Jewish people." Nothing pleases him more than a goy who says that the Jewish people is different from all other peoples. Ha'etzni refers to the biblical figure Bileam, the fortune-teller who was engaged by Balak, the king of Moab, to curse Israel:

He said: *am l'vadad yishkon u'va'goyim lo yitchashav.* [Num. 23:9; "a people that dwells apart, not reckoned among the nations." In Hebrew the word *goyim* also means *nation*]. This shows us that the goyim also say that we are different. I was proud of the statement of De Gaulle about the Jews even though most Jews consider it an insult. [Right after the Six-Day War, de Gaulle called the Jews "proud, dominant, and elitist."] The new Israelis like Shulamit Aloni and Yossi Sarid want to be just like the other peoples, but we have our own traits, we are different, and the goyim say that too. I don't say that we're better or that we're a superior race; we aren't even a race, but we have been chosen to suffer. They say of our law that it will be as *'le'or goyim'* [literally, "a light unto nations"; Isaiah 49:6: "I will also make you a light unto nations, that My salvation may reach the ends of the earth."]. But that dates from the time when polytheistic pagans worshipped more than one god and therefore didn't know absolute good or evil. The Jewish faith is *'le'or goyim'* because it starts from one God and therefore from absolute truths.

The *Tanakh* is our identity and is the essence of our consciousness. If you take that away, the Jewish people will stop being Jewish and will become like the supporters of the left-wing Meretz party who have renounced God.

Not in their worst dreams did the settlers think that their revenge in 1999 would produce a government in which Yossi Beilin, Chaim Ramon, and Shimon Peres of the Labor Party and Yossi Sarid of Meretz would hold key positions. "We no longer know who is for us and who is against us," says Ha'etzni (born in Schleswig-Holstein) a few minutes later in his living room, which is filled with German language history books, novels, and philosophy books. Hebron can be seen in the distance. Ha'etzni continues:

> The party leaders assert publicly that they don't want to be Jews. Some Jews love Jews who foul their own nest, like Shulamit Aloni. She wants to rely on the ten seats of the Arabs who receive their orders from the Palestinian leader Arafat. Just explain to Aloni that it's absurd for representatives of Arafat to be in the Jewish government. She has converted to the "church of the nonbelievers," the "Peace church." She is the one who is Messianic, not we. They believe in an impossible peace. Everyone now thinks that they, and with them the Israeli Israelis, won the 1999 elections, but Barak won with a Jewish Israeli Knesset. [He begins to count:] The right wing in Israel, which has families with ten children, gained sixty seats. Left wing Israel, which has families with three dogs and a child, also gained sixty. Minus the ten Arab seats, the number of Jewish seats comes to fifty; after all, we're talking about the Jewish state. Israeli Arabs are Arabs, and so are Palestinians—and they're proud of it. Just like Jews are proud of being Jewish. Arabs and Jews together, as Israelis in a state for all citizens, form a characterless mishmash in which Jews no longer are Jews and Arabs no longer are Arabs. We on the West Bank fight for the preservation of the Jewishness of the state.
>
> As part of this struggle I dedicated myself to Jewish access to the Temple Mount in 1967 when Moshe Dayan placed Islamic holy places under Jordanian supervision right after the war. After all, the Jewish Holy of Holies is located on the Temple Mount in the Al Aksa mosque. We got access to the Mount, that is to say that we are allowed to read a newspaper there, but we're arrested as soon as we read verses from the Psalms. It's a disgrace! For me it's about our rights and not about the unrealistic plan to build the Third

Temple. We don't need it—we wouldn't have any sacrificial services even if the Second Temple were still standing. God isn't waiting for the smell of lamb—He wants *Eretz Yisrael*; it says so in the Prophets.

"They arrest me as soon as I appear on the Temple Mount with a prayer shawl," says Messianic settler Yehuda Etzion, smiling, in his home in Ofra, a settlement in the hills of Judea. Etzion (1951) identifies with the biblical land, and his life is dominated by the coming of the Messiah but especially by the building of the Third Temple. "For us Jews, this building is a responsibility that we have to be aware of every minute," says Etzion, who in July 1999 organized the first meeting of "Temple activists" in a hotel in Jerusalem. The purpose of the meeting was to open a "Temple treasure chest." "I save all donations, which will only be traded for gold, until the construction of the Temple can start. Our organization has to counterbalance the situation of the Jewish people that is leading increasingly secular lives and is increasingly cut off from religious duties, and building the Third Temple is the most important of these. The only thing we demand is to be allowed to pray in peace individually—not in a minyan as we wanted originally."

Etzion is dressed in dark blue cotton trousers, wears sandals, and a loose-fitting checked flannel shirt hangs over his *tallit katan*. With his long, yellow-white beard, his long, thin, curly hair that he covers with a large crocheted yarmulke, and his modern sunglasses that cover his temples, he resembles a hippie-like Old Testament prophet. Remarks about the beauty of the biblical landscape make him beam, and he cites the Bible, usually smiling: "Prepare to cross the Jordan . . . into the land that I am giving to the Israelites" [Joshua 1:2]; "Let them make Me a sanctuary that I may dwell among them" [Exod. 25:8]. Etzion feels it is his task to give God a helping hand on the way to complete redemption of the Jewish people, the coming of the Messiah. Etzion, the father of seven children, often thinks of the Messiah whose footsteps he says he can already hear. He wants to break through the Messianic tension that exists in Israel and in this way hasten the coming of the Messiah.

He thinks that the redemption was stopped on the Temple Mount. One of his "helpful" deeds was an attempt, in 1984, to blow up the Dome of the Rock holy place. He paid for this deed with a five-year prison sentence. Etzion still wants this holy place to disappear because he says he knows exactly where the Ark of the Covenant is located, even though scholars are still not in agreement about the exact spot. Etzion shows a map of the Temple Mount where he was last arrested in 1995. This map has calculations that support his theory that the Holy of Holies is in the Al Aksa mosque. This mosque is holy for Muslims because it is from this place that the Prophet Mohammed is said to have ascended to heaven on his winged horse. "The Muslims will lose this mosque," Etzion says confidently and looks lovingly at depictions of the Ark in one of his many leather-bound holy books. "Mohammed was never in Jerusalem," he says as he rushes over to the bookcase from which he takes some holy texts to prove that God wants the Jewish people to build the Third Temple on these few hundred square meters.

Etzion feels that Moshe Dayan, who was commander-in-chief at the time, made the biggest mistake in Jewish history in 1967. Dayan prohibited Jewish prayer on the Temple Mount because he thought that these prayers could unleash a religious war and set the Islamic world against Israel. Israeli law doesn't prohibit praying on the Temple Mount, but since 1967 the police have warned the judiciary about the danger of Jews praying on the Temple Mount. Etzion's attempts to obtain his rights through the High Court always fail. The halakhic authorities, like yeshiva heads and the rabbinate, support the court in this matter; Etzion considers this "cowardly." He takes as an example Rabbi Druckman, who advises his students not to pray on the Temple Mount. Yet there have been disturbances for years whenever Jews try to do this, as was the case in February 1999. "The Jewish right to the Temple Mount" was the headline in *Ha'aretz* a few days after several Jews had recited the most important Jewish prayer, the Shema, there.

"God has chosen us, and we have to cherish and protect this land of Benjamin," says Etzion, pointing to the last expansion of his settlement Givat Zvi. This settlement was named after Zvi, a former inhabitant who died during the *intifada*. According to Etzion's Messianic philosophy, all actions of a Jew have to be in the service of his coming. The Temple Mount is "the flag on our ship that will carry us to the Messianic regime, the Kingdom of Israel. Everything that Jews do, before or after His coming, is connected with God." While maneuvering his rickety car over the dusty roads through the hills of

Benjamin, Etzion points to the back seat of his car and says, "My last book is about Lebanon where one soldier after the other died. This happened because many Jews are not concerned about the Temple Mount. If you neglect your heart, the rest of your body suffers."

Etzion's political activism started in the Bnei Akiva Zionist youth movement.

> When at the end of the Six-Day War in the Har Etzion (Hill of Zion) yeshiva in the Alon Shvut settlement I heard "*Eretz Yisrael beYadenu*" [the land of Israel is in our hands] on the radio, an electric shock went through my body. It was fantastic. We realized that we were citizens of a state that had been enriched with Hebron, Nablus, the Temple Mount, and Old Jerusalem. Many Israelis considered the victory a proof of military skill, but we as yeshiva students were convinced that the true spirit of providence of none less than our Rabbi Kook had caused the Jewish victory. The fact is that a month before, in his traditional speech on Independence day, he had lamented the division of Israel. He was the source of our victory because we prayed and studied with him to prevent this division.

Most Muslims believe that Mohammed ascended with his horse from the Temple Mount to heaven to receive instructions from Allah about Islam. Adnan Husseini, the Palestinian director of the Waqf, the Jordanian organization that administers the Islamic holy places on the Temple Mount, does this from a spacious room where a photo of the late King Hussein and shots of the Temple Mount hang on the walls. His office is located at less than 300 meters from the Dome of the Rock behind the Wailing Wall, in the Arab part of the Old City of Jerusalem.

> In the Holy Book—the unchanging word of God—it says that He has given the mosque to the Prophet. Jerusalem, the religious extension of Mecca, is for us the best way to Paradise. The Jews can only go their own way in our sanctuary if God sends a message. It's a sin to change a mosque into a synagogue like Etzion wants to, and besides, with due respect to Christians and Jews, they are Muslims too. Three *thousand* years ago God told the Jews that the Temple Mount was theirs. But fifteen *hundred* years ago He gave it to us. Now Jews in the Knesset and Jews like Etzion act as if God is only *their* God. There is *one* God for all of us, and he gave his last message to Mohammed, therefore to us. They feel chosen, but God

changed His mind. If they want to remain Jews, that's fine, but they are behind the times just like the Christians.

Some Jews, like Michael Öhrbaum of the Temple Institute in the old city in Jerusalem, believe that the Third Temple will "descend miraculously from heaven." Bent over bound books and peering at computer screens in the cluttered rooms of the institute, Orthodox Jews prepare for the coming of the Messiah. They have engaged an architect to design the temple, and other experts are making the vases and the costumes for the sacrifices in the temple. Quoting Exodus, Öhrbaum explains solemnly that it says,

> "Let them make Me a sanctuary that I may dwell among them" [Exod. 25:8]. But we can't hold a complete sacrifice yet because the red cow, whose ash is supposed to cleanse the Jews, doesn't live in Israel and because the priestly robes and the curtains of the Temple are woven with threads that are dyed with specific colors: light blue, crimson, and scarlet. It's all in Exodus 25, but there is disagreement about the way we can obtain this biblical blue. We make red and all the colors derived from it from boiled snail's blood, but as I said, the scholars and scientists don't know yet how to get the exact color blue. Recently, during the tenth annual meeting of the Temple Institute in Jerusalem, the members of the "Light Blue Organization" made public the results of the third inquiry into the halakhic color. The color is obtained from a snail that lives in the area of Tyre, the most natural habitat of the animal according to the Talmud.

"I call this Messianic fever, which the Jews of Gush Emunim have too," says Prof. Uriel Simon of Bar Ilan University. He specializes in the *Tanakh* and is a member of the religious peace movement Netivot Shalom (literally, "paths of peace") that was founded in 1973.

> We wanted to suppress that fever, which had increased because of the smooth course of building the settlements in the Palestinian territories under the leadership of Gush Emunim. As moderate Orthodox Jews we strove for an agreement between Jews and Palestinians while in the yeshivas a new generation of faithful and rabbis was trained with the idea that *Eretz Yisrael* had the highest priority in Judaism. For the members of Netivot Shalom, the glorification of the land was and is the greatest tragedy and the greatest failure of our religion, because through this, glorification of vio-

lence between Jews and Arabs was legitimized in the name of God. We call this *chilul haShem* [desecration of God's name].

The fanaticism of that time is also based on the Book of Joshua, a problematic book for Jews. We didn't accept then and don't accept now the fact that Gush Emunim is proud of this book and interprets the divine command to "take possession of the land" literally. God said to Joshua that He will "cast out before you" the nations who used to live in Canaan. Secular Jews like Shulamit Aloni even want to remove this book from the *Tanakh* because it can encourage and justify extremist behavior. I'm certainly not proud of the statements made by God in this book, but removing it goes too far. The problem is that the fundamentalist religious teacher explains to his students that Joshua received the divine assignment to murder the Canaanites and other peoples in order to go and live in the Promised Land. He writes on the blackboard "Jews=Joshua and Arabs=Canaanites" while it says in the Bible that the Arabs are not Canaanites. None of the peoples named in Joshua 3—Canaanites, Hittites, Hivites, Perizzites, Girgashites, Amorites, and Jebusites—are related to a present-day people.

I believe in the holiness and in the eternal truths of the *Tanakh*, but I've also been confused by the Canaanites. When God warned the Jewish people about bad behavior, he named the Canaanites as an example to make clear how it shouldn't be: "Do not defile yourselves in any of those ways, for it is by such that the nations that I am casting out before you defiled themselves" [Lev. 18:24]. The Jews would get this land only if they didn't behave like the Canaanites who had defiled the land: "for all those abhorrent things were done by people who were in the land before you, and the land became defiled" [Lev. 18:27].

Uriel Simon continues as he leafs through the *Tanakh*:

From Genesis 15 it appears that the Jews were not allowed to settle unconditionally in the Promised Land. After all, God said to Abraham that they had to wait until He could punish the Canaanites. That wouldn't be possible until after four hundred years when the Canaanites would have committed enough sins. How could God have said all this? This is nothing to be proud of.

But the members of Gush Emunim are proud of the these pronouncements by God, who supposedly freed the land for the Jews. The manner in which it was done is of no importance to them. Netivot Shalom tries to remind the extremists of *Tanakh* texts like

"Thus said the Lord: Would you murder and take possession?" [1 Kings 21:19], or "Hark, your brother's blood cries out to me from the ground!" With these texts we want to emphasize that God disapproves of this politics of bloodshed. But according to the new interpretation of the halakha of the seventies, it is unseemly to recall that God also said: "Justice, justice shall you pursue, that you may thrive and occupy the land that the Lord your God is giving you" [Deut. 16:20]. For Porat and his [supporters] justice is only observing the mitzvot and not the decent treatment of Arabs. According to him there is still no place for the two separate peoples, for the nations that issued from Rebecca's body [Gen. 25:23]— as is expressed so beautifully in Genesis.

This is obvious from their politically symbolic interpretation— that made the Jews into extremists—of the story of Jacob and Esau who had already wrestled in their mother's womb. Recently I read in Porat's paper, *Meat min haOr*, that I came across in my synagogue in Jerusalem, that he still tells his children, grandchildren, and lately also his students and other people who will listen that Jacob and Esau represent the Jews and the Palestinians respectively. The words "One people shall be mightier than the other, and the older shall serve the younger" [Gen. 25:23] have prophetic value for Porat. Many extremists hope for the departure of the Palestinians, symbolized by Esau whose dwelling supposedly was "far from the fat of the earth" [Gen. 27:39]. Esau was told this by his father Isaac after the latter had given the blessing to his younger son Jacob. In Porat's point of view he had made Esau, the Palestinians, inferior to Jacob, the Jews. It comes down to the fact that for the extremists the words "But I have made him master over you: I have given him all his brothers for servants" [Gen. 27:37] legitimize the settlement policy and strengthen the extremists in their conviction that the land belongs only to the Jews.

The question raised by this story is who is the true heir of Abraham. Isaac and Esau were hunters who had no interest in the spiritual destiny of the people. Rebecca and Jacob were sensitive to this, and Jacob in particular wanted to make Canaan into the land of Israel. But that has nothing to do with the present situation, and who says that Jacob symbolizes the Jews and that violence is permitted? Unfortunately a public stand has never been taken against that position. In the eyes of the extremists everything went well until the attempts of the government of Shimon Peres and Yitzhak Rabin to stop the *intifada* resulted in the signing of the Oslo accords. [Later followed by the Wye and Camp David agreements]. "Oslo" was a great tragedy for the religious Zionists and certainly for those who had made settling into a mitzvah. Their hope that God would bring peace in the end was undermined."

According to Simon, who sympathizes with the modern-Orthodox party Meimad, the greatest problem of the religious Zionists is the balance that they must try to find between religion and Zionism, between religion and democracy. The National Religious Party is always balancing between two thoughts and is therefore always obliged to compromise. The compromises of the party are not attractive for Simon because their liberalism is not pure. Many Zionists feel that it's Zionism that is not pure. Therefore the party isn't democratic enough for some and not religious enough for others. Meimad has this problem to a certain extent, but according to Simon this party is more democratic, more moderate, and operates from a less linear religious viewpoint. The continuation of peace negotiations is fully supported by Meimad, which is prepared to give up land in exchange for peace.

The mayor of Elkana, a settlement near Tel Aviv, is Marcel Gans, who is originally from Amsterdam. He is not charmed by the idea of giving the Palestinians an independent state. He settled in Israel in 1968 and studied economics and management at the Hebrew University of Jerusalem. Until 1998 he was financial director of various companies, and in 1998 he was elected as mayor of Elkana where he has lived since 1979. He has a Zionist background, grew up with the Greater Israel idea, and wears a crocheted yarmulke. He considers "Oslo" a "dangerous step that will lead to a Palestinian state, a poor state where crazy things will happen—after all, poverty leads to excess. Because the Palestinians are too dependent on us, I'm for autonomy. That way we can control them better." Gans picks up the telephone. From his conversation it becomes apparent that two Arab boys have just stolen two bicycles from the settlement. Gans adds,

This is a problem, but Jews steal bicycles too. The real problem is that the Palestinians have not yet distanced themselves from the goal of destroying the Jewish state. Besides they've not proven themselves too well recently.

We started just like they: everything that we have here we've built ourselves. Jews trust in God, but they also take the initiative themselves and Rabbi Kook inspired us. I think that they don't take control sufficiently. I don't know if it's the wrong mentality or if it's due to the religion, but the Islamics are passive. I don't know. The best proof of this are the Palestinian refugee camps that have existed over there for fifty years in Syria, Jordan, and here. The surrounding Arab lands and the Palestinian Authority itself have invested too little money in the camps; they're not developed. The Palestinians still work in Israel while they should have set up factories there with money from the oil profits of the Arab lands. They have the wrong mentality and wrong ideas about how a state should be set up. If you don't plan your own garden, who will do it?

Mayor Gans isn't worried that his settlement will be endangered by the withdrawals. On the walls of his room hang not only portraits of the famous Rabbi Kook but also detailed maps of Elkana. In his secretary's office hangs a photo of Rabbi Kook with one of his pronouncements showing the importance of the connection with and love for the Holy Land. "We would like to have this area too," says Gans, pointing to an area that is a practice terrain for the Israeli army at present. "I'm discussing the matter with the army, but the expansion will take a while because we need authorization, signatures, and permits. We're not like the Palestinians who build illegally. As mayor I can make sure that we buy land from Arabs, but if someone in the settlement wants to sell his house to an Arab because he offers more, I can't prevent that. We can't oppress people, they are all God's creatures."

Mayor Gans's influence on the peace process is limited. Every month he meets with other Yesha mayors, a total of twenty-three, to discuss the strategy of the negotiations with Barak about "Wye." According to Gans, the atmosphere is less elated than during the time of Netanyahu who, despite signing the Wye accord, would certainly have fought to the bitter end.

We are at a deadlock in the National Religious Party. We have five seats [they are now in the opposition], but we have no power. I think that we have to strive to hold on to our acquisitions and to strengthen the existing settlements. Things went wrong after the Six-Day War. We shouldn't have oppressed the Palestinians. Ultimately they are profiting from our occupation. If we hadn't settled here, they would have lived in even greater poverty, they would have slaughtered one another, and they wouldn't have had the aspiration to establish their own state. They don't want to admit it, but it's true. At the time we didn't realize that it would have been better to push them in the direction of autonomy in order to prevent the awakening of Palestinian nationalism.

Zionism failed in some aspects according to Gans. He feels that the lack of consensus leads to it not being strong enough within:

> After the elections it always turns out that the division of votes for the two candidates for prime minister is more or less equal. There is no one in Israel who can call for a consensus. This shows, for example, in Premier Barak's decision to govern with Shas. We have certainly built a beautiful state. The standard of living is four times higher than thirty years ago, but even after fifty years we haven't defined our identity, and we haven't fixed our borders. We should be clearer about how the state should look in the year 2001. The Arabs have a clear goal: Jews out. We never say that they should leave.

Gans's pessimism can't be detected in Benny Kashriel, the previously mentioned mayor of Ma'aleh Adumim (since 1992) who has been the chairman of Yesha since 1999. According to him, the new postideological age that has already dawned will be accepted in wider circles on the West Bank in 2001 and in the following years. The new era means the expansion of the existing 147 settlements—that number is sufficient according to Kashriel, who doesn't wear a yarmulke. It also means concentrating on encouraging the Jewish settlement on the West Bank, which, according to Kashriel, will in a few years look just like other parts of Israel as regards facilities, employment, and places of entertainment. Ma'aleh Adumim should become like Tel Aviv: "We want to triple the number of Jews living on the West Bank by offering quality life and quality time: we will concentrate on the development of municipal amenities that make life pleasant, like indoor sport facilities, swimming pools, and places of entertainment."

Kashriel explains, "The core of settling in Israel has recently moved from the kibbutzim to the settlements in Judea and Samaria. The people in Yesha are often officers; they have the best functions in the army—it used to be the *kibbutznikim* [inhabitants of a kibbutz]. Left-wing Israel is still afraid of this development, but that will change because not all of us are extremists. The time of Chanan Porat's religious Zionism is past." Kashriel himself settled in 1983 on the West Bank for ideological reasons:

In those years by settling in Yesha we expressed the fact that a good Zionist Jew, who usually wore a yarmulke, went to live there because of his belief in the holy Jewish trinity of Gush Emunim: *Am-Yisrael*, *Torat-Yisrael*, and *Eretz Yisrael*. This still occurs, and we pursued the same goal as Porat, namely settling in the Biblical land, but we are less religious and less extremist in our opinions.

I'm moderate and pragmatic, and I'm a traditional Jew. I look at television on Saturday, I try to drive the car as little as possible on Saturday, and I don't eat pork. I believe in God and that this is the land of the people of Israel. You don't need a yarmulke to love Israel and to be a good Zionist. Jabotinsky and Herzl didn't wear a yarmulke either.

This is why Kashriel is a member of Likud and not of the National Religious Party:

From an ideological point of view I have no problem at all with the National Religious Party, but from a religious point of view I do. This party seems to think that a yarmulke is needed to be a good Zionist. They want to accomplish their Zionist task through religion. It's impossible to achieve anything in the National Religious Party without a yarmulke. I would never be able to become a leader of the National Religious Party.

Just because without a yarmulke I'm considered as a moderate pragmatist, I was chosen as the chairman of Yesha. I represent the new direction and I can make our wishes known to the government ministers who are against Yesha and explain to them that the West Bank is important to Israel because of security considerations. We form first of all the "East [*sic*] security belt" of Israel—especially for places like Hadera, Netanya, and Petach Tikvah that are near the border of Palestinian territories. Secondly Yesha is important because a third of Israeli water is here. The third reason is religious in nature: Ma'aleh Adumim is in Judea, the land of the Jewish tribe Judah. It's impossible in Israel to separate the state from religion. Israel was a Jewish nation and it will always remain that, but we have to be able to distance ourselves from old ideals and for some people that's difficult.

For example, the Jews in Hebron wouldn't be able to live there if they weren't ideologically motivated. We in Ma'aleh Adumim, where 75 percent of the inhabitants are secular, say that they're crazy. They live in a ghetto there, under poor circumstances, and the need for quality life has clearly not penetrated yet. They still live in the old religious Zionist era that has reached an all-time low according to me. They and the inhabitants of such places as Kfar Etzion, Ofra, and Kyriat Arba don't want to have anything to do with the development of the Palestinian territories, and they don't talk with the Palestinians. But now we live in another era, we must try to cooperate. This can be done by making agreements with the Palestinians about the division of water and by talking with them about environmental management, like waste processing. My contact with Palestinians, which dates from my time as deputy chairman of Yesha, doesn't mean that I agree with "Oslo" and "Wye," but in the end I accept—and that's typical of the post-ideological era—that these accords were agreed to by the Knesset, and that we live in a democratic state. We go along with our time, but it must not come to a Palestinian state with a Palestinian army and a Foreign Ministry. If they want peace, they don't need an army. They have their own flag.

According to Kashriel, not all mayors are as moderate as he, and he adds that it depends with whom he is compared: "For Yossi Sarid I'm an extremist, but compared to Ha'etzni, who represents almost no one except himself, I'm a moderate." Kashriel picks up a list of all mayors and adds up the number of secularists, Orthodox, and *haredim* among them, and he names the settlements.

Gaza has one mayor, and in Judea and Samaria there are a total of twenty-two. Among them there are nine secularists, ten Orthodox, and three *haredim*. The latter are from the three ultra-Orthodox settlements Beitar Ilit, Kyriat Sefer, and Immanuel, but they aren't ideologically motivated because they won't accept Judea and Samaria until the Messiah comes. My goal—Jewish settlement in Judea and Samaria and offering good social services in the settlements—has nothing to do with the Messiah and redemption. The Messiah will come, but the hope that he will come sooner by settling in the Biblical land is a false hope.

As proof of his more moderate position, Kashriel tells how he saved several settlements through negotiations.

Between the fall of Netanyahu's government and Barak's taking office, forty-two new settlements were built. Barak wanted to vacate them, and the settlers announced demonstrations because they had no intention of giving up even one settlement. I asked them to hold off because I first wanted to try to save the majority of these new settlements through negotiations with Barak. It was difficult to prevent all demonstrations, but in the end I was able to save thirty-seven settlements with negotiations without too many clashes.

"Religious Zionism has always known low points and high points, but the present low could, according to some people, mean the absolute end of the ideology and perhaps the end of the National Religious Party," says Prof. Eliezer Don-Yehiya of Bar Ilan University in Ramat Gan. For twenty years he has been studying the role of the Orthodox in politics and he wears a crocheted yarmulke.

There was a crisis and also a deep feeling of disappointment in some religious Zionist circles. The big problem of the present religious Zionist ideology is that the traditional role of the National Religious Party seems to be finished. In the fifties and the sixties religious Zionists felt that they were a beleaguered minority, and during those years a party that fought to give shape to the religious Jewish identity of the state was needed. It's paradoxical that the party that should represent religious Zionists is so bad off while the Jews who identify with the National Religious Party have succeeded in Israeli society: they are represented in every professional group, they have their own educational system, and they have guaranteed the Jewish character of Judea, Samaria, and Gaza. Their success is the failure of the party. Additional weakening of the National Religious Party which is now waging a defensive war, is no problem for many religious Zionists. The more extreme have voted for Ichud Leumi while the moderates turned to Meimad, and others emphasize economic and social questions and voted for the Labor Party or for Likud.

Still, Don-Yehiya sees one disadvantage: There is a great demand for religious Zionist education. If the party were to abolish itself, this form of education—which he feels is the pride of many National Religious Party members—could not be maintained. An important question is whether the young people will fill the national religious vacuum. He doesn't think that this will happen. The traditional religious nationalist fervor has not, to be sure, completely disappeared, but he doubts that someone like Chanan Porat will succeed in strengthening it. At the moment it seems to Don-Yehiya that the role of the extreme right is finished and that a new era has dawned:

The unique combination of religion and political radicalism that drove many religious Zionists doesn't appeal to the new generation that was born on the West Bank. They think that their parents' Messiah is false, and many are taking off their yarmulke. The increasing *she'ela* [literally: "question." What is meant here is turning away from the faith, as was discussed in chapter 5) in religious Zionist circles is related to the fact that "the revolution has been institutionalized." This means that for the new generation born on the West Bank it's normal to live and grow up there. They will strive for the "normalization" of the West Bank.

Yet, according to Don-Yehiya, no one knows exactly what course the National Religious Party will take, or how representative Benny Kashriel really is of Yesha. Don-Yehiya continues: "According to Kashriel the post-ideological era has dawned—and that's true in all of Western Europe. But no one knows how the extremists, who still believe that the Jewish presence on the West Bank will bring redemption and the coming of the Messiah closer, will react the moment when Barak goes too far in giving up territory in their eyes. Everything is still uncertain."

After Ariel Sharon's visit to the Temple Mount at the end of September 2000 and the ensuing second *intifada*, this observation remains valid. It turns out that despite all the apparent changes on the surface, the core of the conflict is the same: for lack of consensus about the identity of the Jewish state and lack of true political, social, and religious unity, the general paralysis will continue.

EPILOGUE

"THEY [THE SECULARISTS] HAVE YIELDED GROUND to the Orthodox, but the latter have not gained ground thereby, nor
have they made any inroads among the nonobservant. This policy
was in the nature of a delaying action, and the time gained enabled
the new state to consolidate itself and to strengthen its social cohesion. It has also afforded an opportunity for the development of a
Jewish culture within a climate of a broad national consensus."

With these words the jurist Zalman Abramov (1908–1996) ended
his book *Perpetual Dilemma* in 1976. In this work, which is considered
a standard work in academic circles and still is strikingly topical, the
author analyzes the connection between traditional Judaism and the
Jewish state. In other words, this book discusses the struggle about
the place of traditional Judaism in modern Israel, a struggle that
started in the very first hours of the existence of the state. Abramov,
who received an honorary degree in Hebrew Letters and was asso-
ciate editor of the *Encyclopedia of Zionism and of Israel*, uncovered the
roots of the religious problem in Israel by placing it against the back-

ground of a century of Jewish history. In this respect *A People Who Live Apart* could be considered a sequel to *Perpetual Dilemma*.

In 1976 Abramov already emphasized that in Israel few subjects have produced as much tension and hatred as religion. This is still true for present-day Israel, just as many of his observations are still valid for the current situation in Israel. However, this is not true in terms of the preceding excerpt from his book: today the secularists give in much less easily to the wishes of the *haredim*, who have won the struggle in the eyes of many Israelis. The ultra-Orthodox control (mostly in the financial sense) the lives of the secular, and in addition they don't perform military service. Strengthening the "social cohesion" among Jewish Israelis is totally out of the question, nor is there the "climate of a broad national consensus" mentioned by Abramov.

This observation doesn't mean that Abramov, who was a member of the Knesset Commission for Law and Constitution for seventeen years and who from 1963 to 1972 represented the Knesset at the Council of Europe in Strasbourg, made a wrong analysis. Rather, it indicates a change in Israeli society. The conclusions in *Perpetual Dilemma* are dated, in part, because after the publication of this book a very crucial development took place: upon taking office in 1977, Menachem Begin of Likud brought the Orthodox and the ultra-Orthodox to the center of power. This development ultimately led to the loss of common factors—being Jewish, concern for preserving Jewish unity, and the struggle against the Arabs—that had kept the Jews together until that time. Instead Israeli society polarized very rapidly, and over the course of the years three almost irreparable rifts arose in Israeli society.

The first split arose in the seventies in the coalition of the secular Zionists of the Labor Party and the religious Zionists of the National Religious Party. This coalition had lasted since 1948, but after the Six-Day War in 1967 it started to show its first cracks because of differences of opinion about the West Bank, which was occupied in that year. Since that time the National Religious Party has been radicalized and has become increasingly sympathetic to the ideas of Menachem Begin of Herut (the predecessor of Likud), who made a case for keeping Judea and Samaria. In this way the political developments and the territorial problems increasingly distanced the National Religious Party from the Labor Party. To be sure, the latter party had approved the establishment of the first settlements, but that was in large part the result of their inexperience in this area. Moreover, the National Religious Party exerted pressure on the Labor Party, which wanted to maintain the coalition. Yet the latter party adopted a more moderate line, while the National Religious Party became increasingly activist about the retention of the occupied territories. The split that occurred between these two parties has never healed, and the chance that this may still happen is small because of the nature of their differences of opinion.

The split between secular Israelis and *haredim* also occurred after Begin took office because he made it possible for the ultra-Orthodox community to become stronger. This community came out of its isolation and started to demand its part in political decision making and in the organization of public life. The ultra-Orthodox received their part of public money, which it used to strengthen its own community and to expand the Status Quo. Since the appearance of the *haredim* on the public stage, the secularists have turned away more and more from them, and in this way a second unbridgeable gap has come about in Israeli society. One of the most important causes of the origin of this rift was Begin's abolition of the limitation on the number of yeshiva students who were entitled to be exempted from military service. This number increased rapidly in the following years with the result that the number of inactive men rose, and therefore more money (more taxes for the secular) was needed for the yeshivas.

A third rift, the one between Sephardic and Ashkenazi Jews, came about with the formation of the ultra-Orthodox Sephardic Shas party in 1984. The total subordination of the national interest to the interests of the Sephardic community makes this party unreliable in the eyes of many secular Ashkenazi Jews. By keeping all options open and by not defining its form of Zionism concretely, it is in theory possible that Shas might, in the future, support the Arab parties in their struggle against Zionism. (This has in the meantime happened once.) The danger of this opportunism, which is fed by a feeling of inferiority and is justified by religious arguments, is that it is difficult to anticipate its limits. Moreover, the prominent presence of Shas and its rapid growth have led to the radicalization of Shinui and Meretz, small left-wing parties that have recently sounded more antireligious.

Abramov's argument, which dates from the period before the

developments outlined above and therefore concerns a less polarized, more harmonious society, is an ode to what he calls the "politics of compromises," which, according to him, made it possible for
the new state to consolidate itself. However, among the secularists
the readiness to make compromises with the ultra-Orthodox
changed—especially after 1977—into the realization that unity had
been artificially maintained for all these years. These days they consider Israeli political compromise an admission of weakness and a
sign of disintegration rather than a virtue or a sign of consolidation.

Secular extremists in particular are more outspoken today about
the need to separate religion and state. In their eyes the ultra-
Orthodox have crossed the boundaries and have emerged as win-
ners from the struggle. The Status Quo, to which the secularists
attribute a religious rather than a national value, would have to be
replaced by a full-fledged constitution. The secularists feel that
without a constitution in which this separation has to be set down,
Israel will never become a democratic state and will therefore never
become a normal country. Despite this changed attitude of the secularists, in the press and in parliament the debates with the Orthodox
about the Status Quo—and therefore debates about the separation of
religion and state—are still conducted according to the same old
pattern. As Abramov observed, today it is still true that these "arguments proceed along parallel lines that never meet."

In order to clarify the issues about separating religion and state in
Israel, I have divided this epilogue into four parts, in imitation of
Abramov: one part is about the background of the conflict between the
secularists and the Orthodox; the second part will clarify the standpoint of the Orthodox; the third part will clarify the standpoint of the
secularists; finally, the fourth concluding part will look into the future.

THE RELATIONS BETWEEN ORTHODOX
AND SECULAR JEWS IN A HISTORICAL PERSPECTIVE

The most radical change in Jewish history took place in the spiritual
life of the people. It developed from a religious community in a pluralistic society into the independent Jewish state of Israel. During
this development (which started during the *Haskalah*), Jews who

neglected to observe the Jewish law caused a crisis in the Orthodoxy because they announced at the same time that they didn't want to distance themselves from the Jewish people. These secular Jews, who hardly existed before the *Haskalah*, were a contradiction in terms for Orthodox Jews.

In Jewish societies in the diaspora, where there was no "Jewish" authority to solve problems of Jews among themselves, the Orthodoxy reconciled itself to a certain extent to pluralism. In Palestine the dialogue between Orthodox and secular Jews was made impossible by the old *yishuv*, which retreated into a spiritual world out of fear of renewal. Tensions really started to escalate in the young state of Israel when traditions had to be adapted to the new reality of a sovereign Jewish state. One of the tasks of the politics of this state was precisely to solve the religious problem that has always been on the political agenda since the existence of the state of Israel. The Orthodox wanted to participate in this task because they feared not being able to continue their Orthodox life in modern society. (In this connection Abramov observed that Judaism is the only victim of this entwining of religion and state. According to him it is because of political interference that Judaism didn't manage to develop into a creative force in the spiritual life of the Jewish state.) The tolerance and intellectual discussions from the diaspora seem to have disappeared completely in Israel. It's true that congresses have recently been organized in Israel that have as their goal to bring the Orthodox and the secularists closer, but it is impossible to say if there is a real conciliation or mutual understanding.

Israel is an exceptionally fragmented and complex society where traditionally religious and modern nonreligious Jews, often from different countries, have to come to an agreement about the Jewish identity and the Jewish content of the state. Meanwhile it has become clear that the above-mentioned factors of the past can't close the rifts that have developed between different groups of Jews over the years.

THE ORTHODOX VIEWPOINT IN THE RELIGIOUS QUARREL

For the Orthodox it is out of the question that Israel, the land of the Jewish people, whose nationalism has gained a theological dimension, should ever become a normal country. By "normal" they mean a non-Jewish state for all citizens in which religion doesn't have a privileged position. After all, God chose the Jewish people from all the nations, and because of the uniqueness of Jewish history, religion has become a part of the structure of the Jewish state. Separating these elements would conflict with the unique and particularistic character of Jewish identity. Besides, many Orthodox Zionists are aware that their time-honored slogan "the land of Israel for the people of Israel in accordance with the Torah of Israel" is an inaccessible goal: the halakhah can't meet the needs of a modern state.

The Orthodox can still participate in Israeli politics without scruples because there is no constitution yet. However, a number of Basic Laws have been adopted through the years, and only four more Basic Laws need to be approved in order to have a constitution. Therefore the moment when Israel should be able to accept a constitution has come closer, but because of the composition of successive governments the approval of these four Basic Laws will be long in coming.

For the orthodox the law of God is the true basis for a political party, and it is legitimate to strive to achieve religious goals by democratic means through political parties. From the Orthodox point of view it is also justified to use the compelling force of the state to give that same state a religious content. It was precisely because of the need for religious laws and the safeguarding of the Status Quo that the Orthodox originally began to participate in politics.

In this they succeeded more or less until the seventies. In 1976 Abramov concluded that the position of the Status Quo, which at that time still served a national goal, was not in danger: "its position is firmly secured for the foreseeable future." At the same time he observed that the Orthodox often had "a feeling of uneasiness" because it was rather embarrassing that it was necessary to appeal to nationalist sentiments to attain a religious goal. For them this meant the beginning of the end of traditional Judaism. These days the ultra-Orthodox therefore have the feeling that they were betrayed by the secular Zionists because the latter neglected traditional Judaism in the new state right from the beginning. They, the ultra-Orthodox, have through the years indeed had to give up a lot of their traditional life in order to be able to survive in Israel. The Status Quo has been eroded, and this has given them a feeling of having become a threatened minority in their own state. They and not the secularists are the ones who have lost in the modern state of Israel.

The murder of Yitzhak Rabin in November 1995 and the comparison of Meretz leader Yossi Sarid to the biblical figure of Haman in April 2000 by Rabbi Ovadia Yossef express this feeling of the Orthodox of having been betrayed by the secular Zionists. The large ultra-Orthodox demonstration in February 1999 is another example of this. In the opinion of the Orthodox it's a question of *k'fiah hilonit* rather than *k'fiah datit*, as the *hilonim* claim.

THE SECULAR VIEWPOINT IN THE RELIGIOUS QUARREL

Through the years, secular extremist Israelis have started to feel increasingly that they are the losers in the modern Jewish state where the ultra-Orthodox have attained increasingly more space. The strongly antireligious rhetoric of Meretz, and in particular the election slogans of Shinui against the *haredim* in 1999, express this feeling of being threatened. More than ever it seems that socially and economically they want to make Israel into a European country, that is to say, a state for all citizens where Judaism plays no role or a minimal one. They emphasize the desire to be a free person in a free country, and the argument that preserving the Status Quo is the price to be paid to prevent a *Kulturkampf* (culture war) is one that in their eyes was disposed of long ago. They no longer consider the Status Quo as a necessary evil, but rather as an out-of-date agreement that limits the citizens in their freedoms. The moderate secularists, who form the majority in the Knesset, nevertheless want Israel to remain a Jewish state.

An important cause of the dissatisfaction of the secularists is the fact that the state finances religious education. Abramov points out that in the early years of the state the secularists thought that this was "completely justified." Today they feel it is unacceptable because—and this is the most problematic provision of the Status Quo for the secularists—the ultra-Orthodox are exempted from military service. Through the years this privilege has contributed to the above-mentioned split between the Orthodox and the secularists because of the increasing disparity between the demands the *haredim* make of the state and their contributions to society. The secularists' reasoning is that the state of Israel makes it possible for a whole community to study with secular tax money without participating in the labor process.

During the first decades of the existence of Israel, when the discussion about military service hadn't yet taken place because the number of ultra-Orthodox yeshiva students was limited, the halakhic family laws caused the "greatest conflicts" according to Abramov. The most extreme secularists—this is less true for the moderate secularists—still think it's unjust that Jewish marriage and Jewish divorce were forced on them. This part of the Status Quo has recently come under increasing pressure because of the non-Orthodox movements in Judaism and the increased number of non-Jewish Russian immigrants who are citizens without being able to marry in Israel. The secularists have therefore pinned their hopes on the latter in their striving for the legalization of civil marriage. However, until now the secular politicians have not yet made a proposal to introduce civil marriage in Israel.

In addition, the Sabbath was established as a national day of rest in 1948 in the Status Quo; this has been a source of annoyance for the secularists during the last decades. Although it is legally permitted in very few cities, more and more places of entertainment are open to the public on the Sabbath. Some municipalities feel compelled to adapt the law to reality. Other communities turn a blind eye to the Sabbath openings.

In 1998 a number of secular and religious Knesset members tried to solve the above-mentioned controversy. The result was a new Status Quo, adapted to the modern era, but because of the many compromises, none of the politicians wanted to be associated with it. The result is that the present situation continues, and the call by a minority of secular extremists for the separation of religion and state becomes ever louder.

A Look into the Future

As long as the secular Jewish Israeli population (80 percent) remains internally divided about the Arab question (the peace negotiations with the Palestinians and with Syria and Lebanon), no effective solutions will be found for the internal religious problems. The most urgent of these problems, the exemption from military service for the *haredim* and the halakhic family laws, cause the greatest split in Israeli society. However, the above-mentioned difference of opinion about the "Arab question" between the two largest secular parties, the Labor Party and Likud, results in a political constellation that gives the ultra-Orthodox parties a disproportional amount of influence. For fear of losing their support, the Labor Party politicians don't want to burn their fingers on the religious problem. This support will remain essential in order to form a coalition that will enable the Labor Party or Likud to carry out their foreign strategy with regards to the peace negotiations.

As long as the borders with the Arab countries haven't been fixed permanently, the Labor Party and Likud (which balance each other more or less) will remain dependent on the ultra-Orthodox. The fact is that the ultra-Orthodox parties are easy coalition partners because they go along with the foreign policies of the Labor Party or Likud as long as they are guaranteed that their specific wishes will be met. In this way the Labor Party and Likud can work out their foreign political plans undisturbed while the ultra-Orthodox community strengthens itself with the means it receives in exchange for its political support. This system preserves the three social rifts and will continue as long as the "Arab question" dominates the political agenda. It isn't until these diplomatic problems are solved that the Labor Party and Likud, which differ hardly at all about socioeconomic and domestic problems, will be able to close ranks, making possible the discussion of subjects that involve the Status Quo.

Until that time this paralyzing situation will continue. The dissatisfaction of the majority of Israelis about the above-mentioned privileges enjoyed by the Orthodox will increase, as will the frustration about the impossibility of drawing up a constitution. Although these democratic imperfections hamper very few people in their daily lives (there are Basic Laws and a Supreme Court), these are the very subjects that moderate secular Israelis would like to see arranged differently in their country. In contrast to the extremist secular leftist, European-oriented minority of Meretz, they would like Israel to preserve its Jewish identity. In a constitution they would not want to restrict the rights of the Orthodox, but they would like to establish constitutionally that the *haredim* also have to fulfill military service and that there be religious freedom in their country, which in this case would mean the existence of Jewish pluralism. After all, in Israel there is freedom of religion for Christians and for Muslims, but not for Jews: Jewish civil marriage is not legal, and the non-Orthodox movements have no official religious authorities.

Attempts to solve the domestic problems that have now disappeared from the political agenda because of the second *intifada* often used to get stuck—and will likely do so in the future—in compromises of governmental commissions that overshot their goal. An example of this is the Ne'eman Commission (set up in 1996 to involve the non-Orthodox movements in carrying out conversions), which decided that only Orthodox rabbis may carry out conversions of converts taught by non-Orthodox rabbis. A second example is the Tal Commission, which was set up at the end of the nineties to advise the government about how to have the *haredim* integrate into society through military service. This commission advised the government against a three-year military service for yeshiva students but suggested instead to give these twenty-three-year-old students a year's time to choose between continuation of their Talmud study or a four-month military service as preparation for job training. In the case of both of these commissions, the new situation differs little from the old one.

The proposal of the Tal Commission is, according to some Jews, a step on the way to gradual adaptation of the *haredim* to secular existence, and this may take generations. However, opponents feel that "Tal" is problematic because these twenty-three-year-old married men, who often have two children and usually have no secular knowledge, have to make a crucial decision within one year: stay in the yeshiva and continue to study or go into the service and look for work afterward. The secular members of the population will applaud the choice of the latter possibility, but for convenience's sake they overlook the fact that there is fear of the army in ultra-Orthodox circles, and that the army, for various reasons, does not now have (and most likely in the future will not have) any urgent need for *haredi* soldiers. The second choice will mean that the yeshiva student will not only lose his financial and social advantages as well as the security offered by the yeshiva, but will above all experience a huge change of lifestyle. The first possibility will be the safest for most yeshiva students, but for many families it will mean continued poverty.

The number of yeshiva students who look for contact with the outside and will in this way face these two choices will increase in the coming years. The *haredim* will increasingly be confronted by modernity, partly because of the introduction of the computer, which has led to a crisis that is unequaled in their history. The greatest problem is not the lack of flexibility to face modernity but the lack of knowledge and means to bridge the gap that has developed over the years between the secular and the ultra-Orthodox worlds. For this reason, the call for instruction in secular subjects like math, computer science, and English will become louder in the coming years. Besides, some people feel that the state of Israel will eventually no longer be able to bear the ever-increasing financial pressure of the ultra-Orthodox community. It is difficult to know if there will be a revolution in *haredi* society, or even an explosion as some think, or a gradual change.

According to some, this crisis indicates the victory of secularism. They feel that the reality in Israel is secular, and even Orthodox Israelis live in a secular society where nonreligious values dominate. Every year more and more places of entertainment will be open on the Sabbath, and every year more and more secular Jews will show less interest in *Tisha be-Av*, the most important Jewish day of mourning. And the "Western" Valentine's Day will take an important place next to the "Jewish Valentine's Day," *Tu b'Shevat*.

On the other hand, heads of yeshivas and rabbis speak of an increasing number of yeshiva students and an increasing demand for *Yiddishkeit*. As long as the government of Ariel Sharon is in power, the Likud minister of education will do her best to introduce Jewish "values and standards" in the educational system. In addition to these developments, the interest in Jewish sources will continue to increase, even on a small scale, among secular Jews. This interest has developed partly as a result of Yitzhak Rabin's murder by Yigal Amir and the assault by Baruch Goldstein in Hebron, after which the authority of many rabbis decreased and many secular Israelis no longer accepted Orthodox rabbis as the only true representatives of the Orthodox culture of their grandparents. They want to appropriate the Jewish heritage for themselves. Some of these Jews, who study in special institutes, call themselves humanistic, pluralistic Jews. It is possible that during their search some of them will end up in the Reform movement, a movement that we shouldn't lose sight of in the coming years. Recently this movement has become better known: many secular young people who see no benefit in the traditional Jewish wedding ceremony and don't want anything to do with religion and Orthodox Judaism have started making use of the Reform wedding ceremony, which, incidentally, is not recognized by the state.

The Reform movement will also have to be accommodating to the need of many non-Jewish immigrants to become Jewish. It is therefore possible that in the future there will be an increase in the number of Jews who will be converted to Judaism by the Reform movement and in the number of marriages performed by the Reform movement. Criticism of the Reform movement, which according to some should not be called a religious movement, will continue unabated. However, it is difficult to say at the moment whether this movement—and the same is true for the Conservative movement—will gain a foothold among the Israeli Orthodox.

The number of non-Jews who are Israeli citizens will continue to increase in the future. For this it is important to take into account not only the Israeli Arabs but also the foreign workers (primarily Romanian and Filipino guest workers) and the non-Jewish immigrants from the former Soviet Union. From time to time attention will be fixed on this last group—as happened on July 1, 2001, when a Palestinian suicide bomber killed a number of halakhically non-Jewish young people. The discussion about the growing number of non-Jewish Israeli citizens and about the problems around their funerals will certainly flare up from time to time, but it will also die down again, causing the discussion to temporarily end. It is likely that many of those involved will resign themselves to the shortcomings of the Israeli democracy.

But we should not expect that civil marriage will be provided by law for all Jews in the near future. There will always remain fierce opponents of this "abnormal" situation, but it is not inconceivable that it, as well as the civil ceremony on Cyprus, will be considered "normal" in the future. However, because in the future more and more non-Jewish citizens will live in Israel—but also because of the arrival of large groups—it is conceivable that for them the possibility of a legal civil marriage will be arranged. However, this will not be possible for Jews who can marry in a halakhic manner because of the Orthodoxy's fear of assimilation through mixed marriage. The question remains if it is still possible to prevent real assimilation in Israel.

In order to let the non-Jewish Russian immigrants become established, the conversion question will remain on the political agenda. The Orthodoxy will probably insist on holding on to halakhic conversion because it doesn't want to let the Reform and Conservative movements control its implementation. In the future, the center of these non-Orthodox movements within Judaism will probably remain in the United States, and in Israel equal rights for this small group will remain controversial. In decisions in this matter, Israel will have to take care not to alienate American Jewry with pro-Orthodox measures. However, pro-American decisions will cause problems with the Orthodox parties of the coalition.

It is doubtful whether secular conversion, in which the wish to belong to the Jewish people is the only condition for becoming Jewish, will be supported among the secular population. At this time the prevailing idea is that Jews have a unique identity and that someone who wants to become Jewish has to accept a number of fundamental tenets of Judaism. He or she must no longer adhere to another faith, will have to study Judaism, and will have to celebrate the Jewish holidays—although everyone can do this in his or her own way. A man who wants to become Jewish has to be circumcised in addition. The result of all this is that in the future the number of non-Jewish residents who are Israeli citizens will increase because the non-Jewish Russian immigrants in particular don't want to become Jewish.

The fear that the state will in the long run no longer have a Jewish character will certainly increase among Orthodox Jews. This is evident from the policy of the Orthodox minister of the interior, Shlomo Benizri of Shas, who was appointed by Prime Minister Sharon in March 2001. In May of that year he announced, without articulating his fear in so many words, that "the two hundred thousand illegal guest workers harm the [Jewish] image of the society." Then he announced his plan to deport 500 illegals per month. A fellow party member who is also a member of the commission for guest workers chaired by Benizri added that "expelling five hundred illegals is only a drop in the ocean" and that he "would develop a plan for deporting at least four thousand illegals per month."

The Law of Return will be up for discussion with some regularity in the coming years, but it won't be abolished as the secularists wish, nor will it be adapted as the *haredim* wish.

During the coming years all Israel's attention will probably be focused on the West Bank. The moderates on both sides will be more vocal, but their viewpoints won't be new in Israeli society. Many right-wing religious Israelis will persist in the notion that the left-wing secular ideas are finished and that "Oslo" was an error, an agreement that was signed by naive people who now have to wake up. They will also persist in the viewpoint that the true and sincere Jew is strong, not afraid, and continues to build.

According to these rightists, the second *intifada* and the difficult circumstances in which the residents of the West Bank live will lead to a greater unity of the Jewish people. This doesn't mean that the population of Hebron and Ma'aleh Adumim will agree with the residents of Tel Aviv, but as Jews they will be confronted with a common enemy. Nonetheless—and this is a paradox—the number of Jewish Israelis who are convinced that the residents of the West Bank cause much harm to the Jewish state will also increase in the coming years.

The question remains whether the role of political Zionism is finished or whether the second *intifada* has blown new life into this movement. According to many Orthodox residents of Yesha, living and praying on the West Bank is an integral part of Jewish identity and giving up parts of that territory is a sign of weakness.

Despite the Jewish unity emphasized by many inhabitants of Yesha, the new split in Israeli society between the Jewish elite of the West Bank and the Israeli elite will continue to exist. Jews who live within the borders of 1967 hardly ever visit their relatives and friends on the West Bank, and they feel that things in Israel have gone the wrong way since 1967. They are of the opinion that Israel should give up as many settlements as possible as soon as possible and must endorse the establishment of a Palestinian state.

Until now Israel has remained a unique state with characteristics that make it impossible to compare this country to other states from a political, social, or historical point of view. Until now the country has not been "normalized." Not only because the Orthodox can obstruct certain initiatives that are aimed at "normalization" but also because the majority of secular Israeli citizens want Israel to preserve its Jewish identity. The Orthodox and the secularists simply have different expectations regarding the manner in which this "Jewishness" should be expressed.

The demand for this "Jewishness" and the confrontation between tradition and renewal will continue to occupy the Jews as long as—elaborating on their past—they have the need to define their identity and the meaning of their existence. The particularistic element is deeply rooted in the Jewish state and for the time being the question will remain whether Israel can ever be compared to any other country. During a long period in their history Jews were the object and not the subject. After all, they were not involved in political decision making and their attention was focused on the society that would give shape to a separate way of life that kept them separated from other peoples. In this way the Jewish people was able to keep its unique character and its individuality. Today it can still be rightfully said of Israel: "This is a people that will dwell apart and not count itself among the nations."

AFTERWORD

EVENTS IN ISRAEL HAPPEN IN RAPID succession. In writing a book about the country it is therefore practically impossible to keep close track of the developments. This makes writing about a subject, like the *Kulturkampf*, that is closely related to current events a perilous undertaking. The rift between the Orthodox and the secularists in Israeli society has actually increased since I started writing this book. Nevertheless, the core of the problem has remained the same.

The tension in the government coalition between Shas and Meretz has increased, and both parties have adopted increasingly confrontational positions and become less ready to compromise. Prime Minister Ehud Barak stirred up bad feelings among the secular part of the population because he made more efforts to keep Shas in the coalition. He wanted above all to make peace with the Palestinians, and for this he needed the support of Shas, which had no objection to peace negotiations when the coalition was formed. Meanwhile it has become evident that Shas is quite capable of obstructing the progress of peace negotiations with the Palestinians.

(For that matter it is unclear at the moment if declaring the Palestinian state will actually happen before September 13, 2000, as intended.)

Partly as a consequence of these developments, the government of Barak, who took office in 1999, has collapsed: one after the other Shas, Meretz, the National Religious Party, and Israel ba'Aliyah left the coalition. This was how Barak came to be at the head of a minority government, and from that time on he held at least ten ministerial posts. He lost the trust of both Orthodox and secular Israel. New elections will probably be called after the summer recess of the Knesset.

Just as the unexpected election of the new president, the Sephardic Orthodox Moshe Katsav (and not the secular Shimon Peres), in July 2000 was typical of the capriciousness and complexity of Israeli society and politics, in the same way the unpredictability of the election results and of the future of Israel will be the only constant. The *Kulturkampf* will remain its living proof.

Amsterdam
September 1, 2000

INTERVIEWS

M
ANY PEOPLE AGREED TO BE INTERVIEWED on the record for this book. I am very grateful for their help; below are their names in alphabetical order, followed by their titles and their functions when they were interviewed.

SHULAMIT ALONI, lawyer, lecturer at Ben Gurion University in Beer-sheba, former Knesset member for Meretz and former minister of culture, art and education under Prime Minister Itzhak Rabin.

PROF. MORDECHAI ALTSCHULER, Slavist, professor at the Hebrew University in Jerusalem.

MORDECAI ARNON, well-known actor who became Orthodox.

NOAM ARNON, chairman of the Jewish community of Hebron.

RABBI EHUD BANDEL, chairman of the Conservative movement in Israel.

DANIEL BEN SHIMON, journalist for *Ha'aretz* and author of two books about the elections of 1996 and 1999.

RABBI MICHAEL BOYDEN, head of the Reform community in Ra'anana.

AVRAHAM BURG, head of Sochnut until May 1999, chairman of the Knesset under Prime Minister Ehud Barak.

YOSSEF BURG (died in February 1999), minister of social services during the government of Ben Gurion and prominent member of the Mizrachi diaspora movement.

CHAIM CHESLER, chairman of the Soviet Jewry division of the Sochnut, financial director of the Sochnut since June 1999.

PROF. ASHER COHEN, political scientist at Bar Ilan University.

AVRAHAM AND YAFFA COHEN, a couple that couldn't marry in Israel because he is a "Cohen" and she is a divorced woman.

CHAIM COHEN (died in 2002), former president of the Israeli Supreme Court.

ARYEH DAYAN, journalist and author of "The Source of Shas."

PROF. SERGIO DELLA PERGOLA, demographer at Hebrew University.

PROF. ELIEZER DON-YEHIYA, political scientist at Bar Ilan University.

DOV ELBOIM, philosopher and journalist who left ultra-Orthodox Judaism.

SARIT ELLENBOGEN, anthropologist at the Brookdale Institute; is doing a study of Russian immigrants.

BENNY ELON, Knesset member of the religious Zionist Tekuma party under Prime Minister Ehud Barak.

YEHUDA ETZION, a Messianic Jew, founder and chairman of the Chai veKayam (literally, "live and survive") Messianic movement.

RABBI YITZHAK EZRAHI, head of the Mir yeshiva.

PROF. YEHUDA FRIEDLANDER, vice-chancellor of Bar Ilan University.

PROF. MENACHEM FRIEDMAN, sociologist and anthropologist at Bar Ilan University and author of a number of books about the ultra-Orthodox community.

MARCEL GANS, originally from the Netherlands, mayor of Elkana.

AVIRAMA GOLAN, reporter for Ha'aretz.

ELYAKIM HA'ETZNI, lawyer and resident of Kyriat Arba; in the eighties he was a Knesset member representing the small extreme-right-wing Tehiya party.

PROF. MOSHE HALBERTAL, historian and professor at Hebrew University in Jerusalem and lecturer at the Shalom Hartman Institute; specializes in Jewish philosophy.

RABBI YOSSEF HECHT, Hasidic rabbi and follower of the Lubavitch rebbe, lives in Eilat.

ADNAN HUSSEINI, head of the Jordanian Waqf institute, which supervises the Islamic holy places on the Temple Mount.

PROF. BENJAMIN ISH-SHALOM, philosopher and director of the Morasha institute for applied Jewish studies and director of the conversion institute.

BENNIE KASHRIEL, mayor of Ma'aleh Adumim and chairman of Yesha.

DAVID LANDAU, editor-in-chief of the English-language edition of *Ha'aretz*.

TOMMY LAPID, Knesset member for the secular Shinui party under Prime Minister Barak.

RABBI ISRAEL MEIR LAU, Ashkenazi Chief Rabbi of Israel.

PROF. CHARLES LIEBMAN, political scientist at Bar Ilan University.

PROF. ALEX LUBOTSKY, Knesset member for Moledet under Prime Minister Benjamin Netanyahu, then professor of mathematics at Hebrew University.

RABBI MICHAEL MELCHIOR, minister of diaspora affairs.

SARA POLISHUK, teacher of Judaism at the *ulpan* for Russian immigrants in Ashdod.

CHANAN PORAT, Knesset member for the National Religious Party under Prime Minister Benjamin Netanyahu; interim for Emunim under Prime Minister Barak; presently former Knesset member.

RABBI MEIR PORUSH, minister of housing under Prime Minister Benjamin Netanyahu.

RABBI MENACHEM PORUSH, prominent rabbi of Agudat Israel and organizer of the ultra-Orthodox demonstration in February 1998.

MENACHEM RACHAT, journalist of the *Ma'ariv* daily; has written a book about Shas.

RABBI ELIYAHU RAFAELI, secretary of Rabbi Reuven Elbaz.

RABBI AVRAHAM RAVITZ, Knesset member and party leader of United Torah Judaism under prime ministers Benjamin Netanyahu and Ehud Barak.

PROF. AVIEZER RAVITZKY, professor of Jewish philosophy and history at Hebrew University.

PROF. AVI SAGI, philosopher at Bar Ilan University.

PROF. ELIEZER SCHWEID, professor of Jewish history at Hebrew University in Jerusalem.

TOM SEGEV, journalist for *Ha'aretz* and historian.

CHANANYA SHACHOR, funeral director.

ALICE SHALVI, head of the Pelech orthodox girls' school in Jerusalem.

YAIR SHELEG, journalist for *Ha'aretz*.

NADAV SHRAGAI, journalist for *Ha'aretz*.

DUDI SILBERSLAG, Hasidic journalist and director of a news agency.

PROF. URIEL SIMON, professor of *Tanakh* at Bar Ilan University.

MARINA SOLODKINA, Knesset member for Israel ba'Alyiah immigrant party under prime ministers Benjamin Netanyahu and Ehud Barak; deputy minister of immigration and integration.

EHUD SPRINZAK, political scientist at Hebrew University.

ZERAH WAHRHAFTIG (died in 2002), lawyer and one of the signers of the Declaration of Independence; Israel's first minister of religious affairs.

PROF. HILLEL WEISS, professor of Hebrew literature at Bar Ilan University.

PROF. ZVI WERBLOWSKY, professor of cultural history at Hebrew University.

A. B. YEHOSHUA, writer and lecturer in the study of literature at Haifa University.

GLOSSARY

aguna—a woman who has not received a *get* from her husband.

Agudat Israel; Aguda—Ashkenazi ultra-Orthodox party, founded in Katowice in 1912.

aliyah; going on aliyah—literally, ascent (to *Eretz Yisrael*); originally, going to Jerusalem; later, a way to indicate different waves of immigration to Israel.

Ashkenazi Jews; Ashkenazim—Jews of Western, Central, or East European origin, originally Yiddish-speaking.

ba'al t'shuvah—literally, "master, owner of the answer"; name for someone who has become Orthodox.

bar/bat mitzvah—religious coming of age of Jewish boy/girl.

Baruch—literally, "blessed"; first word of many Jewish prayers.

beEzrat haShem—literally, "with the help of God."

ben Torah—literally, "son of the Torah"; an obedient religious Jewish boy.

Bnei Akiva—religious Zionist youth movement, founded in 1929.

Bnei Brak—ultra-Orthodox suburb of Tel Aviv.

bracha; plural: *brachot*—praise, blessing.

Chabad—contraction of *chochma* (wisdom), *bina* (insight), and *da'at* (knowledge); Messianic movement within Hasidism in which mystic and rational elements are joined.

chozer bish'elah—literally, "returned to the question"; an Orthodox Jew who has become secular.

Cohen—literally, "high priest"; indicates the descent from Aaron, the first high priest; common last name that brings with it the inconvenience that, according to Jewish law, a male Cohen is not allowed to marry a divorced woman or a woman who has converted to Judaism.

Council of Sages—ultra-Orthodox Torah scholars who make political decisions.

dati; plural: *datim*—religious Jew who has adapted his or her way of life to modern times.

Degel haTorah (Degel)—Ashkenazi ultra-Orthodox party that arose in 1988 from Agudat Israel.

diaspora—Jews living in dispersion or exile from the land of Israel; the Jewish community outside Israel.

din moser—literally, "sentence of the informant"; halakhic condemnation that permits killing a Jew who is suspected of giving confidential information to goyim.

din rodef—halakhic condemnation that permits a Jew to kill a Jew; a *rodef* is someone who by actions or politics has created the circumstances that justify his or her murder.

Eretz Yisrael—the land of Israel; term used by right-wing Orthodox Israelis to emphasize that the Gaza Strip, the West Bank, and in some cases parts of Jordan and/or the Sinai belong to Israel; the ultra-Orthodoxy uses this term to emphasize that it will not accept *Medinat Yisrael* until the Messiah comes.

Gemara—written account of discussions among rabbis, part of the Talmud.

get—letter of divorce that is supposed to be handed by the husband to his wife in the presence of a rabbinic court.

goy; plural: goyim—literally, "nation"; non-Jew.

Greater Israel—the idea that Judea, Samaria, and Gaza belong to the state of Israel and that giving up these territories is a sin.

Green Line—provisional eastern border of Israel; this border was drawn up after the Six-Day War in 1967 when Israel occupied the West Bank and Gaza.

Gush Emunim—founded in 1974, the apolitical wing of the National Religious Party that was aimed at the occupation of *Eretz Yisrael*.

halakhah—literally, "way, path, or going"; the entire body of rules and requirements that encompasses Jewish life in all of its facets.

halukkah—system of financing that supported the Jewish communities in the four holy cities of *Eretz Yisrael* with charitable collections made abroad, mainly in the period before World War I.

Halutz; plural: *halutzim*—pioneer who, before the establishment of the state of Israel, worked in agricultural settlements.

Hanukkah—festival of lights that takes place in November, December, or January and has as its only ritual the lighting of candles or oil wicks.

hardal, plural: *hardalim*—contraction of *haredim datim leumim*; literally, "ultra-Orthodox religious Zionists"; term that is used to indicate a new group started by ultra-Orthodox Jews who have become more nationalist and Orthodox Zionists who have become more ultra-Orthodox.

hared; plural: *haredim*—literally, "god fearing"; Orthodox who has adapted his or her life very little to modern times.

HaShem—God

Hasid; plural: Hasidim—literally, "faithful"; *haredi* ultra-Orthodox who adheres to Hasidism.

Hasidism—mystical movement or popular religious movement with mystical features and charismatic leadership, originated in the second half of the eighteenth century in Poland.

Haskalah—Jewish Enlightenment; intellectual movement that brought modern European culture to Jews (1750–1880).

hiloni; plural: *hilonim*—a term used by Orthodox Jews to indicate secular Jews.

Histadrut—contraction of *HaHistadrut HaKelalit shel HaOvedim haIvrim b'Eretz Yisrael*: the federation of Jewish workers in *Eretz Yisrael*; labor union founded in 1920 by Ben Gurion.

huppah—wedding canopy; wedding ceremony.

intifada—Palestinian revolt that broke out in 1987.

Israel ba'Aliyah—literally, "Israel on aliyah"; party for Russian immigrants, founded in 1995.

Kabala—literally, "tradition"; mystical doctrine in Judaism that had great influence on Jewish spirituality after the twelfth century.

Kadosh haBaruch—God the Holy One.

kashrut—regulations regarding clean and unclean food; ritual slaughter; salting meat; and the mixing of meat, milk; and cutlery and other kitchenware. These precepts stem from the Mosaic laws (see Genesis 32; Leviticus 11:3, 11:13–19, 17:10–14; Exodus 23:19, 34:26; Deuteronomy 14:21).

k'fiah hilonit—literally, "secular tyranny"; recently, a term used in Israel to express displeasure of the Orthodox about the behavior of the secularists. Also see: *k'fiah datit*.

k'fiah datit—literally, "religious tyranny"; in the nineties, a term used in Israel to express displeasure of the secularists about the behavior of the Orthodox. Also see: *k'fiah hilonit*.

kiddush—sanctification of the Sabbath and other holidays with a blessing over the wine; all the prayers and acts that sanctify the Sabbath.

kipa; plural: *kipot*—yarmulke; a head covering worn by men as a sign of respect for and obedience to God; in Israel, often a sign of religious identity.

Knesset—Parliament of Israel.

Kookists—supporters of the first chief rabbi of Palestine, Yehuda Kook, who encouraged cooperation with secular Jews.

kvutsa galuyot—ingathering of the exiles.

Law of Return—went into effect in 1950 and is based on the principle that every Jew is a potential citizen of the state of Israel; intended to give expression to the right to exist of the Jewish state.

Likud—right-wing political party founded in 1977; it was made up of various small right-wing parties, among which was Menachem Begin's Herut party.

Mapai—initials of Mifleget HaPo'alei Eretz Israel; literally: "the workers' party of *Eretz Yisrael*"; founded in 1930 in Palestine from the union of two small workers' parties.

Mapam—initials of Mifleget HaPo'alim HaMe'uhedet; literally, "united workers' party"; a left-wing Zionist workers' party that was founded in 1948.

masorti—traditional Jew; term used in Israel in contrast to "secular" or "Orthodox" Jew.

Mea Shearim—literally, "one hundred gates"; the ultra-Orthodox district in Jerusalem.

Medinat Yisrael—literally, "the state of Israel"; for the ultra-Orthodox living in *Eretz Yisrael*, this won't exist until after the coming of the Messiah.

Meretz—literally, "energy"; left-wing political party that originated in the Ratz party (founded in 1972), and with that party participated in the 1992 elections.

mezuzah—literally, "doorpost, an upright post"; a tube containing some texts from the Bible, attached to the doorway of a house (see Deuteronomy 6:9).

mikvah; plural: *mikvaut* or *mikvot*—ritual bath in which ritually impure persons or objects are immersed.

minyan—the ten men needed to hold a service in the synagogue; in the liberal communities women are also counted.

Mishnah—literally, "teachings or repetition"; one of the most important classic Jewish writings, composed around the year 200. The halakhah of that time was organized by subject in the Mishnah. The Mishnah has served as the basis for all subsequent discussions about the halakhah.

mitnachel; plural: *mitnachlim*—derived from the biblical Hebrew word *nachala* which means "heritage"; a term generally used to refer to extremist Jews who live in Samaria, Judea, or Gaza. See also *mityashev*.

mityashev; plural: *mityashvim*—literally: "to settle"; neutral term that is used to refer to Jews who live in Samaria, Judea, or Gaza.

mitzvah; plural: mitzvot—good deed, a religious command. The mitzvot are the commandments of the Torah and also the religious commands (such as the Sabbath, prayers, laws governing food) and the ethical commands (rules about relations among people).

Mizrachi—religious Zionist movement founded in 1902 as a religious party within the World Zionist Organization; in Israel it became the National Religious Party.

m'shumad (the time bomb of Ben Gurion); plural: *m'shumadim*—literally, "someone who is destroyed"; a Jew who has converted to another religion.

m'sirut nefesh—literally, "total devotion, with total submission"; halakhic term.

Netivot Shalom—literally, "paths of peace"; a left-wing Orthodox peace movement founded in 1973.

Neturei Karta—literally, "guardians of the city (Aramaic)";

extremely Orthodox Jews, primarily from Jerusalem, who consider the establishment of the state of Israel a sacrilege and hence do not recognize the state of Israel.

oleh hadash; plural: *olim hadashim*—literally, "new immigrant"; refers only to Jews who have settled in Israel.

Pesach—Passover; the holiday that celebrates the liberation from Egypt (see Exodus 12:1–28, Deuteronomy 16:1–8), celebrated in March or April.

pikuach nefesh—literally, "the preservation of life"; saving the life of a Jew takes precedence over the rules of the Torah.

Purim—literally, "lots"; holiday that commemorates the deliverance of the Jews from Haman, as described in the Book of Esther; celebrated in February or March.

Rosh Hashanah—Jewish New Year, celebrated in September or October.

Sabbath—seventh day of the week; biblical day of rest that starts after sundown on Friday and ends after sunset on Saturday.

sabra—literally, "cactus fruit"; someone who was born in Israel (Palestine).

safek yehudim—literally, "questionable Jews"; non-halakhic Jews.

sal klita—literally, "absorption basket"; the (financial) advantages received since the nineties by Russian immigrants upon their arrival in Israel.

Seder—literally, "order"; the celebration that commemorates the exodus from Egypt; a ceremonial meal that takes place at home during the first two nights of Pesach.

Sephardic Jews—originally from the Iberian peninsula and other countries around the Mediterranean.

shaliach; plural: *shlichim*—literally: "emissary"; someone who is sent abroad by the Sochnut to support the Jewish communities in foreign countries.

Shalom Achshav—literally, "Peace Now"; a peace movement founded in 1987.

Shas—contraction of Sephardim Shomrim Torah; literally: "Sephardic Jews who listen to the Torah"; political party for ultra-Orthodox and traditional Sephardic Jews—founded in 1984.

sh'elah—literally, "question." See also *chozer bish'elah*.

Shema—central prayer of Jewish liturgy; the text of this prayer is composed of three Bible passages: Deuteronomy 6:4–9, 11:12–21, and Numbers 15:37–41. This prayer is said twice a day.

Shinui—political party that in the 1999 elections obtained six seats with a strongly anti-*haredi* platform.

shofar—ram's horn trumpet that is sounded on the Jewish New Year, on Yom Kippur, and on other solemn occasions.

shtetl—Yiddish for "small city"; until World War II place of residence of Jews in Eastern Europe (Russia, Poland, Lithuania, and the eastern part of the Austro-Hungarian monarchy).

Shulchan Arukh—literally, "the prepared table"; codified collection of rules of life, compiled in the sixteenth century.

siddur—literally, "order"; the Jewish prayer book.

Sochnut—the Jewish Agency.

sofer—scribe who specializes in writing the Torah scrolls, among other things.

Sukkot—Feast of Tabernacles; to commemorate God's protection during the passage through the desert (see Leviticus 23:33–44).

tallit; plural: tallitot—literally, "prayer robe"; usually a woolen or linen scarf or shawl that is worn during prayer. Fringes (see tzitzit) are attached to each corner.

Talmud—literally, "study or doctrine"; the most important classic Jewish document; a collection of written summaries of classic rabbinical discussions about the practical applications of the Mosaic Laws.

tefillin—small leather boxes with leather straps attached; the boxes contain, among other things, the text of the Shema. They are worn on the left arm and the head during prayer.

Torah—literally, "doctrine or teaching"; Mosaic Law, the Five Books of Moses that contain the Jewish teachings.

Torah min ha'shamayim—literally, "the Torah from heaven"; conviction in Orthodox Judaism that the Torah, given by God to Moses on Mount Sinai, cannot and may not be altered by human beings.

t'shuvah—answer, repentance. See also *ba'al t'shuvah*.

tzitzit—fringes that, according to the Torah, have to be fastened to the corners of the tallit in order to be reminded of the commandments (see Numbers 15:37–41).

ulpan—school where new immigrants can learn Hebrew in a short period of time.

United Torah Judaism—ultra-Orthodox Ashkenazi party that consists of the Degel and Aguda parties.

Yesha—acronym for Judea, Samaria, and Gaza; the name of the collective government of these territories.

yeshiva—school for Talmud studies at different levels.

yishuv—literally, "settlement"; Jewish community in Palestine. The pre-Zionist community is called the "Old Yishuv" and the community that developed after 1880 is called the "New Yishuv."

Yom Kippur—Day of Atonement, a day of change in attitude, atonement, and fasting. This day, the most important holy day of the Jewish year, usually falls in September or October (see Leviticus 23:27–32).

BIBLIOGRAPHY

Abramov, S. Zalman. *Perpetual Dilemma: Jewish Religion in the Jewish State.* Foreword by W. Gunther Plaut. London: Associated University Presses, 1976.

Aviad, Janet. *Return to Judaism: Religious Renewal in Israel.* Chicago: University of Chicago Press, 1983.

Avnery, Uri. *Israel without Zionists.* New York: Macmillan, 1968.

Ben-Chorin, Shalom. *De verkiezing van Israël. Een theologisch-politieke beschouwing.* Baarn, the Netherlands: Ten Have, 1994.

Ben Gurion, David. *Years of challenge.* Tel Aviv: Massada Press, 1963.

———. *Ben Gurion Looks Back in Talks with Moshe Pearlman.* London: Weidenfeld and Nicolson, 1965.

Bouman, Salomon. *Israël contra Zion.* Amsterdam: Mets. Gent: Scoop, 1998.

Cohen, Asher, and Bernard Susser. *Israel and the Politics of Jewish Identity: The Secular-Religious Impasse.* Baltimore/London: The Johns Hopkins University Press, 2000.

Cohn-Sherbok, Lavinia, and Dan Cohn. *A Popular Dictionary of Judaism.* Richmond: Curzon Press, 1995.

Edersheim-Levenbach, Ella, and Theodor Herzl. *Profeet van de staat Israël.* Amsterdam: De Bezige Bij, 1959.

Elon, Amos. *The Israelis: Founders and Sons*. Jerusalem: Adam Publishers, 1981. (Original publisher: London: Weidenfeld and Nicolson, 1971.)

———. *Jerusalem, City of Mirrors*. Boston: Little, Brown and Company, 1989.

Evers, Lou. *Jodendom voor beginners*. Amsterdam: Forum, 1999.

Friedmann, Georges. *Fin du peuple juif?* Paris: Gallimard, 1965.

Goldberg, Michael. *Why Should Jews Survive? Looking Past the Holocaust Toward a Jewish Future*. Oxford: Oxford University Press, 1995.

Hazony, Yoram. *The Jewish State: The Struggle for Israel's Souls*. New York: Basic Books, 2000.

Heilman, Samuel. *Defenders of the Faith: Inside Ultra-Orthodox Jewry*. New York: Schocken, 1992.

Huppert, Uri. *Back to the Ghetto: Zionism in Retreat*. Amherst, N.Y.: Prometheus Books, 1988.

Israel Yearbook and Almanac. Vol. 53. Jerusalem: IBRT Translation/Documentation, 1999.

Jaffe, Benjamin, comp. *A Herzl Reader. Background material for discussions on Theodor Herzl, the Jewish Problem and Zionism*. Theodor Herzl Centenary. Jerusalem: The Youth and Hechalutz Department of the Zionist Organization, 1960.

Landau, David. *Piety and Power: The World of Jewish Fundamentalism*. New York: Hill & Wang Pub., 1993.

Leibowitz, Yeshayahu. *Het geweten van Israël*. Translated from the Hebrew by Ruben Verhasselt. Amsterdam: Arena, 1993.

Liebman, Charles S., and Eliezer Don-Yehiya. *Civil Religion in Israel: Traditional Judaism and Political Culture in the Jewish State*. Berkeley: University of California Press, 1983.

Liebman, Charles S., and Eliahu Katz, eds. *The Jewishness of Israelis: Responses to the Guttman Report*. SUNY Series in Israeli Studies. New York: State University of New York Press, 1997.

Liebman, Malvina W. *Jewish Cookery from Boston to Baghdad*. Miami: Seemann, 1975.

Melkman, Jozeph. *Israël*. Amsterdam: Elsevier, 1949 (2d ed., 1950).

Orr, Akiva, *Israel: Politics, Myths and Identity Crises*. Pluto Middle Eastern Series. London: Pluto Press, 1994.

Pearl, Chaim, and Reuben S. Brookes. *Wegwijs in het jodendom*. Translated and adapted by Henriëtte Boas and Ja'acov Colthof. Amsterdam: Nederlands-Israëlietisch Kerkgenootschap, 1993.

Polak, Inez, Thomas Simon, and Ina Friedman, eds. *Israël in vredesnaam. De politiek van een geharnaste democratie*. Haarlem, the Netherlands: Becht, 1992.

Ravitzky, Aviezer. *Messianism, Zionism and Jewish Religious Radicalism*. Translated from the Hebrew by Michael Swirsky and Jonathan Chipman. Chicago Studies in the History of Judaism. Chicago: University of Chicago Press, 1996.

Rosenberg, Roy A. *The Concise Guide to Judaism: History, Practice, Faith.* 1990; reprint. New York: Meridian Books, 1994.

Sartre, Jean-Paul. *Réflexions sur la Question Juive.* Paris: Morihien, 1946.

Segev, Tom. *1949: The First Israelis.* Edited by Arlen Neal Weinstein. Translated from the Hebrew. New York: Henry Holt, 1986.

———. *The Seventh Million: The Israelis and the Holocaust.* Translated from the Hebrew by Haim Watzman. New York: Hill & Wang Pub., 1993.

Siegel, Dina. *The Great Immigration: Russian Jews in Israel.* With a preface by Emanuel Marx. New Directions in Anthropology, vol. 11. New York: Berghahn, 1998.

Sprinzak, Ehud, and Larry Diamond, eds. *Israeli Democracy under Stress.* An Israel Democracy Institute Policy Study. Boulder: Lynne Rienner Publishers, 1993.

———. *The Israeli Right and the Peace Process, 1992–1996.* Davis Occasional Papers, no. 59. Jerusalem: Leonard Davis Institute for International Relations, Hebrew University of Jerusalem, 1998.

———. *Brother against Brother. Violence and Extremism in Israeli Politics from "Altalena" to the Rabin Assassination.* New York: Free Press, 1999.

Unterman, Alan. *Dictionary of Jewish Lore and Legend.* London: Thames & Hudson, 1991.

Vries, S.Ph. de. *Joodse riten en symbolen.* 2d ed. Amsterdam: De Arbeiderspers, 1968.

Yehoshua, A. B. *Naar een normaal Joods bestaan.* Translated from the Hebrew by L. Waterman. Amstelveen, the Netherlands: Amphora, 1983.

INDEX